TAKE COMMAND OF THE ENGLISH LANGUAGE!

Whether you are speaking or writing, vocabulary is the key to successful communication. And never before has it been so important for a college-bound student. A strong vocabulary will make a difference on how well you do on your required college entrance exam and where you finish in your graduating class. Don't waste time. Begin increasing your word power with this invaluable revised edition—expanded by 10 lessons to include more of the words neccssary to compete on a college level. It's the quick, easy, enjoyable way to build the vocabulary you need. You'll discover:

- Well-constructed lessons—all depicting a theme for complete understanding
- Definitions of terms with sentences to clarify usage
- Quizzes, tests, and a sentence completion section to reinforce the meanings
- Quotes from the classics to illustrate word usage—all in review test form
- Glossaries of words that relate directly to subjects in areas such as Social Studies, Arts, Language and Literature
- And much more!

When You've Got A Great Vocabulary, You've Got The Advantage!

ESSENTIAL VOCABULARY for COLLEGE-BOUND STUDENTS

ESSENTIAL VOCABULARY for COLLEGE-BOUND STUDENTS

MARGARET ANN HALLER

Prentice Hall
New York • London • Toronto • Sydney • Tokyo • Singapore

Second Edition

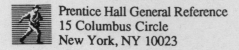

Prentice Hall General Reference
15 Columbus Circle
New York, NY 10023

Copyright © 1987, 1985 by Margaret A. Haller
All rights reserved
including the right of reproduction
in whole or in part in any form

An Arco Book

Arco, Prentice Hall, and colophons are
registered trademarks of Simon & Schuster, Inc.

Library of Congress Cataloging-in-Publication Data

Haller, Margaret A.
    Essential vocabulary for college-bound students.
    "An Arco book."
    Includes index.
    1. Vocabulary. I. Title.
PE1449.H24   1987   428.1   87-17439
ISBN 0-671-86759-8

Manufactured in the United States of America

6   7   8   9   10

CONTENTS

INTRODUCTION

The aim of this book is to help you increase your vocabulary for college quickly and enjoyably. It is designed for you to use on your own and at your own speed. Each of the sixty lesson-chapters defines and illustrates nine to fifteen words and provides a number of exercises to help you practice the new words and fix them in your memory. The six review tests show how various authors have actually used the vocabulary you have learned. Each lesson can be completed easily in one sitting. You will probably find that one lesson is enough to absorb at one time. Pace yourself and you'll learn more effectively.

At the back of the book, following the lessons and answer keys, you will find glossaries of additional terms that you are especially likely to encounter in introductory college courses in the humanities (the arts, languages and literature, and the social sciences). In all, this book covers over a thousand words and phrases that the college-bound student ought to know.

Some of the lesson-exercises will ask you to look things up for yourself. For this you will need a good desk dictionary, one with a pronunciation key and an etymology (word history) for each entry. There are several good, reasonably priced desk dictionaries on the market, including *Webster's New World Dictionary,* the *American Heritage Dictionary of the English Language (New College Edition),* and the *Random House College Dictionary.* A good dictionary is indispensable for college work. If you don't already have one, invest in one now and begin to make a habit of using it.

You have probably heard that the best way to increase your vocabulary is to read—to read a lot and to read many different kinds of writing. It is true that nearly all of the words we know we have learned unconsciously, simply by hearing and seeing them used again and again. By learning words in context, we learn not only what they mean but how they are used. Even if we can't define them precisely, we are likely to feel confident about using them ourselves. This does not mean, however, that you can't increase your vocabulary by conscious effort. This book will guide you in doing just that. It will give you a feeling for how unfamiliar words are used by illustrating them in sentences. It will help you form a habit of learning new words, of analyzing them and associating them with words you already know, and of consulting the dictionary. You will then find that your subsequent reading will reinforce what you have learned and make these new terms part of your permanent vocabulary.

LESSON 1

One way to remember a new word is to associate it in your mind with another word you already know. Often an unfamiliar word will be related to familiar terms through a common root. This is where knowing the etymology (origin) of a word comes in handy. For instance, you already know *verb,* the name of one kind of word, and *verbal,* "expressed in words." Both come from the Latin root *verbum,* meaning "word." The same root gives us a word you may not know,

verbatim—word for word, expressed in precisely the same words. *The lawyer requested the defendant to repeat his comments verbatim.*

Once you realize that an English word containing *verb* always has something to do with words, it becomes easy to remember the meaning of *verbatim.*

Another example: The common word *line* can help you fix in your mind less common words in the same word family, such as:

delineate—to outline, sketch out, depict, describe. *The artist quickly delineated the general contours of the figure.*

rectilinear—having straight lines, forming a straight line. *The rectilinear paths create long vistas from one end of the garden to the other.*

lineage—direct line of descent from an ancestor. *Only one local family can trace its lineage back to the first European settlers.*

The Latin base *clud* or *clus* means "shut" or "close." Among the many English words deriving from this root are *include, exclude,* and *conclusion,* as well as:

recluse—person who deliberately shuts himself away from the world, one who leads a solitary life. *The man had become a recluse, rarely going out and refusing invitations from his former associates.*

preclude—to shut out as a possibility, make impossible. *Losing all our savings at the track will preclude our taking a vacation this year.*

seclude—to shut away from others or from observation, make isolated or private. *The cabin was in a secluded spot, out of sight of the road.*

Duc or *duct* is a Latin stem meaning "to lead." It is at the root of many familiar terms, including *deduct, produce, conduct,* and *reduce.* It also gives us:

abduct—(lead away) to kidnap, steal a person. *The heiress was abducted from her home and held for ransom.*

traduce—(lead across) to expose to public scorn, defame, slander. *He had traduced his former partner by spreading lies that he was a crook.* The Latin ancestor of *traduce* meant "to lead as a spectacle, to display publicly as a disgraceful object."

conducive—leading to, helping, tending to promote. *Mother found the waterbed conducive to a restful sleep.*

Answers to the following exercises are on page 198.

EXERCISE I Synonyms. Circle the letter of the word or phrase closest in meaning to the given word.

1. delineate: a) lead up to   b) straighten up   c) draw an outline   d) scheme

2. preclude: a) make impossible   b) open   c) make likely   d) come before

3. conducive: a) attentive   b) leading to   c) without curves   d) prophetic

4. abduction: a) investigation   b) ransom note   c) subtraction   d) kidnapping

5. seclude: a) silence   b) shut off from view   c) apprehend   d) leave out

6. rectilinear: a) righteous   b) vertical   c) circular   d) in a straight line

7. traduce: a) publicly deny   b) publicly defame   c) defend openly   d) hide away

8. lineage: a) grandchildren   b) drawings   c) line of descent   d) yardage

9. verbatim: a) verbose   b) word for word   c) in sign language   d) like a proverb

10. recluse: a) one who lives in willing isolation   b) prisoner   c) patient   d) alienist

EXERCISE II Circle the letter of the best choice to complete each sentence.

1. If going out to eat precludes your seeing a movie, a) you will see the movie   b) you will probably be late for dinner   c) you won't be able to do both   d) you will do neither

2. A rectilinear sketch is drawn   a) all with straight lines   b) larger than life   c) sloppily   d) with arabesques

3. To repeat a conversation verbatim, a person must have   a) a loud voice   b) typing skills   c) an excellent memory   d) hypnotic powers

4. Traducing a friend is a kind of   a) retreat from intimacy   b) loyalty   c) testimonial   d) betrayal

5. To abduct a child is to take him or her away   a) illegally   b) on short notice   c) to private school   d) by court order

6. An environment conducive to physical well-being is   a) chronic   b) luxurious   c) healthful   d) noxious

7. A secluded meeting is held in   a) a public forum   b) a private spot   c) an emergency   d) a classroom

8. In delineating a problem, one   a) blames others for it   b) makes it harder to understand   c) resolves it   d) indicates its nature and scope

9. A racehorse's lineage includes his   a) inoculations   b) sire and dam   c) owner   d) record of earnings

10. A recluse likes to live   a) in seclusion   b) exclusively   c) in abduction   d) by traducing society

EXERCISE III Antonyms. Draw a line connecting each word with the word or phrase most nearly its *opposite*.

1. seclude
2. recluse
3. preclude
4. traduce
5. verbatim
6. conducive
7. rectilinear

curved 1
in paraphrase 2
social butterfly 3
make inevitable 4
preventive 5
uphold the honor of 6
expose to view 7

Using Roots

The root meaning, or etymology, of a word is hardly ever precisely the same as its meaning in current usage. Knowing where a word comes from doesn't tell you exactly what the word means now or how to use it. For example, you might figure out that *deduct* comes from *de* (away) and *duct* (lead). But how do you learn that one can deduct a number from a total, or an expense from a taxable income, but not a cow from a barn? The quickest way is to look up the precise definition of *deduct* in a good dictionary. The surest way—and this is probably the way you learned *deduct*—is to read it and hear it over and over again in context.

What good, then, is knowing etymologies? Once you've learned a word, roots can help you fix it in your memory. The familiar root, which connects the new word to words you already know, can be a clue to remind you of what the word means.

LESSON 2

Vocal, "having to do with the voice," comes from *vox,* the Latin word for "voice." There's a related verb in Latin—*vocare,* "to call." *Vox* and *vocare* have given rise to lots of English words. Knowing that the *voc* root means "voice" or "call" will make it easier to remember the meanings of:

vocation—a calling, a career or lifework, especially one to which a person feels dedicated. *Like many others, he had chosen medicine as his vocation out of a desire to help people and to receive a lot of recognition.*

avocation—hobby, work done for pleasure and interest rather than profit. *By profession she's an engineer, but her avocation is flying.*

vociferous—making a noisy outcry, shouting. *The class was vociferous in its objection to the surprise quiz.*

irrevocable—not able to be called back or undone. *The decision was irrevocable: there was no turning back once the letter was mailed. Irrevocable* is formed from the verb *revoke,* "to call back."

evocative—calling forth, tending to remind, suggestive. *To me nothing is more evocative of spring than the scent of fresh lilacs.* The adjective comes from the verb *evoke,* "to call up as a mental image."

equivocate—to mislead, especially to tell the truth in such a way that it is misunderstood. *The government equivocated in reporting that unemployment had declined; the number of people looking for work had declined, but only because many job seekers had given up looking.* The adjective for something deliberately ambiguous, for something that equivocates, is *equivocal.*

Another Latin word, *similis,* is already familiar to you through the English word *similar. Similis* means "like." It is the root of a whole family of English words, including:

similitude—state of being similar, likeness, image or counterpart. *The three types of zebra may not be as closely related as their apparent similitude has led naturalists to assume.*

verisimilitude—appearance of truth. *The set designer reconstructed the presidential car with great verisimilitude.*

assimilate—to absorb and make part of something larger, become like and be incorporated into an entity or system. *In time, each generation of immigrants becomes assimilated into the American population.*

facsimile—an exact copy. *To be certain of the original punctuation, the editor studied a facsimile of the author's manuscript.*

simile—a verbal comparison using *like* or *as.* *"My love is like a red, red rose" is a classic simile.*

Answers to the following exercises are on page 198.

EXERCISE I Synonyms. Draw a iine connecting each word with the word or phrase that means most nearly the same.

1. assimilating   summoning up
2. simile   appearance of accuracy
3. irrevocable   kind of comparison
4. equivocating   clamorous
5. avocation   line of work
6. similitude   resemblance
7. facsimile   perfect reproduction
8. evocative   making like something else
9. vociferous   hobby
10. verisimilitude   deliberately misleading
11. vocation   impossible to call back

EXERCISE II Choose the best word to complete each sentence. Write it in the blank.

1. For most people, sports are a(n) _____; very few can make a living as athletes.

similitude   avocation

vocation   facsimile

2. The _____ of the portrait is striking; one feels convinced that this is how the man really looked.

assimilation   simile

verisimilitude   avocation

3. A photocopy is a(n) _____ of an original page.

   facsimile

   avocation

   vocation

   assimilation

4. The proverb "There's no use crying over spilled milk" means that the past is
   _____.

   equivocal

   irrevocable

   facsimile

   vociferous

5. An organism grows by _____ nutrients.

   assimilating

   revoking

   evoking

   equivocating

6. He looked on teaching not merely as a job but as a _____ to
   which he could happily devote his life.

   facsimile

   verisimilitude

   similitude

   vocation

7. An effective stage set need not be elaborate; it need only be _____
   of the appropriate mood.

   vociferous

   an avocation

   evocative

   a similitude

8. "She eats like a pig" is an example of a(n) _____.

   vocation

   evocation

   verisimilitude

   simile

9. Not wanting to admit that he hadn't read the book, he made a(n)
   _____ response.

   assimilated

   equivocal

   vociferous

   irrevocable

10. A family resemblance often includes a _____ of manners and
    speech.

    similitude

    vocation

    verisimilitude

    simile

11. The shouting of the hecklers broke out again in a(n) _____ din.

    irrevocable

    vociferous

    equivocal

    evocative

EXERCISE III Circle the letter of the best choice to complete each sentence.

1. A picture is evocative of the countryside if it   a) is a photograph
   b) reminds you of being in the country   c) is by Van Gogh   d) is a
   cityscape

2. Equivocating is a way of   a) hedging   b) deliberating   c) doodling
   d) intimidating

3. A vociferous crowd is not   a) riotous   b) riled up   c) enthusiastic
   d) quiet

4. While a vocation provides a living, an avocation is pursued   a) relentlessly
   b) under duress   c) for pleasure   d) for tax purposes

5. A similitude to the truth is called   a) a simile   b) an aversion   c) a lie
   d) a verisimilitude

6. A student assimilates information by   a) talking   b) asking questions
   c) buying books   d) studying

7. A facsimile reproduces an original text   a) in every detail   b) in a
   condensed version   c) with annotations   d) in paraphrase

8. A simile is a figure of speech that   a) insults people   b) makes a
   comparison   c) copies something exactly   d) is rarely used

9. If a mistake is not irrevocable, it   a) can be analyzed   b) is fatal   c) can
   be corrected   d) is noticeable

LESSON 3

A **figure of speech** is a way of speaking that is out of the ordinary or nonliteral. A **simile**, defined in Lesson 2, is one kind of figure. If I say that my aunt was coming down the street like a ship under full sail, I probably mean that she was moving fast, bearing down on me, and looking large and awesome. You, as a listener, understand that saying my aunt looked like a ship was a figure of speech.

A **metaphor** is another figure of speech. Like a simile, a metaphor makes a comparison, but it does so without using *like* or *as*. If I tell you that as a child Angela was an ugly duckling, I am using a metaphor. I do not mean that Angela was formerly an unattractive young duck, complete with feathers and webbed feet. As a listener, you understand what I mean—that Angela was awkward or odd-looking as a child but that she grew up to be beautiful, like the ugly duckling who grew into a swan. You know that this is figurative, not literal, language.

We use figurative language all the time without thinking about it. For instance, budgets are "slashed," issues are "sidestepped," costs "skyrocket," and eaters "pig out." Many words have taken on permanent figurative meanings in addition to their literal ones. You should know both the literal and figurative uses of the following words:

caustic—biting, burning, stinging. *The surface of the wood had been marred by some caustic chemical. Her caustic comments hurt the other girl's feelings.*

abrasive—scraping or rubbing; annoyingly harsh or jarring. *Sandpaper has an abrasive surface. The high-pitched whine of the machinery was abrasive to my nerves.* The adjective *abrasive* comes from the verb *abrade,* "to scrape, wear away by rubbing." *Abrade* is used only in the literal sense: *sandpaper abrades wood.*

volatile—tending to evaporate quickly, turning to vapor easily; very changeable or fickle. *A volatile liquid must be stored at low temperatures. A volatile temper is quickly aroused and quickly soothed.*

rabid—having rabies, violent, maddened; fanatically devoted to a belief or cause. *Bitten by an infected squirrel, the dog turned rabid. The man's rabid devotees looked on him as a holy prophet.*

myopic—nearsighted; shortsighted. *His myopic vision made the distant lamps appear as huge globes of colored light. Their failure to make long-term plans was myopic.* The noun for "nearsightedness" is *myopia.*

insular—pertaining to an island; narrow-minded or prejudiced as a result of cultural isolation. *Puerto Rico is an insular commonwealth. She made the insular assumption that people of other cultures were somehow wrongheaded or misled.*

scabrous—rough to the touch, scabby; rough or impolite, especially concerning sex, improper. *The heat had made the varnish bubble up, giving the desk a scabrous surface. The comedian's scabrous jokes made some members of the audience blush.*

profound—very deep; intellectually or emotionally deep, thorough. *They descended into a profound and narrow ravine. Socrates is our archetype of a profound thinker.*

Answers to the following exercises are on page 198.

EXERCISE I Synonyms. Circle the letter of the word or phrase closest in meaning to the given word. The meaning may be literal or figurative.

1. abrasive: a) blatant b) grubby c) blithering d) grating

2. myopic: a) not looking ahead b) blind c) wearing glasses d) unpredictable

3. scabrous: a) sprightly b) risqué c) cadaverous d) unhealthy

4. profound: a) irreligious b) circumspect c) deep d) submerged

5. caustic: a) dissatisfied b) burning c) scouring d) causal

6. insular: a) tropical b) of an island c) using insulin d) padded

7. rabid: a) raving b) racist c) vagrant d) irritated

8. volatile: a) piquant b) unstable c) rushed d) charming

EXERCISE II Circle the letter of the best choice to complete each sentence.

1. Myopia can be rectified by a) censorship b) corrective lenses c) psychoanalysis d) travel

2. A volatile substance will a) remain solid at high temperatures b) be viscous c) be inert d) quickly turn from liquid to gas

3. An insular territory is a) peninsular b) autonomous c) surrounded by water d) uncivilized

4. A scabrous surface is characteristic of a) a wound b) the sea c) silk d) felt

5. A rabid devotion is a) listless b) excessive c) estimable d) wary of commitment

6. Evidence of abrasion by glaciers is found in   a) underground springs   b) river deltas   c) scratches on rocks   d) prehistoric legends

7. An example of a caustic substance is   a) pumice   b) pewter   c) lye   d) mineral water

8. A profound insight is not   a) trivial   b) of lasting importance   c) a sign of intelligence   d) an intellectual act

9. Figurative language is not   a) common in everyday speech   b) proper   c) intelligible   d) intended to be taken literally

10. A metaphor is a kind of   a) falsehood   b) implied comparison   c) mistake in grammar   d) shortsighted error

EXERCISE III Fill in the blanks from the list of words below.

myopic	caustic
rabid	insular
abrasive	volatile
profound	scabrous

1. His flippant put-downs and cutting sarcasm gave him a reputation for _____ wit.

2. Foaming at the mouth, the _____ animal had to be shot.

3. The proposal to build a new school is _____ because it does not take into account projected shifts in population over the next ten years.

4. Even her supporters admitted that she had a(n) _____ personality; her tactless and opinionated manner undoubtedly cost her some votes.

5. With no firsthand experience of the world beyond their own village, they were _____ in their views and somewhat mistrustful of outsiders.

6. His _____ stories embarrassed acquaintances who weren't accustomed to ribald conversation.

7. The woman felt that her grief was too _____ to be expressed in words.

8. The patient's mood was extremely _____ — he was overjoyed one moment and plunged into gloom the next.

LESSON 4

As we saw in Lesson 3, words are frequently used in more than one way, but the ways are usually related. Over centuries of use, words have been stretched to fit looser or more figurative contexts. But while they are applied more loosely or more figuratively, they may still retain their older meanings. You should be aware of the range of meanings for the following words:

gall—to chafe, irritate the skin by rubbing; to annoy, vex, or humiliate. *The ill-fitting saddle galled the horse's back. It galled the children to hear the praise lavished on their worthless and obnoxious cousin.*

espouse—to marry; to adopt as a cause, advocate or devote oneself to a cause or belief. *Henry VIII is often best remembered for having espoused six wives and for having beheaded two of them. A hopeless romantic, she loved to espouse lost causes.* You can see the relation of *espouse* to *spouse.* The figurative use is now more common than the literal meaning "to marry."

apprehend—to catch or catch on, to seize physically or grasp mentally. *Police apprehended the suspect. I could not apprehend what he was trying to tell me.* The Latin verb *prehendere,* the source of our *apprehend,* was also used by the Romans in the double sense of physical and mental grasping. The same root gives us *prehensile,* "able to grasp," as the tail of a monkey, which wraps around branches. The noun *apprehension* means three things: 1) a catching, 2) understanding, 3) fear or dread.

breach—a breaking, an opening or gap; a failure to keep the terms of a promise or law. *Troops poured in through a breach in the fortified wall. When they failed to deliver the goods, they were guilty of a breach of contract. Breach* isn't from Latin; it originates from the same Old English word that gave us *break.*

provincial—of a province, rustic, of the country; narrow-minded or unsophisticated in outlook. *The mayor of the town was engaged in a feud with the provincial government.* An opposite of *provincial* used in one sense is *urban* and in another sense the opposite of *provincial* is

urbane—suave, smoothly well-mannered, and sophisticated. *The man's urbane conversation gave others the impression that he had traveled widely.* Both *urban* and *urbane* come from the Latin root *urbs,* "city." It was traditionally assumed that polished and sophisticated manners could only be learned in the city.

consonance—a sounding together, harmony, agreement. *Their consonance of opinion in all matters made for a peaceful household. Sonare* in Latin is "to sound." *Consonance* literally means "sounding with," but is used more generally to refer to any kind of harmonious agreement.

confluence—a flowing together; a crowd or throng. *Cairo, Illinois is located at the confluence of the Ohio and Mississippi Rivers. There was a large confluence of shoppers waiting for the store to open. Fluere* in Latin means "to flow." The same root gives us *influence,* literally a "flowing in."

11

maelstrom—a whirlpool; a violently agitated, uncontrolled, and turbulent condition or state. *The ship was twisted in the maelstrom. Caught up in a maelstorm of rage, he struck out blindly. Maelstrom* comes from an archaic Dutch name for a whirlpool in the Arctic Ocean off the coast of Norway. Originally the name of a specific whirlpool, it has been expanded to cover any whirlpool and, even more loosely, any violently turbulent state.

Answers to the following exercises are on page 198.

EXERCISE I Synonyms. Keeping in mind the range of meanings of each word, circle the letter of the word or phrase closest in meaning to the given word.

1. consonance: a) identity b) lack of conflict c) reunion d) fluorescence

2. breach: a) antipathy b) atrophy c) gap d) battle

3. espouse: a) distort b) support as a cause c) sympathize d) bless

4. apprehend: a) make clear b) opt c) expose to view d) take into custody

5. confluence: a) a crowding together b) a separating c) euphony d) appreciation

6. provincial: a) genteel b) with a proviso c) sham d) unsophisticated

7. gall: a) rein in b) muzzle c) vex d) alter

8. maelstrom: a) violent confusion b) plague c) high velocity d) aggression

9. urbane: a) obtuse b) abstruse in thought c) polished in manner d) uncommunicative

10. espouse: a) wed b) eschew c) legalize d) court

11. provincial: a) forested b) popular c) belonging to provinces d) temporal

EXERCISE II Fill in the blanks from the list of words below.

urbanity	apprehension
confluence	espousal
maelstrom	consonance
breach	

1. As the tornado brushed by the house, the peaceful home became a(n) _____ of flying objects and shattering glass.

2. Before the _____ of the suspect, the whole community was rife with fear.

3. The candidate's _____ of strict pollution standards appealed to voters who felt that the environment was being irreparably damaged.

4. Failing to thank people properly for gifts is a(n) _____ of etiquette.

5. At the _____ of the two rivers we parted company with the other

canoe and paddled up the smaller branch.

6. A person of such _____ is not easily flustered by a sudden change in plans.

7. I felt sure, judging from the complete _____ of their views, that they would become fast friends.

EXERCISE III Circle the letter of the best choice to complete each sentence.

1. Apprehension can mean both understanding and   a) aggravation   b) fearful foreboding   c) penalty   d) preparation

2. A breach of regulations is a kind of   a) concordance   b) reprimand c) authorization   d) disobedience

3. A provincial outlook usually results from   a) lack of broad experience b) too much education   c) curiosity   d) expensive tastes

4. Maelstrom literally refers to   a) lightning   b) a tornado   c) a whirlpool   d) massive confusion

5. The opposite of gall is   a) soothe   b) enervate   c) demur   d) melt

6. In a confluence, people   a) converge in a mass   b) scatter   c) babble d) march in formation

7. According to its root meaning, urbane manners belong to   a) ancient peoples   b) young sophisticates   c) cityfolk   d) émigrés

8. In the older meaning of the word, a man espoused   a) a cause   b) a wife   c) a country   d) principles

9. Consonance is achieved by   a) monotony   b) focusing a lens c) dissension   d) blending sounds pleasantly

LESSON 5

The words in this lesson are all nouns (names) for people's characters and feelings.

mettle—degree of spirit of courage, worth of character. *She proved her mettle by risking her life to rescue her companions.* The adjective *mettlesome* means "high-spirited" or "fiery."

contrition—sincere remorse, regret for one's actions. *They were overwhelmed by contrition when they realized the damage they had caused.*

veracity—truthfulness, honesty. *The author's veracity was called into question by evidence that some dates had been changed.*

acumen—sharpness of mind, keen mental perception. *The business acumen of many early industrialists contributed to their success.*

diffidence—shyness, lack of assertiveness. *His diffidence before such a distinguished visitor prevented him from expressing his own views.*

fortitude—moral or emotional strength to endure hardship or misfortune. *It takes fortitude to do one's duty in the face of universal disapproval.* From the Latin *fortis* (strong), *fortitude* is closely related to *fortify* (make strong), *fort* (a stronghold), and *forte* (a strong point).

hypocrisy—acting in contradiction to what one professes, feigning to be what one is not, playing a part in order to deceive. *It is sheer hypocrisy for you to condemn her for remaining silent when that is exactly what you would have done under the same circumstances.*

lassitude—feeling of weariness, languor. *The heat created a lassitude among the tourists that caused them to postpone sightseeing.*

petulance—petty fretfulness. *Petulance is her most annoying trait: she tends to whine and sulk when things go wrong.*

sobriety—soberness, trait of being moderate (especially in the use of alcohol), or sedate and serious in one's conduct. *The Puritans placed high value on qualities such as sobriety and industriousness, qualities essential to their survival in the New World.*

temerity—foolish audacity, recklessness, rashness. *After the teacher's lecture on paying attention, only John had the temerity to ask him once again to repeat the assignment.*

Answers to the following exercises are on pages 198 and 199.

EXERCISE I Antonyms. Circle the letter of the word or phrase most *opposite* in meaning to the given word.

1. lassitude: a) reprimand b) intense vigor c) strong preference
   d) emotional equilibrium

2. contrition: a) sorrow b) wearing away c) lack of compunction d) guilt by association

3. diffidence: a) bold self-assurance b) similitude c) secretive manner
   d) knowledge

4. hypocrisy: a) humaneness b) consistency of word and deed c) depravity
   d) resistance to reform

5. fortitude: a) spinelessness in the face of adversity b) love of conflict
   c) ingenuousness d) betrayal to an enemy

6. sobriety: a) self-denial b) laziness c) drunken abandon d) self-reliance

7. mettle: a) stupidity b) weak character c) clairvoyance d) flamboyance

8. acumen: a) inebriation b) intellectual inadequacy c) sincerity d) poor manners

9. temerity: a) daring b) subtlety c) awesomeness d) timidity

10. petulance: a) impudence b) patient attitude c) prostration d) craven conduct

11. veracity: a) dishonesty b) efficiency c) small appetite d) false modesty

EXERCISE II Choose the best word to complete each sentence. Write it in the blank.

1. The editorial accused the mayor of _____ in knowingly promising improvements that he will not be able to deliver.

sobriety	lassitude
hypocrisy	acumen

2. One expects such _____ from children, who do not have the maturity to cope easily with disappointments.

petulance	fortitude
mettle	contrition

3. The doctor's fine _____ in psychological matters makes him a good judge of when people are lying.

veracity	acumen
temerity	mettle

4. The patient complained of abnormal _____ and loss of appetite.

lassitude	diffidence
fortitude	sobriety

5. Only a fool would have the _____ to insult a short-tempered gunslinger.

diffidence	mettle
temerity	hypocrisy

6. The thoroughbred had the _____ appearance of a born champion.

hypocritical	mettlesome
diffident	petulant

7. Her conservative clothes, measured speech, and calm face give an impression of complete _____.

petulance	temerity
sobriety	contrition

8. If he's always told us the truth before, why should we doubt his _____ now?

sobriety	hypocrisy
contrition	veracity

9. The sailors endured the poor rations and cramped quarters with patient _____.

temerity	acumen
lassitude	fortitude

10. _____ makes an individual defer to the opinions of others.

Veracity	Diffidence
Acumen	Fortitude

11. The student expressed her _____ in a formal note of apology.

contrition	veracity
lassitude	petulance

EXERCISE III From memory, try to complete the following sentences with words from this lesson. The first letter of each answer is given before the blank. Write your answers in the blanks.

1. She has the [a] _____ to tell when a client is really ready to make a purchase.

2. The child felt such [c] _____ for breaking her sister's doll that she offered to buy her another one just like it.

3. Although she is very interested in the subject, her [d] _____ keeps her from participating in the class discussion.

4. The Biblical Job, who undergoes every kind of misfortune, exemplifies [f] _____.

5. People who publicly condemn conduct they themselves indulge in privately are guilty of [h] _____.

6. The exhausting ordeal left the travelers with a feeling of [l] _____; it took several days for them to recoup their energy.

7. A natural disaster tests the [m] _____ of everyone caught up in it.

8. He reacted with spiteful [p] _____, blaming the others for their mutual predicament and refusing to lift a finger to help himself.

9. I had expected a famous and venerable historian to be a model of [s] _____; instead he was a tipsy gentleman with a whimsical sense of humor.

10. The boss was annoyed that his secretary had the [t] _____ to interrupt him when he had ordered that he not be disturbed.

11. [V] _____ is an essential attribute of a good journalist; he or she has an obligation to report events accurately.

LESSON 6

The following are ten nouns for naming people.

savant—a wise and learned person, scholar of exceptional knowledge or wisdom. *The professor was a savant of psychological research who enjoyed an international reputation for brilliance.*

pedant—a person who makes a needless display of learning or who is preoccupied with trivial points of scholarship. *The lecturer was a pedant who made several allusions to literary works with which his audience was unfamiliar.* Both a *savant* and a *pedant* are people of learning. *Savant*, however, is a positive term, often connoting wisdom along with exceptional knowledge. A *pedant*, on the other hand, lacks judgment or a sense of proportion about expressing or applying his learning.

connoisseur—a person with special knowledge or judgment in some matter of taste or the arts. *A connoisseur of wines has a cultivated and discriminating palate.* Although we borrowed it from French, *connoisseur* goes back to the Latin *cognoscere*, "to know." Like the previous entries, *connoisseur* connotes a kind of knowledge, but a knowledge of aesthetic or sensual experiences rather than of scholarly matters.

martinet—a rigid and petty disciplinarian. *The captain was a martinet who considered an unpolished button an example of criminal negligence.*

novice—a person new to a job or activity, someone inexperienced. *A novice in the job, she needed more time than an experienced worker to complete the same tasks.*

curmudgeon—a churlish, grumpy, unfriendly person. *The old curmudgeon was so difficult to get along with that no one could stand to work for him.*

incumbent—a person holding public office or church office. *The young vicar was given the benefice when the incumbent retired.*

skeptic—a person who doubts, especially one who questions or suspends judgment on beliefs commonly accepted. *A skeptic will not be convinced without substantial evidence.* Also spelled *sceptic*.

misogynist—woman-hater, usually a man. *Although he corresponded affectionately with a lady he addressed as Stella, Jonathan Swift was in general a misogynist.*

vixen—shrewish, mean, bad-tempered woman. *He spent evenings in the pub complaining about his vixen of a wife.* A *vixen* is literally a female fox. Used figuratively of a woman, it is similar in meaning to *shrew*, another animal term. It is slightly more polite than *bitch*, which literally means a "female dog."

Answers to the following exercises are on page 199.

EXERCISE I Antonyms. Circle the letter of the word or phrase most *opposite* in meaning to the given word.

1. martinet: a) puppet b) indecisive person c) fastidious eater d) someone careless about procedure

2. novice: a) veteran b) layman c) elderly person d) candidate

3. pedant: a) kind person b) one who conceals his learning c) self-sacrificing person d) slob

4. vixen: a) knowledgeable person b) mousy girl c) stupid woman d) ugly person

5. skeptic: a) serious thinker b) trustworthy individual c) loyal friend d) credulous person

6. savant: a) ignoramus b) specialist c) scholar d) stickler for discipline

7. misogynist: a) gregarious person b) philosopher c) lover of women d) lover of animals

8. incumbent: a) nonprofessional b) competent worker c) elected official d) person not presently in office

9. curmudgeon: a) amiable person b) loud talker c) person easily deceived d) sane person

10. connoisseur: a) person of learning b) native citizen c) spectator
    d) person with unsophisticated tastes

EXERCISE II Fill in the blanks from the list of words below.

savant	misogynist
skeptic	martinet
vixen	novice
connoisseur	pedant
curmudgeon	incumbent

1. The _____, although his name is likely to be more familiar than his opponent's, has the disadvantage of being blamed for whatever is wrong.

2. In the old-fashioned stereotype, a schoolmaster is a(n) _____ who insists that pupils be in the classroom precisely on time, seated at their desks with their hands folded.

3. As a(n) _____ of the ballet, he never failed to attend the local premiere of a new work.

4. The book is the work of a(n) _____ —both encyclopedic in its erudition and strikingly original in its approach.

5. The _____ had no friends and showed no desire to make any.

6. She was a nagging _____, always critical of her spouse and scornful of her neighbors.

7. At the time we thought she was just a(n) _____, but later we were glad that we had been forced to learn all those trivial dates and obscure facts.

8. Since he is only a(n) _____ at skiing, this slope may be hazardous for him.

9. A(n) _____ is happiest when he can avoid female company.

10. Doubting Thomas was the _____ among the followers of Jesus.

EXERCISE III Circle the letter of the best choice to complete each sentence.

1. A motto for skeptics is a) Show me b) Excelsior c) Live free or die d) Don't look back

2. When you ask a question, a pedant will give you a) an equivocal answer b) a blank stare c) a succinct response d) more information than you need

3. A misogynist a) is usually a woman b) shouldn't marry c) is thoroughly professional d) is an accomplished cook

4. A curmudgeon will probably not be a) hospitable b) hostile c) recalcitrant d) peevish

5. A savant is generally   a) unpredictable   b) a charlatan   c) under a doctor's care   d) highly educated

6. As a term for a woman, vixen is   a) flattering   b) voracious c) derogatory   d) inconsequential

7. A student who is a novice at college life is probably   a) on the Dean's List   b) a graduating senior   c) a freshman   d) very active in clubs

8. When her term expires, the incumbent will   a) be paroled   b) retire from the stage   c) renew the loan   d) run for higher office

9. A martinet is offended by   a) punctilious decorum   b) minor infractions   c) injustice   d) demonstrations of affection

10. A connoisseur of painting probably   a) visits museums   b) paints c) despises Impressionism   d) knows nothing about perspective

Most unflattering names—like slob or martinet—can be applied to people of either sex. But English also has a large vocabulary of derogatory terms used solely to describe women. Check your dictionary for the definitions of:

slattern	_____
slut	_____
harridan	_____
virago	_____
hoyden	_____
termagant	_____

This misogynistic list reveals a lot about sexual politics in traditional English culture. All the above terms were invented to censure the many women who over the centuries have failed to display the supposedly feminine virtues of docility and good housekeeping. There are no equivalent terms used solely for men: men have never been particularly blamed for being bold, sloppy, scolding, quarrelsome, or noisy.

LESSON 7

The dozen adjectives below can all be used to describe people.

effusive—overflowing with emotion, expressing feeling to excess. *The new attendant concealed her nervousness behind an effusive friendliness.*

dispassionate—detached, objective, free of strong feelings or bias. *When his resentment subsided, he was able to take a more dispassionate view and realize that he too was at fault.*

contumacious—refusing to obey, obstinately resistant to authority. *The tutor despaired of ever controlling his spoiled, contumacious pupils.*

Gcul avenncular

beleaguered—under seige, surrounded, beset by hostile people or forces. *During the delay, the beleaguered railroad conductor was bombarded with questions and complaints from the irate passengers.*

avuncular—like an uncle, in the relationship of an uncle. *He was moved by avuncular concern to offer his nephew advice.*

impecunious—poor, without money, especially as a permanent condition. *In* Tess of the D'Urbervilles, *the Durbeyfields are an impecunious family of many children and precarious income.*

jubilant—very happy, joyful in a triumphant or excited way. *The jubilant populace took to the streets to celebrate the revolution.*

facetious—not serious, amusing, joking at an inappropriate time. *We were too upset by the results to be entertained by Claire's facetious commentary on the election.*

corpulent—fat, fleshy, obese. *Constant indulgence in rich foods had made him corpulent.*

splenetic—fretfully spiteful, peevish. *The heat, the cranky children, the pressure of a heavy workload—all contributed to the woman's splenetic outburst. Splenetic* is related to *spleen;* it was once thought that anger originated in the spleen, just as the heart was the seat of love.

pensive—thoughtful, especially in a sad or moody way. *She was quiet and pensive all afternoon, thinking about the old days and her late husband.*

indolent—lazy, tending to avoid work or activity. *An indolent student will often learn just enough to get by.*

Answers to the following exercises are on page 199.

EXERCISE I Synonyms. Draw a line connecting each word with the word or phrase that means most nearly the same.

1. dispassionate	inactive by choice
2. beleaguered	lost in thought
3. impecunious	penniless
4. facetious	besieged
5. splenetic	unemotional
6. indolent	overjoyed
7. corpulent	disobedient
8. effusive	very overweight
9. pensive	peevish
10. contumacious	joking
11. jubilant	like an uncle
12. avuncular	too demonstrative

EXERCISE II Fill in the blanks from the list of words below.

pensive	effusive
corpulent	avuncular
beleaguered	dispassionate
jubilant	contumacious
splenetic	indolent
facetious	impecunious

1. In later years the great actor lost his trim figure and became quite
   _____.

2. He worked hard, but his work paid little; he was a(n) _____
   man, always in debt.

3. Though _____ by the pranks and derision of his classmates, the
   boy persisted in his eccentric behavior.

4. A(n) _____ crowd thronged the avenue to welcome home the
   victorious team.

5. Please don't take my _____ remarks seriously; I was only joking
   to cheer you up.

6. Since we hardly knew them, we were somewhat embarrassed by their
   _____ greeting; they treated us like long-lost brothers.

7. At one side of the canvas stood a(n) _____ figure, seeming lost
   in thought amid the bustle of the carnival.

8. I like to stay active even during vacations; a workaholic cannot bear to be
   _____.

9. Although he never wished for children of his own, he had a(n)
   _____ fondness for his sister's brood.

10. By putting aside her own personal stake in the outcome, Jane made a(n)
    _____ appraisal of the case.

11. Grumpy with exhaustion and disappointment, he lashed out at his friend
    with _____ recriminations.

12. This horse is a(n) _____ animal that delights in doing the very
    opposite of what you ask.

EXERCISE III Antonyms. Circle the letter of the word or phrase most *opposite*
in meaning to the given word.

1. pensive: a) unreflecting b) hale c) affable d) idiotic

2. jubilant: a) slavish b) suicidal c) obsequious d) jocund

3. splenetic: a) cheerful b) distraught c) orderly d) vicious

4. indolent: a) respectful b) well-off c) energetic d) well-rested

5. effusive: a) immoderate b) recessive c) fragile d) reserved

6. avuncular: a) like a relative b) oracular c) like a stranger d) geriatric

7. facetious: a) bantering b) insistent c) politically sound d) unnecessarily
   solemn

8. contumacious: a) sneering b) pliant c) pleasurable d) laughing

9. dispassionate: a) passive b) highly emotional c) revivified
   d) compassionate

10. corpulent: a) emaciated b) spiritual c) spirited d) healthy

11. beleaguered: a) independent   b) disconnected   c) free from attack
    d) protected from competition

12. impecunious: a) wealthy   b) subservient   c) not fussy   d) not curious

EXERCISE IV Circle the letter of the best choice to complete each sentence.

1. A dispassionate account does not   a) use emotionally loaded terms   b) pull
   punches   c) give the facts   d) concern matters of importance

2. Her jubilant face told me that she had   a) lost her keys   b) lost her temper
   c) won a victory   d) run a race

3. A splenetic person is frequently   a) ill   b) dispassionate   c) penitential
   d) discontent

4. He is somewhat older than I, but his avuncular manner   a) is infantile
   b) makes him seem younger   c) makes him less outgoing
   d) exaggerates the difference

5. As a teenager she was much too indolent to   a) go without makeup
   b) cave in to parental demands   c) play tennis   d) talk on the
   phone for hours

6. An indolent life and a passion for desserts can lead to   a) effusiveness
   b) corpulence   c) facetiousness   d) contumely

7. A beleaguered person feels   a) hemmed in   b) demanding   c) compulsive
   d) unconstrained

8. A worker can be impecunious because he does not know how to   a) make
   friends   b) let off steam   c) budget his finances   d) run an office

9. A contumacious individual resists   a) improvement   b) dieting
   c) authority   d) fighting

10. In a pensive mood, one   a) fritters   b) ponders   c) gibbers   d) chatters

11. People often become more effusive when they drink because they are
    a) more likely to take offense   b) accident-prone   c) more sensual
    d) less inhibited about their feelings

12. Facetious talk is intended to   a) wound   b) play for time   c) amuse   d) be
    profound

LESSON 8

Here are twelve more adjectives, words that describe or limit nouns.

ephemeral—short-lived, passing quickly. *As an adolescent he had an intense but ephemeral passion for collecting postcards. Ephemeral* is derived from a Greek word meaning "for a day." An *ephemerid* is a May fly, an insect whose adult life lasts only a day.

feasible—able to be performed or executed by human means or agency, practicable. *It is feasible to complete the project by July.*

germane—pertinent, on the subject at hand. *The facts were not germane to the argument.*

impeccable—faultless, perfect. *Successful comedy depends on impeccable timing.*

moribund—dying. *The moribund tree put out fewer and fewer leaves each spring.*

putative—supposed rather than known, reputed. *His putative wealth was exaggerated by his ostentation.*

specious—deceptively plausible, only seeming to be good or correct. *He defended his opinion with specious arguments that could be refuted by anyone familiar with the facts.*

inherent—inborn, existing as a basic or natural characteristic, not learned or acquired. *A love of hunting is inherent in cats.*

obligatory—required, binding morally or legally, having the nature of an obligation. *He feels nothing in common with his family, yet he makes an obligatory visit to them once or twice a year.*

superfluous—extra, beyond what is necessary. *It was clear from the group's boredom that his lengthy explanations were superfluous.* The Latin prefix and stem *super fluere* literally mean "over flow." The *fluere* stem also gives us *fluent* (flowing), *fluid* (something that flows), and

mellifluous—(literally, honey-flowing) very sweet and smooth, honied. *Her best feature as an actress is her mellifluous speaking voice. Mellifluous* is always used to describe things sweet to the ears, not to the tastebuds.

recumbent—lying down, resting. *The painting depicted the goddess recumbent on a sumptuous couch, attended by her son Cupid.*

Answers to the following exercises are on page 199.

EXERCISE I Antonyms. Circle the letter of the word or phrase most *opposite* in meaning to the given word.

1. moribund: a) seasonal b) budding c) decaying d) evergreen

2. obligatory: a) fast-paced b) insufferable c) disinterested d) optional

3. impeccable: a) marred b) contrary c) lined d) sinful

4. feasible: a) effortless b) impossible to effect c) predictable
   d) momentous

5. recumbent: a) out of office b) not required c) standing at the ready
   d) causing panic

6. superfluous: a) repressed b) essential c) inordinate d) dammed up

7. specious: a) valid b) remarkable c) humorous d) biological

8. inherent: a) acquired b) insufficient c) creative d) genetic

9. ephemeral: a) real b) prized c) durable d) artificial

10. germane: a) ancestral b) irresponsible c) insipid d) irrelevant

11. mellifluous: a) bittersweet b) rasping c) acoustic d) sour-tasting

12. putative: a) salacious b) hypothetical c) known with certainty
    d) concealed from view

EXERCISE II Fill in the blanks from the list of words below.

superfluous	ephemeral
germane	moribund
putative	specious
mellifluous	impeccable
feasible	inherent
recumbent	obligatory

1. The topic was well-defined and the writing _____. The instructor
   found nothing to criticize in the essay.

2. In the 1930s Hollywood's Hayes Office imposed industry-sponsored censorship on American films. It became _____ for good guys to
   win and bad guys to be punished.

3. The concerto is a lush, romantic work ideally suited to the _____
   tones of the violin.

4. He spent two hours of the afternoon _____ on the living-room
   sofa with a book in his hand, fast asleep.

5. The fame of personalities in the news is _____; in a few years, or
   sometimes weeks, most of them are forgotten.

6. The junta's _____ motive in holding elections was to encourage
   political participation, but some observers believed the junta was merely
   trying to ferret out the opposition.

7. Since funds have been cut drastically, the program is _____.
   Without renewed support it will undoubtedly cease operation by the end
   of the year.

8. Artful makeup and indirect lighting gave the ailing celebrity a(n) _____
   appearance of health.

9. Since we need only three yards for the costume, the rest of this material
   is _____.

10. Mandy had taken a lot of notes on revivalism in America but not all the information was _____ to the more limited scope of her paper.

11. Defining social goals is not enough; we must come up with _____ plans for realizing them.

12. All healthy human infants seem to have a(n) _____ aptitude for learning any language they are exposed to.

EXERCISE III Circle the letter of the best choice to complete each sentence.

1. A mellifluous sound is typical of _____.
   a) bees   b) freight trains   c) tympani   d) accomplished flutists

2. _____ is an inherent trait of some individuals.
   a) Ignorance   b) Soccer-playing   c) Brown hair   d) Criminal behavior

3. When making a pie, the cook _____ the superfluous crust.
   a) kneads   b) rolls out   c) trims off   d) brushes with butter

4. A recumbent figure usually does not look _____.
   a) overweight   b) anxious   c) relaxed   d) sensual

5. A moribund love is _____.
   a) fading away   b) clinging to hope   c) eternal   d) star-crossed

6. To be impeccable in appearance, a person must choose clothes _____.
   a) for the beach   b) with special care   c) instinctively   d) according to the price tags

7. A germane contribution to a debate is one that _____.
   a) changes the subject   b) confuses the opposing side   c) addresses the issue   d) uses unfair tactics

8. If I _____ something, it becomes obligatory.
   a) say I might do   b) promise to do   c) dread   d) prophesy

9. If an agreement is merely putative, it is _____.
   a) only a rumor   b) likely to be published in full   c) legally binding   d) temporary

10. If a person's schedule is not feasible, he or she is _____.
    a) difficult to contact   b) likely to be a success   c) able to relax   d) liable frequently to be late

11. An ephemeral sadness _____.
    a) is gone momentarily   b) leaves deep scars   c) is only pretended   d) indicates a melancholy streak

12. Specious reasoning does not _____.
    a) convince anyone   b) sound plausible   c) stand up to analysis   d) stick to the subject

LESSON 9

The words in this lesson and the next are verbs, words that show action.

debilitate—enfeeble, weaken. *Constant excesses will debilitate even the strongest constitution.*

impeach—challenge one's honesty or reputation, call before a tribunal on a charge of wrongdoing. *President Nixon resigned before he could be impeached by the Senate for high crimes and misdemeanors.*

abate—lessen in intensity or amount, diminish. *After an hour or two the storm abated and the sky began to clear.*

nullify—make void or without effect. *The new contract nullifies all previous agreements between the two parties.*

jettison—cast overboard. *They had to jettison the cargo to lighten the plane.* Jettison comes from the Latin verb *jactare,* "to throw." Originally, cargo was jettisoned in order to lighten a ship in an emergency. By extension, *jettison* can mean to throw away any kind of dead weight or useless burden.

exacerbate—make worse, aggravate. *A generous portion of french fries is sure to exacerbate an upset stomach.*

procrastinate—delay doing something, put off without reason. *Since you'll have to get it done eventually, you might as well stop procrastinating and get started.*

mitigate—lessen, make milder, less severe, or less serious. *The fact that they were not at fault for the accident did not mitigate their grief over it.*

recapitulate—relate in brief, summarize, repeat in a condensed version. *In five minutes he recapitulated the complex plot of Hitchcock's* Spellbound.

construe—interpret, analyze. *His attitude was construed as one of opposition to the proposal, although he claimed to have no opinion.*

berate—scold vehemently, rebuke harshly and at length. *The teacher who berates his class is rationalizing his own shortcomings.*

obliterate—demolish, destroy all trace of. *The building had been obliterated; we could not even be sure exactly where it had stood.*

Answers to the following exercises are on page 199.

EXERCISE I Synonyms. Circle the letter of the word or phrase closest in meaning to the given word.

1. jettison: a) preserve b) float c) fly d) dump

2. debilitate: a) take strength away from b) reiterate c) make louder d) take for granted

3. recapitulate: a) instigate b) repeat in full c) summarize d) execute

4. mitigate: a) improve b) radicalize c) soften d) make drowsy

5. abate: a) pay back   b) grow mild   c) deactivate   d) agree with

6. procrastinate: a) conform   b) be optimistic   c) predict the future   d) postpone action

7. construe: a) consume   b) translate   c) strain   d) interpret

8. exacerbate: a) worsen   b) overstate   c) clear up   d) endure

9. nullify: a) soothe   b) minimize   c) make ineffective   d) restrict

10. berate: a) chastise verbally   b) argue convincingly   c) insist strongly   d) address

11. obliterate: a) put off   b) wipe out utterly   c) dismantle   d) forget

12. impeach: a) repeal   b) vote against   c) formally accuse   d) convict in the Senate

EXERCISE II Choose the best word to complete each sentence. Write it in the blank.

1. The effect of the sleeping pill was _____ by three cups of coffee.
    exacerbated   nullified
    recapitulated   construed

2. There were gaps in the manuscript where the writing had been _____ by rot and water damage.
    procrastinated   jettisoned
    debilitated   obliterated

3. In a desperate attempt to keep the tiny craft afloat, the survivors _____ all nonessential items.
    abated   nullified
    jettisoned   obliterated

4. The defendant's youth and unbalanced mental state were considered to _____ the seriousness of his crime.
    mitigate   nullify
    impeach   exacerbate

5. The man is a complete mystery to me: I don't know how to _____ anything he says and I can never tell if he's joking.
    recapitulate   mitigate
    construe   obliterate

6. As volcanic activity _____ , rescue workers were able to move into the area.
    obliterated   abated
    procrastinated berated

7. People often _____ out of anxiety. They put off doing a task because they don't have confidence that it will turn out well.
    procrastinate jettison
    impeach   construe

8. We found the hot weather so _____ that we collapsed after lunch and stayed in our hammocks the rest of the day.

    berating   mitigating
    recapitulating   debilitating

9. The Secretary of State's rash public pronouncements only _____ a tense and delicate international situation.

    abated   procrastinated
    jettisoned   exacerbated

10. The children had learned to tune out their older sister, who _____ them endlessly over trivial and unavoidable mishaps.

    construed   abated
    berated   debilitated

11. A(n) _____ is not a conviction, but a formal accusation brought against someone in public office.

    mitigation   impeachment
    obliteration   nullification

12. Although she could not remember everything that was said, the student was able to _____ the highlights.

    impeach   berate
    exacerbate   recapitulate

EXERCISE III From memory, try to complete the following sentences with words from this lesson. The first letter of each answer is given before the blank. Write your answers in the blanks.

1. Thanks to the medicine, the fever [a] _____ and the patient was able to sleep peacefully.

2. Because they were three hours late and hadn't bothered to call, I lost my temper and [b] _____ them for their rudeness.

3. The defense claimed the money was a legitimate campaign contribution, but the jury [c] _____ it as a bribe.

4. The desertion of so many soldiers was [d] _____ to morale.

5. The rash is [e] _____ by scratching; the more you scratch, the worse it will get.

6. The senator was [i] _____ by the grand jury on charges of influence-peddling.

7. To lighten their packs, the hikers [j] _____ the cooking equipment and the tent.

8. Jim's regret when his companions left was [m] _____ by his pleasure at having the cabin all to himself again.

9. Her clumsy play in the opening round [n] _____ whatever psychological advantage she may have had.

10. The space station had been [o] _____ . Not even debris remained.

11. Fay has been [p] _____ on the research paper for a month and now has only a week to get it written.

12. At the end of the class, the professor quickly [r] _____ for us the political events of the decade.

LESSON 10

rescind—formally cancel or take back. *They rescinded their offer of aid when they became disillusioned with the project.*

matriculate—enroll, especially as a candidate for a degree in a college or university. *Bruce will matriculate in an associate degree program at the college in September.*

bequeath—leave as a legacy or inheritance. *The woman bequeathed her house to her only daughter.* Something bequeathed is called a *bequest.*

impute—attribute, ascribe, charge with. *The difficulties were imputed to his negligence.* The things imputed are usually negative, such as faults, crimes, or misfortunes.

perambulate—walk about, stroll, especially for the purpose of observing or inspecting. *They perambulated the borders of the property to check that the gates were secure.*

enunciate—pronounce clearly. *He could not enunciate certain sounds because of a speech impediment.*

prevaricate—mislead, lie. *He prevaricated when he said he hadn't been to the movies: he had gone there but then had left almost immediately.* Like *equivocate* (see Lesson 2), *prevaricate* usually does not mean to lie outright but rather to mislead, to bend or evade the truth. Its root in Latin means literally "to walk crookedly."

impugn—cast doubt on someone's motives or truthfulness. *Do not impugn his testimony unless you can substantiate your charges.*

regale—entertain, delight or refresh with something pleasing. *Our friends regaled us with funny stories of their adventures.*

extricate—free from an entanglement. *Carefully removing each prickly branch, she extricated herself from the briars.*

Answers to the following exercises are on page 200.

EXERCISE I Choose the best word to complete each sentence. Write it in the blank.

1. Not blaming the little girl herself, we _____ her rudeness and rowdy behavior to parental neglect.

bequeathed	regaled
imputed	impugned

2. The story Vera told was true for the most part, but the detective suspected she was _____ to conceal some evidence.

prevaricating	perambulating
enunciating	matriculating

3. The physician felt that the anxious patient was somehow _____ his competence or judgment by raising so many questions.

impugning	regaling
imputing	perambulating

4. That provision of the law was _____ by a later act of the legislature and so it is no longer in effect.

impugned	extricated
regaled	rescinded

5. The regulations as published in the catalogue stipulate that no student may _____ unless he or she has been formally accepted into a degree program.

prevaricate	matriculate
enunciate	extricate

6. Although he was no longer in love, the young man had become so deeply involved with the woman that he saw no way of _____ himself gracefully from the relationship.

perambulating	prevaricating
matriculating	extricating

7. The last will and testament left numerous small _____ of money and memorabilia to employees and friends.

prevarications	rescindings
imputations	bequests

8. We dropped in for an hour at our neighbors', where we were _____ with chocolate mousse and pleasant conversation.

rescinded	enunciated
regaled	extricated

9. The best way to become acquainted with the soul of a city is to spend a few days _____ its various neighborhoods.

perambulating	rescinding
impugning	bequeathing

10. Some sounds are naturally more difficult to _____ than others; in every language the baby word for *mother* is a very easy combination.

matriculate	enunciate
impute	bequeath

EXERCISE II Circle the letter of the best choice to complete each sentence.

1. One extricates oneself from   a) a positive outlook   b) a long walk   c) pleasant pastimes   d) a sticky situation

2. One way to impugn a person's objectivity is to   a) suggest she is blinded by self-interest   b) call her fair-minded   c) recall the past   d) commend her motives

3. After a day of perambulating, a person is likely to have   a) tired eyes   b) a hoarse throat   c) sore feet   d) little appetite

4. Excellent enunciation is of the utmost importance to   a) actors b) novelists   c) private investors   d) professional models

5. To impute a mistake to someone is to   a) condone it   b) assign responsibility for it   c) invite a repetition of it   d) cover up the truth

6. When you are regaled by the company you are with,   a) you wish you were somewhere else   b) accidents are rife   c) time passes quickly   d) a spat is likely

7. People generally bequeath their possessions   a) at tag sales   b) to make money   c) to avoid taxes   d) to their relatives

8. A person who matriculates becomes   a) a liar   b) a graduate   c) a student   d) an employee of a college

9. A prevarication is usually   a) an animated tale   b) a partial falsehood c) deleted   d) translucent

10. A promise that has been rescinded has been   a) withdrawn   b) confided c) sabotaged   d) reaffirmed

EXERCISE III Antonyms. Draw a line connecting each word with the word or phrase most nearly its *opposite*.

1. prevaricate	become enmeshed
2. bequeath	be sedentary
3. enunciate	praise
4. rescind	promulgate
5. impugn	slur one's words
6. regale	bore
7. perambulate	keep as one's own
8. extricate	stick to the truth

Perambulate derives from the Latin roots *per* (through) and *ambulare* (to walk). You can fix it in your mind by associating it with the more familiar *amble,* another English verb from the same root. Latin *ambulare* also gave rise to the French *hôpital ambulant* (moving or "walking" hospital), which in turn became our *ambulance.* Check your dictionary for the definitions of these additional descendents of *ambulare:*

ambulatory   _____

funambulist   _____

somnambulist   _____

EXERCISE IV Circle the letter of the best choice to complete each sentence.

1. One is likely to see a funambulist   a) at night   b) in a circus   c) in the countryside   d) in a hospital

2. A patient who is bedridden   a) is not ambulatory   b) needs an ambulance   c) is a somnambulist   d) ambles about the hospital

3. A somnambulist suffers from a form of   a) pneumonia b) dizziness   c) sleep disturbance   d) intense lethargy

4. One can impugn a man's veracity by calling him   a) a funambulist   b) a perambulator   c) an extricator   d) a prevaricator

5. To enunciate a word is to   a) swallow it   b) deny its truth   c) say it distinctly   d) bequeath it

6. A funambulist needs   a) a superb sense of balance   b) legal counsel   c) a sedative   d) to be regaled

REVIEW TEST I

1.   *That which is past is gone, and irrevocable; and wise men have enough to do with things present and to come. . . .*
                                                                    —*Francis Bacon*

Bacon states that the past   a) is not remembered   b) cannot be called back
        c) was better than the present   d) is without blemish

2.   *The nature of the wounds upon her own person entirely precludes the idea of self-destruction.*
                                                                    —*Edgar Allan Poe*

According to this sentence, suicide in this case is   a) germane   b) improbable
        c) the coroner's verdict   d) an impossibility

3.   *They said nothing unkind . . . but in a week or two I was my old procrastinating idle self and had soon left the class altogether.*
                                                                    —*William Butler Yeats*

Yeats accuses himself of   a) postponing worthwhile actions   b) disobedience
        c) lying   d) frivolity

4.   *She sought to be eloquent in her garments, and to make up for her diffidence of speech by a fine frankness of costume.*
                                                                    —*Henry James*

The character described is   a) vociferous   b) urbane   c) not effusive in speech
        d) a vixen

Questions 5 and 6
        Yet, for all his hardy sobriety and fortitude, there were certain qualities in him which at times affected, and in some cases seemed well nigh to overbalance the rest.
                                                                    —*Herman Melville*

5. The man described is usually   a) fond of company   b) of steady character
        c) a curmudgeon   d) eager to be liked

6. Fortitude is   a) sharpness of mind   b) soberness   c) reckless courage
        d) strength to endure

7.   *Kant, who had been educated in the rationalist tradition, was much perturbed by Hume's scepticism, and endeavored to find an answer to it.*
                                                                    —*Bertrand Russell*

Hume represents a   a) breach of faith   b) lack of seriousness   c) position of radical doubt   d) tradition of belief

8.   *He enunciated distinctly, with soft precision.*

—*Joseph Conrad*

The character in question   a) pronounced words clearly   b) argued rationally   c) sang softly   d) whistled

9.   *Superfluous wealth can buy superfluities only.*

—*Henry David Thoreau*

Superfluous means   a) inadequate   b) beyond what is necessary   c) bequeathed rather than earned   d) deceptive in appearance

10.   *I thought it prudent not to exacerbate the growing moodiness of his temper by any comment.*

—*Edgar Allan Poe*

To exacerbate moodiness is to   a) make it worse   b) soothe it   c) ignore it   d) impute it to some cause

11.   *The least relaxation of his vigilance, the smallest abatement of his strength . . . put him in jeopardy.*

—*James G. Frazer*

An abatement is   a) an obliteration   b) a diminishing   c) a maturing   d) a repelling

12.   *The English ear has been accustomed to the mellifluence of Pope's numbers.*

—*Samuel Johnson*

According to Johnson, Pope's verse   a) galls the English ear   b) is learned   c) flows sweetly   d) is evocative

13.   *To assert myself thus traduced is not vanity or arrogance. It is a demand of justice. . . .*

—*Edmund Burke*

Here Burke implies that his character has been   a) impugned   b) rescinded   c) regaled   d) construed

14.   *Mary had neither genius nor taste; and though vanity had given her application, it had given her likewise a pedantic and conceited manner, which would have injured a higher degree of excellence than she had reached.*

—*Jane Austen*

Mary tends to   a) be dispassionate   b) primp and preen   c) lack self-confidence   d) bore people with her accomplishments

Questions 15 and 16

There is now your insular city of the Manhattoes, belted round by

wharves as Indian isles by coral reefs—commerce surrounds it with her
surf.

—Herman Melville

15. Melville refers to the fact that   a) Manhattan is only part of a larger city
     b) Manhattan is an island   c) New York is beleaguered   d) New Yorkers
     are provincial

16. With the word *as*, Melville introduces a   a) literal description
     b) recapitulation   c) simile   d) nullification

17.   *Even at the age of twenty-seven Austin Sloper had made his mark suffi-*
     ciently to mitigate the anomaly of his having been chosen among a dozen
     suitors by a young woman of high fashion. . . .

—Henry James

An *anomaly* is something unusual or difficult to explain. To mitigate the anomaly,
     or strangeness, of something is to   a) make it appear more usual
     b) espouse it   c) explain it   d) make it even stranger

18.   *Such unaccountable masses of shades and shadows, that at first you al-*
     most thought some ambitious young artist . . . had endeavored to de-
     lineate chaos bewitched.

—Herman Melville

Delineate here means   a) overcome   b) evoke   c) sketch the form of
     d) apprehend

Answers to the above questions are on page 200.

LESSON 11

The Latin *genus* is a broad term meaning "kind, type, birth, origin, family, race." It comes from a much older root, a prehistoric Indo-European word meaning "to produce, beget." *Genus* has been borrowed unchanged into English; if you have studied biology, you will recall that it means "type" or "kind." But *genus* has been borrowed more than once. It appears in English in a variety of disguises, such as:

generic—pertaining to a race or kind. *Colorblindness is a generic characteristic of some animals. Generic is the adjective form of genus.*

engender—to produce, cause, beget. *Angry words may engender strife.*

degenerate—to decline from a higher or normal form. *The discussion eventually degenerated into a shouting match.*

regenerate—to form or produce again, reconstitute, restore, grow back. *The formerly declining neighborhood was regenerated by the influx of artists looking for studio space.*

genealogy—history of family descent, a family tree. *They were able to trace their genealogy back five generations to a small village in Sicily.*

genocide—the deliberate killing of an entire people. *The native inhabitants of Tasmania were the victims of genocide at the hands of European settlers.*

homogeneous—uniform throughout, all of the same kind. *The entering class was fairly homogeneous; nearly all the students were the same age and from similar middle-class homes.* The Greek prefix *homo* means "same" or "like."

heterogeneous—composed of different types, not uniform. *The ship's crew was a heterogeneous group representing no fewer than twelve nationalities.* The opposite of *homo*, the prefix *hetero* means "other" or "different."

progenitor—direct ancestor, forefather. *According to Genesis, Adam and Eve were the progenitors of the entire human race.*

genre—kind, type, used especially for types of literary or artistic works. *College literature courses are sometimes organized by genre, for instance nineteenth-century poetry or modern drama.* In art, *genre painting* refers to the representation of common, everyday objects in a realistic style. We've borrowed *genre* from modern French and pronounce it more or less in the French style, but like the other words in this lesson its source is the Latin *genus*.

Answers to the following exercises are on page 200.

EXERCISE I Synonyms. Circle the letter of the word or phrase closest in meaning to the given word.

1. homogeneous: a) pasteurized b) composed of like elements c) homosexual d) similar in function

2. degenerate: a) ameliorate b) waver c) disperse d) worsen

36

3. genocide: a) classification b) family tree c) killing of a parent
    d) extermination of a race

4. genre: a) type of art work b) oil painting c) epoch d) zoological
    division

5. generic: a) inordinate b) belonging to a class c) unfamiliar d) sold
    over the counter

6. regenerate: a) create anew b) convoke c) rejoice d) give again

7. heterogeneous: a) pragmatic b) unconventional c) varied in makeup
    d) normal

8. progenitor: a) prevaricator b) superior c) ancestor d) advocate

9. genealogy: a) historical determinism b) lineage c) friendliness d) study
    of inherited traits

10. engender: a) ascribe sexual characteristics to b) serve c) embrace
    d) give rise to

EXERCISE II Choose the best word to complete each sentence. Write it in the blank.

1. The sedimentary rock was a _____ mix of several minerals
    randomly distributed.

    heterogeneous   genre
    regenerate   degenerate

2. Some simple organisms are able to grow back or _____ parts of
    their bodies that have been hurt or destroyed.

    engender   make heterogeneous
    regenerate   degenerate

3. The term _____ was first applied to the Nazis' systematic attempt
    to destroy the Jews.

    progenitor   genocide
    generic   genealogy

4. The Dutch still life, typical of _____ painting, depicted a pitcher,
    a glass, and some fruit assembled on a kitchen table.

    genocidal   genre
    regenerated   genealogical

5. According to ancient myth, life on earth has _____ from a former
    state of innocence and happiness known as Eden or the Golden Age.

    become homogeneous   regenerated
    degenerated   engendered

6. The Romans claimed as their _____ Aeneas, the warrior son of
    Venus who escaped the Greeks at the fall of Troy.

    progenitor   genocide
    genealogy   genre

7. The double blossom is not a fluke of this particular plant but a
_____ trait of the species.

    genre   heterogeneous
    progenitor   generic

8. Shared hardship _____ a feeling of camaraderie that soon ripened
into a friendship.

    engendered   degenerated
    homogenized   made generic

EXERCISE III Circle the letter of the best choice to complete each sentence.

1. An example of a progenitor is a) an uncle b) a great-grandfather c) a hybrid d) a predecessor in office

2. A homogeneous substance is a) gaseous b) uniform c) sterile d) a conglomeration

3. A genealogy is best organized by a) generation b) year c) biological form d) nationality

4. The generic name of a drug identifies its a) brand b) manufacturer c) composition d) efficacy

Borrowing from Latin and Greek

English is not descended from Latin or Greek. The structure of English—its grammar and basic vocabulary—makes it a member of the Germanic language family. But ever since their tribal progenitors invaded Britain in the fifth century, the English have been borrowing foreign words, mostly from Latin (sometimes through French) and Greek.

Throughout the Middle Ages and into the modern era, the chief language of learning in Europe was Latin. Greek was less well-known but likewise highly regarded. Englishmen who wrote and even spoke Latin in their work and studies simply borrowed terms from the classical languages to create for English a kind of educated jargon. Much of the academic and technical vocabulary we use today entered English this way.

It is easy for someone versed in Latin to remember that, say, *munificent* means "generous"; he or she can recognize roots in the word meaning "gift" and "making." Similarly, if you had never seen the word *manlike* before, you would break it down into the familiar elements *man* and *like*. You might have difficulty, though, with *anthropoid*, "manlike," because the the elements that make it up are not English but Greek. For the majority of English-speaking students, who never study classical languages, much of the learned vocabulary of English is a puzzle because the words are built on roots from unfamiliar languages.

LESSON 12

Our word *benefit* contains the Latin root *ben* or *bene,* meaning "good" or "well."
A benefit is a good deed, a favor, or an advantage. The same root also gives us:

benign—(good-type) favorable, kind, doing little or no harm. *Astrologers believe that the stars exert influences, evil and benign, on human lives.*

benefactor—(well-doer) one who does a good deed or confers a benefit. *The young man's uncle acted as his benefactor, paying his tuition and later arranging job interviews for him.*

benediction—(a speaking well) a blessing. *The church service ended with a benediction.*

benevolence—(good will) good will, kindness. *Her many acts of charity earned her a reputation for benevolence.* The adjective is *benevolent.*

The opposite of ben or bene is mal—"bad" or "ill." Once you have learned the above words, you should be able to guess the meanings of *malefactor, malediction,* and *malevolence. Mal* is at the root of many other words as well, including:

malice—(bad intention) desire to do evil or injury. *The face of the wicked queen in* Snow White *is a blend of beauty and malice.* The adjective is *malicious.*

malignant—(bad-type) very harmful or dangerous. *It was feared that the widespread spraying of the weedkiller would have a malignant effect on wildlife in the area.*

malinger—to pretend to be ill in order to avoid work or responsibility. *The child, upset by her family's move to the new neighborhood, malingered in order to put off her first day at the new school.*

malady—illness. *Researchers were unable to find the cause of the mysterious malady which had attacked several of the hotel's residents.*

malaise—(bad ease) a vague uneasiness, discomfort, or unhappiness. *A cold often begins with muscle ache and a general malaise.*

malpractice—(bad practice) harmful, incompetent, or neglectful conduct in a professional activity. *The attorney managed the case so ineptly that the client sued him for malpractice.*

From benevolence and *malevolence,* you can guess that the Latin root *vol* means "will." It comes from the word *volo* (I will, I want) and gives us our word *voluntary.* Associating it with *voluntary* can help you remember the meaning of

volition—deliberate choice, act of will, power to will. *No one forced them to come here; they came of their own volition.*

It should be obvious from benefactor and *malefactor* that the root *fac* or *fact* means "do." It derives from the Latin verb meaning "to do" or "to make" and is at the root of many familiar English words, such as *factory* (a place where things are made), *fact* (something done), and *manufacture* (originally, to make by hand). The same root gives us

factotum—(do everything) an employee with miscellaneous duties. *As chief facto-tum of the plant, he knew everything that went on.* The *totum* part of *factotum* comes from the Latin word for "all" or "everything," the same word that gave rise to *total* and *totality.*

Answers to the following exercises are on page 200.

EXERCISE I Fill in the blanks from the list of words below.

malicious   malady
volition   benefactor
benign   factotum
malaise   benevolent
benediction   malefactor

1. The physician diagnosed the _____ as measles.

2. The crowd gathered in the square to receive the _____ of the bishop.

3. In the film *Svengali,* Trilby loses all power of _____ and be-comes a mere puppet in the hands of the hypnotist.

4. Since the biopsy showed the lesion to be _____, there was no immediate need for an operation.

5. The accused _____ in this crime has already been convicted twice of armed robbery.

6. Charles, hired as a _____ for the estate, did everything from gardening to chauffeuring to electrical repairs.

7. People are immediately attracted by his cheerful and _____ expression.

8. The busybody had nothing to gain from his _____ gossip but the pleasure of embarrassing people who had done him no harm.

9. An anonymous _____ gave the library a large donation, which allowed it to stay open on Sundays.

10. His depression resulted in a _____ that lasted nearly a month; al-though he was not actually sick, he did not feel well.

EXERCISE II Synonyms. Circle the letter of the word or phrase closest in meaning to the given word.

1. malignant: a) helpful b) injurious c) ugly d) weak

2. malediction: a) prediction b) guess c) ailment d) curse

3. volition: a) awareness b) generosity c) free will d) eagerness

4. benevolent: a) kind b) willful c) rational d) mean-spirited

5. malinger: a) misbehave b) feign illness c) work willingly d) fall sick

6. malpractice: a) professional misconduct b) laziness c) lack of professional success d) ignorance

7. benign: a) unfortunate b) risky c) good d) genuine

8. malefactor: a) do-gooder b) poor worker c) philanthropist d) criminal

9. malodorous: a) accursed b) disorderly c) evil-smelling d) cruel

10. malice: a) evil intent b) anger c) mischief d) incompetence

11. malevolence: a) pettiness b) disgust c) ill will d) charity

12. benediction: a) speech b) clear pronunciation c) pleasant greeting
   d) blessing

Write your own definitions in the blanks for the underlined words below. Check your dictionary if necessary.

What does it mean to say:

that a machine is *malfunctioning*?   _____

that a person is *malcontent*?   _____

that a comment is *malapropos*?   _____

that a government is *totalitarian*?   _____

Shades of Meaning

The Latin-based *benefactor* is almost precisely equivalent in its root meaning to the English expression *do-gooder*. However, the two words don't mean the same, since *do-gooder* has a negative connotation. A benefactor does something that improves the lives of other people. A do-gooder meddles in other people's business under the pretext of helping them, out of a smug belief in his or her own moral superiority. The difference is like that between a *good person* and a *goody-goody*. Which one you think a person is—a benefactor or a do-gooder—depends on what you think of that person's motives and of the supposed benefit.

LESSON 13

Twelve adjectives:

conciliatory—tending to placate or to gain good will. *After the quarrel he sent flowers as a conciliatory gesture.* This adjective is formed from the verb *conciliate*, meaning "to placate, overcome hostility or win good will by friendly behavior."

insidious—secretly dangerous, tending to entrap. *The casino games were insidious; before he realized it, he had gambled away all of his savings. Insidious* derives from the Latin prefix *in* (in) and the verb *sedere* (to sit). Together they mean "to sit in wait for," or, as we would say, "to lie in wait for."

stringent—severe, strict, compelling. *The speaker presented stringent arguments for the unwelcome cutbacks.*

meticulous—showing careful attention to detail, very precise. *The sewing on the jacket was so meticulous that one could hardly see the stitches.*

fastidious—hard to please, too critical or sensitive, squeamish, delicate to a fault. *He considered her fastidious because her feelings were offended by trifling defects and errors.* Meticulous denotes a concern with details, and it is usually a positive trait, though it can be overdone. *Fastidious,* on the other hand, virtually always has a negative connotation. It implies an inability to accept or cope with the minor disappointments, mistakes, messiness, confusion, or dirt of life which most people take in stride.

vacuous—empty of meaning or interest, without substance, without purpose. *His vacuous promises were forgotten as soon as they were uttered. Vacuous* is usually used figuratively to describe things that are intellectually or morally empty, not physically empty. Etymologically, it simply means "empty."

soporific—sleepy, causing sleep. *Because of the drug's soporific effect, you should not try to drive after taking it.*

vicarious—experienced secondhand through imagining another person's experience. *The children enjoyed a vicarious sense of power through the exploits of the comic book hero.*

ubiquitous—existing everywhere. *Papaya, ubiquitous in that region, is considered fit only for children and animals.*

turgid—swollen, bloated. *By the end of his life, the mammoth body of Henry VIII was turgid and riddled with disease. Turgid* is one of those adjectives that is used both literally and figuratively. A river swollen by rains is literally turgid; overwritten and bombastic prose is figuratively turgid. *Turgid* generally has an unpleasant connotation. The bellies of starving children are turgid; balloons are merely inflated.

capricious—changing suddenly, willfully erratic. *She is so capricious in her moods that no one can predict how she will take the news.*

incorrigible—beyond reform, not able to be corrected. *Some delinquents are incorrigible.*

Answers to the following exercises are on page 200.

EXERCISE I Antonyms. Circle the letter of the word or phrase most *opposite* in meaning to the given word.

1. soporific: a) inducing coma b) adult c) nonmedical d) enlivening

2. capricious: a) unimaginative b) despotic c) boring d) methodical

3. conciliatory: a) revealing b) ill-advised c) provoking d) difficult

4. incorrigible: a) capable of improvement b) craven c) never arrested d) seldom encountered

5. meticulous: a) radical b) careless c) languid d) revolting

6. vacuous: a) very busy b) pretentious c) intrepid d) deeply significant

7. ubiquitous: a) unprecedented b) unpopular c) rare d) virtuous

8. stringent: a) placid b) lax c) protective d) massive

9. fastidious: a) impeded b) nauseous c) easy-going d) ignorant

10. turgid: a) shrunken b) lucid c) sanitary d) instantaneous

11. vicarious: a) first-hand b) secular c) benign d) unblemished

12. insidious: a) stellar b) suspicious c) slovenly d) harmless

EXERCISE II Choose the best word to complete each sentence. Write it in the blank.

1. The weight given to legal precedents, or earlier judicial decisions, is supposed to prevent arbitrary or _____ interpretations of the law by judges.

        incorrigible   vacuous
        capricious   insidious

2. The woman took _____ pleasure in the accomplishments of her daughter.

        ubiquitous   turgid
        soporific   vicarious

3. Fountains are _____ in Rome: one can hardly turn a corner without spotting one.

        stringent   ubiquitous
        meticulous   capricious

4. Rose's cookies were delicious but _____. I had eaten a dozen before I remembered I was on a diet.

        vicarious   fastidious
        vacuous   insidious

5. Meeting by accident on the street, the former classmates exchanged a few polite but _____ comments and went about their business, forgetting each other immediately.

        vacuous   incorrigible
        conciliatory   capricious

6. The college, being small, prestigious, and well-endowed, has very _____ requirements for admission.

        insidious   stringent
        soporific   turgid

7. Although the teenager has been in trouble several times already and her parents view her as _____, the social worker thinks she can be helped.

        incorrigible   stringent
        meticulous   ubiquitous

8. Audubon's beautiful wildlife paintings show a _____ attention to anatomical detail.

        conciliatory   fastidious
        vicarious   meticulous

9. A _____ letter, in which he admitted to being somewhat temperamental, led to a reconciliation between the partners.

        soporific   ubiquitous
        vacuous   conciliatory

10. The character of Felix in *The Odd Couple* is so _____ that he obsessively cleans up after the cleaning lady.

    turgid   capricious
    fastidious   insidious

11. It is an overblown, _____ novel of over a thousand pages in which nothing much happens and no one cares.

    turgid   fastidious
    vicarious   conciliatory

12. The music drifting in over the garden had the soothing, _____ sound of a lullaby.

    incorrigible   soporific
    stringent   meticulous

Check your dictionary for the etymology of *incorrigible*. Although the prefix *in* sometimes means "in" (as in *insidious*), it frequently signifies "not." What is the etymological meaning of the following words? Use your dictionary to check your answers.

incongruent   _____
inimitable   _____
inconclusive   _____
incurious   _____

LESSON 14

The following adjectives can all be used to describe people.

dexterous—having manual skill or ease, expert in performing some physical skill. *A dexterous mechanic, she had the tire changed in five minutes.* Also spelled *dextrous*.

parsimonious—stingy, miserly, too unwilling to spend money. *Although wealthy, she was parsimonious and never gave to charity.*

obstreperous—noisy, boisterous, especially in opposition to something. *A crowd gathered as the obstreperous customer demanded his money back.*

amenable—agreeable, open to suggestion. *The director was amenable to the proposed schedule change.*

credulous—inclined to believe on slight evidence. *The credulous woman followed every instruction of the fortuneteller.* Credulous derives from the Latin verb *credere* (to believe), which is also the source of our nouns *creed* (belief) and *credit,* and of the adjective *credible* (able to be believed).

gregarious—fond of company, sociable. *They are a gregarious couple who cultivate many friendships.* Gregarious comes from the Latin word *gregis,* "of the flock or herd." Gregarious people, like herd animals, enjoy the company of others.

imperturbable—not easily excited or disturbed. *His poker game was aided by an imperturbable face.*

lethargic—unusually tired, drowsy, abnormally sluggish. *The convalescent was still lethargic and found conversation exhausting.* The noun form is *lethargy.*

truculent—ferocious, savage, harsh. *The champion affected a truculent manner to intimidate the young challenger.*

recalcitrant—stubborn, refusing to obey, uncooperative. *A recalcitrant child is difficult to teach.*

formidable—causing fear or awe. *The experienced pro was a formidable opponent.* Despite its appearance, *formidable* has nothing to do with our word *form.* It comes from the Latin word *formido,* "fear"; etymologically it means "worthy to be feared." It can be used of things as well as people: *The police confiscated a formidable array of weapons.*

supercilious—proud, haughty, believing oneself to be superior. *The supercilious social attitudes of the aristocracy contributed to the resentment felt by the mercantile middle class.* Latin *supercilium* means "eyebrow." It seems that raised eyebrows have long been used to express disdain or disapproval.

Answers to the following exercises are on page 200.

EXERCISE I Synonyms. Circle the letter of the word or phrase closest in meaning to the given word.

1. amenable: a) thinking profoundly b) recalcitrant c) brooding d) agreeing readily

2. formidable: a) awesome b) repulsive c) correctable d) able to be copied

3. imperturbable: a) superior b) wary c) hysterical d) unflappable

4. gregarious: a) animalistic b) liking to be with people c) shepherdlike d) confident

5. lethargic: a) malingering b) strenuous c) unconscious d) very sleepy

6. obstreperous: a) making a commotion b) vacillating c) too eager to obey d) of childbirth

7. parsimonious: a) affluent b) corruptible c) tight-fisted d) grammatical

8. recalcitrant: a) sowing wild oats b) feigning innocence c) softening d) resisting authority

9. supercilious: a) powerful b) too proud c) abundant d) asinine

10. truculent: a) rough-mannered b) sweaty c) insipid d) saccharine

11. dexterous: a) generous b) manually competent c) formally polite d) faithful

12. credulous: a) easy to deceive b) believable c) religious d) buying on credit

EXERCISE II Circle the letter of the best choice to complete each sentence.

1. A lethargic person wants to _____.
   a) rest b) eat c) feel superior d) be with people

2. Recalcitrant people are _____.
   a) hostile to strangers   b) unwilling to cooperate   c) easy to get along with   d) outspoken

3. An obstreperous crowd is likely to _____.
   a) line up peacefully   b) be unruly   c) be respectful   d) disperse

4. _____ is the act of a credulous person.
   a) Reading novels   b) Dancing on a table   c) Cheating at solitaire   d) Buying the Brooklyn Bridge

5. A large, truculent man is liable to _____.
   a) drive a truck   b) be stubborn   c) pick fights   d) have a lot of money

6. If the person in charge is amenable to a suggestion, the suggestion is likely to be _____.
   a) forgotten   b) implemented   c) rewritten   d) printed

7. A parsimonious individual _____.
   a) is always late   b) gambles   c) preaches sermons   d) counts every penny

8. Gregarious people are not _____.
   a) loners   b) trustworthy   c) physically fit   d) misers

9. A dexterous cook can _____.
   a) read a recipe   b) plan a menu   c) flip eggs without breaking the yolks   d) barely boil water

10. A formidable figure is one that inspires _____.
    a) giggles   b) fearful respect   c) imitation   d) love

11. A supercilious person often feels _____ for others.
    a) contempt   b) sympathy   c) sorrow   d) hope

12. In a crisis, an imperturbable person _____.
    a) talks incessantly   b) faints   c) remains calm   d) cracks jokes

EXERCISE III From memory, try to complete the following sentences with words from this lesson. The first letter of each answer is given before the blank. Write your answers in the blanks.

1. The older boy wore a [s]_____ expression of haughty disdain.

2. He was a rough, [t]_____ savage, given to public brawling.

3. The [r]_____ class refused to do any of the work assigned.

4. The hero of the film never loses his cool through all his globe-trotting adventures; although his life is threatened every three minutes, he remains [i]_____.

5. Even a friendly, [g]_____ host can get tired of houseguests.

6. Disappointed with the movie, some of the kids became so rowdy and [o]_____ that they were thrown out of the theater.

7. Young children are naturally [c]_____: they will believe almost anything you tell them.

8. An experienced, [d]_____ seamstress can make a dress in an afternoon.

9. The combination of exhaustion and a heavy meal left them feeling so [l]_____ that they could hardly drag themselves to bed.

10. The assembled army, bristling with weapons, made a [f]_____ appearance, striking fear into the hearts of the citizens.

11. If you are [a]_____ to the plan, we will go ahead with it.

12. Scrooge, the [p]_____ old man who cares for nothing but his moneybags, is the perfect miser.

LESSON 15

Thirteen more adjectives:

impromptu—spontaneous, not planned or prepared in advance. *Impromptu remarks, spoken on the spur of the moment, often tell voters more about how a candidate really thinks than prepared speeches do.*

salutary—promoting health, conducive to good. *The preacher's anecdote provided a salutary lesson on the perils of dishonesty.*

peremptory—imperative, dictatorial, commanding in an abrupt or offensive way. *He announced his opinions in a peremptory tone, which was extremely rankling to his hearers.*

vapid—tasteless, dull, lifeless, flat. *Their conversation was so vapid and predictable I lost interest in talking to them.*

cursory—hurried, superficial. *Cursory examination of the scene revealed nothing amiss.*

efficacious—able to produce a desired effect. *The drug is efficacious in the treatment of malaria.*

blatant—too noisy or obtrusive, impossible to ignore. *The children's blatant disregard for conventional manners embarrassed their older relatives.*

ingenuous—artless, innocently straightforward or truthful. *As a young man he still had the wide-eyed, ingenuous look of a child.*

adamant—inflexible, hard, unbreakable. *She was adamant in her determination to make the Olympic team.*

complacent—happy with what is, self-satisfied. *She was complacent about her grades, but her parents thought she should have been working harder.*

estranged—alienated, separated, especially emotionally, from what one was formerly close to. *Her estranged husband had moved out six months previously.*

imponderable—not capable of being weighed or measured. *Some skills, for instance* *typing speed, are easy to measure, while others, such as the talent for getting along with fellow workers, are imponderable.*

contentious—quarrelsome, tending to argue too frequently or persistently. *One contentious student can ruin a debate.*

Answers to the following exercises are on page 201.

EXERCISE I Antonyms. Circle the letter of the word or phrase most *opposite* in meaning to the given word.

1. complacent: a) passive b) onerous c) dissatisfied with oneself d) jocose

2. vapid: a) scintillating b) aggravating c) inebriated d) irascible

3. adamant: a) convincing b) convivial c) lackluster d) quick to yield

4. imponderable: a) featherweight b) measurable c) thoughtless d) adroit

5. impromptu: a) decorous b) rehearsed c) extraneous d) extemporaneous

6. efficacious: a) arduous b) not lively c) supine d) ineffective

7. contentious: a) arduous b) not lively c) disconsolate d) desiring to avoid a quarrel

8. estranged: a) native b) in rapport c) removed d) breathing easily

9. blatant: a) subtle b) feckless c) fascinated d) placating

10. peremptory: a) lacking drama b) pleading c) foreseen d) planned

11. salutary: a) doing damage b) salubrious c) saying goodbye d) lubricous

12. cursory: a) printed b) attenuated c) thorough d) beatific

13. ingenuous: a) solitary b) full of guile c) ambitious d) full of ideas

EXERCISE II Fill in the blanks from the list of words below.

salutary	imponderable
estranged	ingenuous
complacent	contentious
cursory	vapid
peremptory	blatant
impromptu	adamant
efficacious	

1. The essay was thorough and technically competent but _____ and colorless; the writer seemed to have no fresh ideas about his subject.

2. She planned to make a(n) _____ review of her notes in the hour before the exam.

3. When the car broke down on a road next to a river, they decided to have a(n) _____ swim and picnic.

4. The days of sun and exercise had a(n) _____ effect; his asthma abated and he looked more relaxed.

5. The coach warned the winning players against becoming _____ and taking the repeat championship for granted.

6. His contempt for his colleagues was _____ ; he made no attempt to conceal his disgust.

7. Maria is _____ from her family; her parents disapproved of her moving out and now she rarely calls them.

8. The man had a(n) _____ manner, which he considered masterful and which everyone else found bossy and offensive.

9. Proven skills and past records aside, there are too many _____ factors to allow one to predict with confidence the outcome of any single game.

10. Very young children are naturally _____ ; they haven't yet learned to edit their remarks for public consumption.

11. He's a(n) _____ soul who loves to meet people of other political persuasions so that he can argue with them.

12. The most _____ remedy for insomnia she'd found was a glass of milk and television—ten minutes of a late-night rerun and she would be snoring.

13. The parents were generally strict and especially _____ about the curfew. The kids had to be home by midnight, no matter what.

EXERCISE III Circle the letter of the best choice to complete each sentence.

1. A blatant display is a) tasteful b) flagrant c) fragrant d) criminal

2. An argument may be salutary if it a) clears the air b) is contentious c) involves partisan feelings d) estranges people who love each other

3. An adamant person is like a a) butterfly b) snake in the grass c) marshmallow d) rock

4. An impromptu conference is a) protracted b) clandestine c) regularly scheduled d) held on the spur of the moment

5. An example of something imponderable is a) sugar b) mass c) loyalty d) an efficacious medicine

6. An ingenuous person usually appears a) preoccupied with his own problems b) too inexperienced to deceive anyone c) complacent with his station in life d) dedicated to evil

7. A vapid personality is a) schizoid b) memorable c) uninteresting d) devious

8. A peremptory manner is to be expected from a a) drill sergeant b) younger sibling c) psychotherapist d) servant

LESSON 16

The items in Lessons 16, 17, and 18 are all verbs, words denoting actions.

expedite—speed, facilitate. *In order to expedite delivery of the letter, you should send it special delivery.*

excoriate—scratch severely, flay, strip off the skin of. *The sharp rocks excoriated her tender feet. Excoriate is frequently used in a figurative sense, as: The play was an excoriating attack on the stupidity and moral blindness of the warmongers.*

augment—increase. *He augments his wealth with every deal.*

promulgate—announce publicly as a law or doctrine. *The revolutionary government promulgated some of the promised reforms.*

militate—operate against, work against. *A poor appearance at the interview will militate against your being hired. Militate is always used with against.*

annul—wipe out, make void. *The Supreme Court can annul a law which it deems unconstitutional.*

circumvent—go around, frustrate by avoiding, outwit. *A technicality allowed people to circumvent the intention of the law without actually breaking it.* The root *circum* is Latin for "around" and *vent* derives from the verb meaning "come."

comprise—include, be made up of, consist of. *The test will comprise the subject matter of the previous five lessons.*

denigrate—blacken, defame, expose unfairly to scorn or hatred. *The lawyer tried to denigrate the character of the witness by implying that he was mentally unstable.*

quibble—evade an issue or confuse an argument by picking on trivial details or playing on words. *We're in agreement on the main points, so let's not quibble over details.*

evince—make evident, display, show clearly. *His curt reply evinced his short temper.*

Answers to the following exercises are on page 201.

EXERCISE I Antonyms. Circle the letter of the phrase most *opposite* in meaning to the given word.

1. annul: a) affirm b) prize highly c) institutionalize d) abet

2. expedite: a) stay at home b) hasten c) delay d) remove

3. comprise: a) fail to apprehend b) overlook c) exclude d) ignore pointedly

4. evince: a) convince b) conceal c) capitulate d) win

5. quibble: a) make a joke b) make a fuss c) argue the main issue
   d) protest

6. militate: a) sign a peace treaty b) support c) enlist d) eschew

7. promulgate: a) procrastinate b) revoke c) rebel d) reconsider

8. denigrate: a) clarify b) be grateful c) blacken d) whitewash

9. circumvent: a) obey to the letter b) entice c) elude d) stifle

10. augment: a) fail to impress b) reduce c) lose money d) add to

11. excoriate: a) be thick-skinned b) be subtle c) soothe with flattery
    d) strip of ornaments

EXERCISE II Circle the letter of the best choice to complete each sentence.

1. One way to evince stupidity is to _____.
   a) act composed b) be careful c) solve intellectual puzzles d) fail to
   understand simple things

2. A _____ promulgates laws.
   a) law-abiding citizen b) scofflaw c) legislature d) court of appeals

3. An excoriating review is _____.
   a) extremely unfavorable b) used for publicity c) judiciously
   balanced d) a rave

4. Our _____ will require that we augment our program.
   a) budgetary cutback b) growth in clientele c) progressive dismantling
   d) chaotic billing methods

5. The monarch wished to have his marriage annulled so that
   _____.

   a) he could get a divorce b) the children would be legitimate c) he
   could remarry d) his wife would be recognized as queen

6. _____ will expedite the processing of claims.
   a) Having fewer adjusters b) Investigating claimants c) Closing
   early d) Consolidating paper work

7. By circumventing a requirement, a person _____ it.
   a) avoids having to fulfill it b) asserts c) invalidates d) lives up to

8. In the debate, he accused his opponent of quibbling when the opponent
   _____.

   a) lost his temper b) asked him to define his terms c) resorted to smear
   tactics d) interrupted him twice

9. To say that a tidy woman is _____ is to denigrate her character.
   a) a good housekeeper b) an ideal wife c) a slattern d) affianced

10. _____ comprises many autonomous states.
    a) A satellite nation b) A federation c) An aggressor d) A
    dictatorship

11. Having _____ will militate against your getting a fellowship.
    a) letters of recommendation b) financial need c) several incompletes d) many A's

EXERCISE III Fill in the blanks from the list of words below.

comprised	circumvented
evinced	quibbled with
promulgated	augmented
excoriated	denigrated
expedited	annulled
militated against	

1. With more streamlined equipment, production capacity could be
   _____ by thirty percent.

2. The professor _____ one or two paragraphs where the argument was overstated, but otherwise found the paper provocative and well-informed.

3. The entertainer sued, claiming that the newspaper had _____ her good name and exposed her to embarrassment and mental anguish.

4. From the pulpit the minister, with righteous wrath, _____ the hoodlums who had attacked an innocent stranger.

5. She _____ the detective's vigilance by escaping out a back window.

6. The student _____ such an eagerness to travel that I was sure he would get to Europe somehow.

7. The surplus of highly qualified applicants and the steady decrease in the number of positions available _____ a significant improvement in salaries.

8. The infallibility of the pope when speaking *ex cathedra* was not _____ as dogma in the Roman Catholic Church until modern times.

9. The anthology _____ the best-known works of about twenty Victorian poets.

10. The computers have _____ simple transactions so that customers no longer have to wait half an hour on line every time they come to the bank.

11. Their commitments to each other were _____ by mutual consent and they parted on friendly terms.

EXERCISE IV Circle the letter of the best choice to complete each sentence.

1. A task completed expeditiously is done   a) surreptitiously
   b) half-heartedly   c) quickly   d) audaciously

2. The denigration of a man's character will probably cause him to
   a) quibble   b) regale his attackers   c) evince anger   d) circumvent legal proceedings

3. To excoriate, something must be   a) augmented   b) very sharp
   c) compromised   d) legally binding

4. Once an agreement has been annulled, it   a) has no force   b) has been promulgated   c) can be augmented   d) is comprised of numerous clauses

5. If many forces militate against passage of a bill, it is likely to be
   a) denigrated   b) promulgated   c) poorly worded   d) defeated

LESSON 17

prognosticate—predict, foretell, forecast. *Market analysts must prognosticate economic fluctuations accurately in order to advise investors.*

maraud—travel about in search of plunder, raid, pillage. *Medieval towns were walled and guarded to protect inhabitants from marauding bandits.*

upbraid—scold, charge with something disgraceful, reproach. *The husband upbraided his wife for her extravagances.*

appraise—set a value on, estimate the worth of. *The price at which authorities appraise a building determines its taxes.*

apprise—give notice to, inform. *The soldier was captured because none could apprise him of the enemy's advance.*

stigmatize—brand, mark as criminal or disgraceful. *His odd appearance and secretive manner stigmatized him as weird; his classmates regarded him with suspicion.* Originally, a *stigma* was a mark branded on or cut in the skin to identify criminals or slaves.

explicate—explain the meaning of, interpret. *The French teacher explicated the grammar of the more difficult passages.* The Latin *ex* means "out" and *plicare* means "fold," so etymologically to explicate is to unfold. Something that can be explicated is *explicable.*

parlay—use one asset to gain more, exploit an advantage for futher gain. *The merchant parlayed a small neighborhood business into a citywide chain of retail stores.*

parley—confer, speak, especially with an enemy for the purpose of settling a dispute or reaching an agreement. *Both sides agreed to a truce in order to parley for the exchange of prisoners.* While *parlay* is based on the word *paro* (equal), parley comes from the French verb *parler* (speak).

wheedle—nag, plead with, or coax in a flattering way. *With soft words the girl wheedled permission from her reluctant guardian.*

renege—go back on a promise or agreement. *Their assurances of good faith were hollow; they reneged on the agreement almost at once.*

desecrate—defile a holy place, make unsanctified, profane. *They desecrated the church by seizing the man who had taken refuge there.*

Answers to the following exercises are on page 201.

EXERCISE I Circle the letter of the best choice to complete each sentence.

1. A person who agrees to parley is ready to   a) negotiate   b) chat   c) make money   d) surrender

2. An appraisal is   a) a notification   b) a conference   c) a kind of tax   d) an evaluation

3. One can parlay   a) an abatement   b) an asset   c) a prediction   d) a detriment

4. Traditional devices for prognostication do not include   a) decks of cards   b) souvenirs   c) crystal balls   d) horoscopes

5. To apprise a person is to   a) reproach him   b) gull him   c) startle him   d) inform him

6. A person who reneges   a) breaks faith   b) confers   c) plunders for booty   d) defiles a sacred place

7. A desecrated temple requires   a) buttressing   b) an orthodox congregation   c) ritual purification   d) acolytes

8. A marauder does not   a) commit outrages   b) steal   c) travel about   d) stay indoors

9. A person who is constantly upbraiding others feels   a) placid   b) aggrieved   c) unkempt   d) lucky

10. One wheedles with   a) blandishments   b) brandishes   c) branding irons   d) lawsuits

11. A stigmatized person is   a) persuasive   b) marked out from the crowd   c) accepted   d) carefree

12. An explication of a joke is   a) an analysis of it   b) a suppression of it   c) obscene   d) humorous

EXERCISE II Antonyms. Draw a line connecting each word with the word or phrase most nearly its *opposite*.

1. apprise   give honor to
2. desecrate   keep a promise
3. maraud   fail to notify
4. appraise   cleanse
5. stigmatize   refuse to confer
6. upbraid   obfuscate
7. parley   thank
8. explicate   recall the past
9. parlay   restore wealth to
10. wheedle   lose an asset
11. renege   be unable to put a price on
12. prognosticate   threaten

EXERCISE III Fill in the blanks from the list of words below.

reneging   upbraiding
parlaying   apprising
marauding   desecrating
prognosticating   parleying
appraising   explicating
stigmatizing   wheedling

1. The thirty-page article was devoted to _____ a single poem of a dozen lines.

2. Softened by the child's _____ , she let him stay up past his bedtime.

3. While you're _____ , tell me whether it's going to rain tomorrow.

4. By _____ the agency of your change of address, you have fulfilled your legal obligation.

5. Social groups often enforce uniformity by _____ nonconformists as insane or evil.

6. By _____ on their contract, they not only inconvenienced the buyers but damaged their credit in the business community.

7. John's mother was constantly berating him about his manners and _____ him for his clumsiness.

8. The youths were guilty of _____ a national monument by painting it with slogans and crude anatomical diagrams.

9. After _____ a modest capital into a small fortune, the entrepreneur retired at forty.

10. He gave the applicant a(n) _____ look, as if she were a side of beef and he a butcher considering a price.

11. If they are _____ for terms, a settlement of the border dispute must be imminent.

12. The province lapsed into lawless confusion as _____ soldiers ran rampant through the countryside.

EXERCISE IV Circle the letter of the best choice to complete each sentence.

1. _____ phenomenon defies explanation.
   a) An inexplicable b) A marauding c) A desecrating d) An unappraised

2. The phrase _____ recalls the original meaning of *stigmatize*.
   a) "lowdown and dirty" b) "hopelessly in love" c) "brand as a liar" d) "star quality"

3. An _____ prognosticates good fortune.
   a) upbraiding b) auspicious omen c) ominous sign d) appraisal

4. He _____ good looks and a pleasant voice into a singing career.
   a) parlayed   b) parleyed   c) appraised   d) wheedled

5. We took the heirlooms to a reliable jeweler to be _____ .
   a) reneged   b) apprised   c) marauded   d) appraised

6. Once captured, the _____ were stigmatized as outlaws.
   a) appraisers   b) marauders   c) explicators   d) wheedlers

LESSON 18

palpitate—flutter, tremble, beat rapidly. *The dog was palpitating with excitement as his master went to get the leash.*

enervate—weaken, debilitate, cause to lose energy or nerve. *A long illness can enervate even the strongest constitution.*

defile—make dirty, pollute, make ritually unclean, sully. *I wouldn't defile my hands with the profits from such cynical exploitation.*

obviate—eliminate as a requirement, make unnecessary. *A few phone calls can often obviate the delay of a protracted correspondence.*

flail—thrash, wave wildly, beat. *The younger child was flailing with his fists, trying to hit the older boy, who held him easily at arm's length. A flail is an old-fashioned farm implement—two sticks tied end to end so that one is a handle and the other can swing freely—used for threshing grain by hand. To flail is therefore to beat, as one beats grain with a flail, especially in a wild or free-swinging way.*

capitulate—surrender, yield. *The city capitulated to the victors without a shot being fired.*

beguile—trick or mislead, especially by pleasant or charming means. *While he pretended to be beguiled by Blanche's flirtatious attentions, Rochester knew that she was only interested in him for his money.*

inculcate—teach, instill, impress on the mind by repetition. *From earliest childhood they had been inculcated with the tenets of the community's beliefs.*

ululate—howl, hoot, wail in lamentation. *The ululating of wolves is perhaps the most haunting sound in nature.*

resuscitate—bring back to life, revive. *Artificial respiration was used to resuscitate the swimmer.*

ameliorate—improve, make or become better. *With the recent influx of wealth into the country, social conditions can be expected to ameliorate.*

wrest—take by violence. *In a bloody coup, a military junta wrested control of the government from the president and his cabinet.*

Answers to the following exercises are on page 201.

EXERCISE I Synonyms. Circle the letter of the word or phrase closest in meaning to the given word.

1. beguiled: a) pleasurably deceived b) widely diffused c) baited d) bated

2. inculcated: a) vaccinated b) dogmatic c) oriented d) indoctrinated

3. wrest: a) grab b) knock down c) hold tightly d) wave with wild abandon

4. obviate: a) neglect b) render nonessential c) make obvious d) become fertile

5. palpitate: a) cry out b) vibrate c) remain unmoved d) touch

6. resuscitated: a) brought to light b) hospitalized c) restored to life d) interred

7. ululation: a) deprivation b) keening lament c) wave-like motion d) grief

8. ameliorate: a) sweeten b) enhance c) deteriorate d) promise

9. enervate: a) make excuses for b) surrender c) devitalize d) madden

10. defile: a) challenge b) straighten c) muddy d) question

11. flail: a) feel deep chagrin b) skin an animal c) sift d) pound furiously

12. capitulate: a) give in b) reiterate c) captivate d) decline

EXERCISE II Choose the best word to complete each sentence. Write it in the blank.

1. They longed to take a vacation somewhere where the air was not _____ with smoke and gas fumes.

    obviated   ululated
    inculcated   defiled

2. I was so terrified I could hear my heart _____.

    ameliorating   enervating
    palpitating   resuscitating

3. The president declared that _____ to the terrorists' demands would encourage others to follow the same violent course.

    resuscitation   defiling
    capitulation   inculcating

4. The square echoed with the _____ of the heartbroken mourners.

    inculcations   ululations
    capitulations   flailings

5. The policeman _____ the pistol from the assailant.

    wrested   capitulated
    flailed   obviated

6. In the distance we spotted three figures on the strand, _____ their arms to attract our attention.

    beguiling   palpitating
    wresting   flailing

7. When she fainted in the waiting room, the patient was _____ with smelling salts.

        resuscitated   defiled

        enervated   wrested

8. The optimistic forecast predicted that the housing shortage would be _____ by the end of the year.

        obviated   wrested

        ameliorated   ululated

9. A notarized signature will suffice; it will _____ the need for you to come in personally.

        beguile   capitulate

        resuscitate   obviate

10. The parents claimed that the cult's methods of _____ its doctrines amounted to brainwashing.

        ululating   palpitating

        beguiling   inculcating

11. _____ by the delightful company, she forgot that she had an appointment.

        Enervated   Beguiled

        Defiled   Ameliorated

12. The survivors were too _____ by their ordeal to eat much; all they wanted to do was sleep.

        ameliorated   flailed

        enervated   palpitated

EXERCISE III From memory, try to complete the following sentences with words from this lesson. The first letter of each answer is given before the blank. Write your answers in the blanks.

1. The patient's condition has [a] _____: his temperature is down and he is able to sit up.

2. The confidence man insinuated himself into the old lady's trust and [b] _____ her out of her savings.

3. In small matters many people will [c] _____ to unreasonable demands for the sake of avoiding a quarrel.

4. A scrupulously honest person feels [d] _____ by having to tell even a justifiable lie.

5. After sticking to a crash diet for over a week, she became too [e] _____ to go to work.

6. The man [f] _____ out in anger at the youth who had taunted him.

7. The father felt it was necessary to [i] _____ in his children a mistrust of strangers for their own protection.

8. The fact that she had worked for the company previously [o] _____ the need for an interview.

9. Picking up the fledgling robin that had fallen from its nest, the boy could feel it [p] _____ in his hand.

10. Heart massage successfully [r] _____ the stroke victim.

11. The campers' sleep was broken by the [u] _____ of the hyenas.

12. Charlene tried frantically to [w] _____ her toy truck from the teacher's grip.

LESSON 19

The items in this lesson are all nouns.

equanimity—calm temper, quality of being even-tempered or of remaining composed. *Unforeseen accidents and hostile questions could not ruffle the speaker's equanimity.*

affinity—relationship, kinship, special liking. *There is a close affinity among the many European languages, such as Spanish, French, and Italian, that are descended from Latin.*

opprobrium—reproach or scorn resulting from disgraceful conduct, infamy. *He deserved all the opprobrium he received for turning his back on a friend.*

proclivity—tendency, inclination, especially for something not approved of. *The child has a proclivity for getting into trouble.*

surveillance—a watching or observation, especially done by those in authority. *The police kept the house of the suspected drug dealers under 24-hour surveillance. Surveillance is a form of spying in which those doing the spying have more power or authority than those being spied upon. It comes from a French word meaning "oversee."*

juxtaposition—a placing close together. *The juxtaposition of the Capitol and the White House was avoided in planning the city of Washington to emphasize the separation of the legislature from the executive branch.* The verb is *juxtapose*, "to place together or in relation."

liaison—a connection, linking. *He had served as a liaison between the Allied command and the local government.* Also borrowed for English from French, *liaison* ultimately derives from the Latin verb *ligare*, "to bind."

chicanery—unethical methods, petty trickery, especially in legal matters. *He accused the winning candidates of chicanery in the election.*

travesty—an imitation of a serious work so as to make it seem ridiculous, a burlesque. *The new production of Shakespeare in modern language is a travesty.*

incidence—the range of occurrence of an effect. *The incidence of reported alcoholism among teenagers is increasing.*

rationale—rational basis, an explanation or justification supposedly based on reason. *They defended their discriminatory policy with the rationale that women were physically incompetent to perform the work. Rationale* used to have an entirely respectable meaning: a rationale was the underlying reason or logical basis for something. It can still be used in this neutral sense. Recently, however, it has acquired a negative flavor in many contexts. A *rationale* is now frequently a false or indefensible reason for something. When people make up plausible but bogus explanations for the things they do, we say they are *rationalizing*.

Answers to the following exercises are on pages 201 and 202.

EXERCISE I Synonyms. Circle the letter of the word or phrase closest in meaning to the given word.

1. opprobrium: a) ridicule b) severe disapproval c) approbation d) lack of enthusiasm

2. liaison: a) link b) trick c) cut d) embassy

3. chicanery: a) political participation b) legal action c) petty tricks d) news reporting

4. incidence: a) an urging b) number of occurrences c) statistic d) disagreement

5. proclivity: a) reluctance b) rashness c) friendliness d) tendency

6. travesty: a) itinerary b) costume c) ludicrous imitation d) insincere response

7. affinity: a) close relation b) engagement c) promise d) endlessness

8. surveillance: a) connection b) illegal harassment c) probation d) official watching

9. rationale: a) a rationing b) a misconceiving c) fundamental reason d) process of thought

10. juxtaposition: a) basis b) a splitting in two c) a placing together d) reconciliation

11. equanimity: a) vivaciousness b) calmness of mind c) creativity d) fairness

EXERCISE II Fill in the blanks from the list of words below.

affinity	equanimity
liaison	travesty
rationale	opprobrium
incidence	juxtaposition
chicanery	proclivity
surveillance	

1. Because of the patient's _____ for drug abuse, the physician hesitated to prescribe even a mild sedative.

2. The landlord was guilty of _____ in trying to insert a new clause into the lease after it had been signed.

3. A suicidal prisoner must be kept under constant _____.

4. Treachery and cowardice in the face of the enemy earned them
   universal _____.

5. Because we have such similar tastes, I feel a great _____ with
   Edith, as if she were my own sister.

6. Since the jury was prejudiced, the defense attorney incompetent, and the
   judge bribed, the case was a(n) _____ of justice.

7. The _____ of cancer was unusually high in the area that had
   been sprayed with Agent Orange.

8. Her _____ was not disturbed by the commotion around her; she
   was an island of calm in a sea of hysteria.

9. The _____ for the increased rates was that fuel costs had risen
   38 percent.

10. The _____ of photographs by the two artists in the exhibit made
    the difference in sensibility obvious.

11. A special officer acted as _____ between the company and
    community organizations.

EXERCISE III From memory, try to complete the following sentences with
words from this lesson. The first letter of each answer is given before the blank.
Write your answers in the blanks.

1. The close [a] _____ of design and color leads me to think that
   the two textiles must have been woven in the same region, perhaps in the
   same village.

2. The [c] _____ involved in her real estate dealings, though not
   actually illegal, was bad enough to embarrass her when it was exposed in
   the newspapers.

3. Richard has the [e] _____ and patience to watch five kids at
   the beach all day without once losing his temper.

4. The [i] _____ of fatal automobile accidents nationwide dropped
   when the 55-mph speed limit went into effect.

5. The [j] _____ of the elegant old mansion and the drive-in
   donut shop created a bizarre look.

6. As spokesperson for the department, she acted as a [l] _____
   with other government agencies.

7. Although he was never legally charged with any crime, he lost his position
   and suffered public [o] _____ for betraying the nation's trust.

8. A [p] _____ for eating when depressed can lead to obesity.

9. They claimed national security as the [r] _____ for their sudden
   attack.

10. Wiretapping is a kind of electronic [s] _____.

11. The plot is so improbable and the prose so ludicrous, I think the author must
    have intended the novel as a [t] _____ of a gothic romance.

EXERCISE IV Circle the letter of the correct choice to complete each sentence.

1. Things that are juxtaposed are not   a) parallel   b) distant from each other   c) akin   d) commonly found

2. A travesty is never   a) publicly acknowledged   b) humorous   c) the result of a proclivity for burlesque   d) respectful

3. Things having an affinity are likely to   a) last   b) lean   c) have a high incidence   d) be similar

4. A rationale purports to be   a) reasonable   b) laughable   c) planned   d) bigoted

5. Most people cannot face opprobrium with complete   a) surveillance   b) anxiety   c) equanimity   d) affinity

6. A liaison is a means of   a) deception   b) communication   c) making money   d) chicanery

LESSON 20

The words in this lesson are frequently misunderstood or confused with each other.

ambiguous—having more than one possible meaning. *The ambiguous wording of some legislative acts requires clarification by the courts.*

ambivalent—having conflicting feelings. *I am ambivalent about the job; although the atmosphere and people are pleasant, the work itself is boring.*

adverse—opposing, contrary. *Adverse winds slowed the progress of the ship.*

averse—having a dislike or reluctance. *The perennial bachelor is averse to matrimony, at least for himself.*

imply—suggest indirectly, say without stating outright. *Although they made no comment, their cool manner implied strong disapproval of the scheme.*

infer—to conclude from reasoning or evidence. *From hints that the student dropped, the instructor inferred that he was having problems at home.*

flaunt—to display freely, defiantly, or ostentatiously. *Flaunting expensive jewelry in public may be an unwitting invitation to robbery.*

flout—to mock, show contempt for. *He flouted respectability by appearing with his lover in public.*

affect—to influence. *The judge did not allow his personal feelings to affect his judgment of the case's legal merits.*

effect—to bring about, cause. *New regulations have effected a shift in policy on applications.*

imminent—about to happen, soon to occur. *With the storm imminent, we brought in the lawn furniture and closed all the windows.*

eminent—outstanding, prominent, distinguished. *She is an eminent scholar of Russian literature and she is widely acclaimed for her work as a translator.*

unique—without like or equal, unmatched, single in its kind. *The statue was valuable because of its unique beauty.* You will see *unique* used loosely to mean "superior" or "unusual," but in formal prose it generally signifies "one of a kind."

disinterested—not involved, unprejudiced. *A disinterested witness is one who has no personal stake in the outcome of the case.* In formal usage, *disinterested* does not mean "uninterested" but rather "impartial."

Answers to the following exercises are on page 202.

EXERCISE I Synonyms. Circle the letter of the word or phrase closest in meaning to the given word.

1. eminent: a) renowned   b) likely   c) threatening   d) profound

2. disinterested: a) thoughtful   b) uncaring   c) unbiased   d) immoderate

3. flaunt: a) waive   b) disregard   c) show off   d) float

4. imminent: a) prominent   b) approximate   c) in close proximity   d) impending

5. ambiguous: a) dense   b) emotionally confused   c) able to use both hands equally   d) open to more than one interpretation

6. flout: a) treat with consideration   b) scornfully disregard   c) be ignorant of   d) recommend

7. unique: a) very good   b) sole   c) coherent   d) cloned

8. infer: a) guess on the basis of evidence   b) comprehend   c) imprecate   d) suggest indirectly

9. averse: a) unwilling   b) detracting   c) dashing   d) contradictory

10. effect: a) influence   b) hurry   c) modify   d) cause

11. ambivalent: a) emotionally torn   b) stubborn   c) intricate   d) mysterious in meaning

12. adverse: a) dilatory   b) working against   c) conditional   d) turned upside down

13. implied: a) concluded   b) hinted at   c) reasoned   d) involved

14. affected: a) brought to pass   b) diseased   c) emphasized   d) changed

EXERCISE II Fill in the blanks from the list of words below.

ambiguous	unique
inferred	ambivalent
flouted	flaunted
implied	disinterested
averse	eminent
imminent	adverse

1. While any number of prints can be made from a single engraving, every painting, good or bad, is _____.

2. The source he quoted in his paper was not an obscure commentator but a(n) _____ authority in the field.

3. That rain had been predicted could be _____ from the fact that two-thirds of the people in the street were carrying umbrellas.

4. Her outrageous conduct _____ her parents' notions of propriety, causing them deep chagrin.

5. The voters, _____ to paying higher taxes, defeated the proposal.

6. The low voter turnout was blamed on apathy and _____ weather conditions.

7. Whenever he returned to his hometown, he _____ his new-found wealth in front of all the people who had derided his ambition.

8. The student was _____ about attending college so far from home; she was both very nervous and very happy at the prospect.

9. Janice said that she thought she had done badly on the test, but her cheerful manner _____ otherwise.

10. Warned by a phone call that an explosion was _____, police evacuated the building immediately.

11. You are prejudiced because the man is your friend, but a(n) _____ observer would say that he is acting unfairly.

12. The note they left was so _____ I couldn't figure out if they were planning to return or not.

EXERCISE III Circle the letter of the best choice to complete each sentence.

1. To affect a person's mood is to a) change it in some way b) dampen his spirits c) create it d) ridicule it

2. Another way of saying *to effect* is a) to affect b) to influence c) to have an effect on d) to put into effect

3. An adverse review is a) glowing b) reluctantly favorable c) negative d) tepid

4. The object of flaunting something is generally to a) inspire disdain b) offend sensibilities c) inspire admiration and envy d) disguise one's real motive

5. When a disaster is about to strike, great misfortune is a) ambivalent b) imminent c) eminent d) ambiguous

REVIEW TEST 2

1. *Though elated by his rank, it did not render him supercilious; on the contrary, he was all attention to everybody.*

    —Jane Austen

The man described is probably   a) truculent   b) arrogant   c) gregarious   d) a malefactor

2. *The news of the morning become stale and vapid by the dinner hour.*

    —William Hazlitt

Another word for vapid is   a) false   b) forgotten   c) brief   d) lifeless

Questions 3 and 4.

On the third day my mother sickened; her fever was accompanied by the most alarming symptoms, and the looks of her medical attendants prognosticated the worst event. On her deathbed the fortitude and benignity of this best of women did not desert her.

—Mary Shelley

3. The looks of the mother's attendants   a) were avuncular   b) foretold her death   c) obviated a cure   d) implied that she was malingering

4. Benignity means   a) patience   b) stamina   c) goodness   d) sense of humor

5. *We commented adversely upon the imbecility of that telegraphic style.*

    —Joseph Conrad

The writer's comments on the style may be imagined as   a) caustic   b) conciliatory   c) amenable   d) vacuous

Questions 6 and 7.

The mates regularly relieved each other at the watches, and for aught that could be seen the contrary, they seemed to be the only commanders of the ship; only they sometimes issued from the cabin with orders so sudden and peremptory, that after all it was plain they but commanded vicariously.

—Herman Melville

6. A peremptory order is   a) not feasible   b) meticulous   c) imperiously commanding   d) ambiguously worded

7. By saying that the mates "commanded vicariously" Melville implies

that   a) they were too stringent   b) someone else really gave the orders
c) they took pleasure in giving orders   d) the crew was obstreperous

Questions 8 and 9.

False facts are highly injurious to the progress of science, for they often endure long; but false views, if supported by some evidence, do little harm, for everyone takes a salutary pleasure in proving their falseness and when this is done, one path towards error is closed and the road to truth is often at the same time opened.

—Charles Darwin

8. The harm of false views is in Darwin's opinion   a) blatant   b) ingenuous
c) ephemeral   d) imponderable

9. A salutary pleasure   a) is enjoyed alone   b) is intellectually demanding
c) enervates scientists   d) has benign results

10.   *His demeanor was exceedingly capricious and even grotesque.*

—Edgar Allan Poe

The behavior of a capricious person is   a) erratic   b) offensive   c) incorrigible
d) beguiling

11.   *I had my formidable goat-skin coat on, with the great cap I have mentioned, a naked sword by my side, two pistols in my belt, and a gun upon each shoulder.*

—Daniel Defoe

The writer's coat is   a) ankle-length   b) furry   c) impressive   d) antiquated

12.   *He must persuade himself that Death can be propitiated, circumvented, abolished.*

—George Bernard Shaw

Circumvented here means   a) delayed   b) evaded   c) eliminated   d) conquered

13.   *The arguments employed are of very different value: some are important and sound, others are confused or quibbling.*

—Bertrand Russell

The arguments of little value mentioned by Russell are either confused or   a) of
minor importance   b) logically unsound   c) out of date   d) turgid

14.   *There is accordingly something outside of the artist to which he owes allegiance, a devotion to which he must surrender and sacrifice himself in order to earn and to obtain his unique position.*

—T. S. Eliot

According to Eliot's statement   a) artists should be amenable to criticism
b) good artists are credulous   c) the position of the artist belongs to him
alone   d) artists should flaunt their independence

Questions 15 and 16.

I began to understand why Starkfield emerged from its six months' siege like a starved garrison capitulating without quarter. Twenty years earlier

the means of resistance must have been far fewer, and the enemy in com-
mand of almost all the lines of access between the beleaguered vil-
lages . . . .

—*Edith Wharton*

15. Capitulating means   a) surrendering   b) negotiating   c) holding out
    d) retreating

16. The narrator describes the villages as if they were   a) averse to surviving
    hardships   b) ameliorating   c) isolated and under siege   d) in a
    federation

Questions 17-19.

We have thus far endeavored rudely to trace the genealogy of the Verte-
brata by the aid of their mutual affinities. We will now look to man as he
exists; and we shall, I think, be able partially to restore the structure of
our early progenitors . . . .

—*Charles Darwin*

17. By his own account, Darwin has tried to describe   a) man's history   b) the
    structure of vertebrates   c) the augmenting of an animal population
    d) the lines of descent of the vertebrates

18. Affinities here means   a) similarities   b) affections   c) traits   d) locations

19. Progenitors are   a) distant cousins   b) anthropologists   c) direct ancestors
    d) early varieties

20.   *An immediate result of the promulgation of the evolution theory*
        was . . . to give an immense impulse to comparative anatomy . . . .

—*James G. Frazer*

Promulgation here probably means   a) general opprobrium   b) wide
    acceptance   c) rational basis   d) tendency

Answers to the above questions are on page 202.

LESSON 21

Ten nouns for naming people:

thrall—slave, serf. *Frank is a thrall to his television set on Sundays during the football season.* There is also the verb *enthrall*, which means "enslave or captivate," as in: *We were so enthralled by the movie that we couldn't go out for popcorn.*

raconteur—skilled storyteller. *A raconteur knows how to time punchlines for maximum effect. Raconteur* has been borrowed unchanged from French. In French a female storyteller is a *raconteuse*, but in English it is acceptable to use the masculine form for everybody.

consort—wife or husband, especially of a monarch. *The consort shares in the honors of the ruler.*

muckraker—reporter or publisher who exposes scandal or corruption in public life. *Thomas Nast was a muckraker who used political cartoons to expose the corruption of New York's Tammany Hall.*

yahoo—man as a filthy, degraded, ignorant, or vicious brute. *Yahoos in the stands yelled obscenities and threw beer bottles at the players.*

pariah—outcast, person scorned and therefore excluded. *Her disreputable, filthy clothes and disoriented manner marked her as one of society's pariahs. Pariah* entered English from India, where it originally referred to a person of a very low, hereditary social caste.

gamin—street urchin, an impoverished and neglected child who lives in the streets. *The gamins of Milan make a living by begging and by petty theft.*

nemesis—person who pursues for vengeance or exacts retribution, one who works tirelessly for another's harm or punishment. *Among the mythic figures of the Old West is the Lone Ranger—friend of the helpless and nemesis of outlaws.* In Greek mythology, Nemesis is the goddess who metes out divine justice to arrogant mortals.

interloper—meddler, an outsider who interferes where he or she has no right or business. *Ten years after the wedding the old woman still regarded her daughter-in-law as an interloper in the family.*

wiseacre—person who deludes himself that he knows everything, a fool. *A wiseacre believes he is impressing people when in fact he is posturing like an idiot.*

Answers to the following exercises are on page 202.

EXERCISE I Synonyms. Draw a line connecting each word with the word or phrase that means most nearly the same.

1.	interloper	teller of anecdotes
2.	gamin	pursuer
3.	wiseacre	meddler
4.	muckraker	exposer of graft
5.	consort	foul brute
6.	yahoo	street ragamuffin
7.	thrall	serf
8.	raconteur	outcast
9.	nemesis	marriage partner
10.	pariah	fool

EXERCISE II Circle the letter of the best choice to complete each sentence.

1. A pariah is   a) a castaway   b) feted   c) elegantly garbed   d) ostracized

2. A wiseacre is   a) enviable   b) a witty conversationalist   c) a self-enchanted buffoon   d) a sage

3. A yahoo seems   a) debonair   b) highly educated   c) subhuman   d) affable

4. A raconteur is generally   a) an entertaining guest   b) a wise counselor   c) a person of no talent   d) painfully shy

5. A nemesis is persistent in   a) meddling in other people's business   b) telling stories   c) digging up information   d) stalking his prey

6. A consort is   a) an outcast   b) someone's spouse   c) a nation's ruler   d) a parent

7. An interloper is similar to   a) a busybody   b) a prizefighter   c) a marriage-broker   d) a jogger

8. A gamin, by definition, is   a) charming   b) an orphan   c) cunning   d) a juvenile

9. A thrall is a person   a) in bondage   b) who seeks thrills   c) of repulsive aspect   d) who has mastered a skill

10. A muckraker is usually   a) a government employee   b) a heavy drinker   c) a reporter   d) a pervert

EXERCISE III From the following list of names, pick a term to match the description given in each of the sentences below. Write the names in the blanks.

yahoo	gamin
raconteur	interloper
consort	nemesis
thrall	wiseacre
muckraker	pariah

1. Their older brother kept the children entertained by his tall tales so that they didn't get cranky during the long delay.   _____

2. Prince Albert was the husband of England's Queen Victoria.

_____

3. Her investigative reports led to the indictment of several public officials for conspiracy to fix prices. _____

4. In one of Boccaccio's stories, a ludicrous doctor from Bologna boasts of his learning and brilliance even while he's being duped by two Florentine painters. _____

5. Though it's none of her affair, Alicia always tries to tell us how to run the council. _____

6. Because of his heretical opinions and demented outbursts, almost everyone in the village crossed the street when they saw him coming. _____

7. She was in the grip of an obsession, unable to break free or to make a rational choice. _____

8. Refusing to give up the chase, the detective swore to pursue the suspect to the ends of the earth. _____

9. The child seemed to have no other home than an alleyway, where she huddled for warmth at night with a handful of other waifs.

_____

10. Hating everything more civilized than himself, he took a mindless joy in slashing the exquisite canvases. _____

Names Borrowed from Literature

The word *muckraker* comes from Bunyan's *Pilgrim's Progress*, a seventeenth-century allegory of Christian salvation immensely popular with generations of English readers. Christiana, the heroine of the second part, sees a man with a muck-rake who only looks downward. When offered a heavenly crown in exchange for his rake, "the man did neither look up nor regard, but raked to himself the straws, the small sticks, and dust of the floor." In 1906 Teddy Roosevelt revived the term by calling someone a *muckraker*, and the word has been used ever since to describe people who dig up political dirt.

Yahoo was coined by Jonathan Swift in his eighteenth-century satire *Gulliver's Travels*. On his last voyage, Gulliver comes ashore in the land of the Houyhnhnms, a race of horses free of passions and blessed with perfect reason. The horses are masters of the Yahoos, a degenerate race of men without speech or reason. Lewd, filthy, and vicious, the Yahoos like to scramble up trees to pelt Gulliver with their excrement. In the end, the odious Yahoos turn Gulliver against mankind for good. When he returns to England, he can't bear to be in the same room even with his own family and spends most of his time out in the stable with his horses.

LESSON 22

The nouns in this lesson name things.

precedent—similar earlier event, especially one used as a model or justification for present action. *The lawyer's brief argued that the legal precedents cited by the opposition were not relevant because of subsequent changes in the law.* The *precedent* is something which has *preceded* present events.

tribunal—any court of law, especially when conceived as a seat of judgment or justice. *An international tribunal convened at Nuremburg to try German leaders for war crimes.*

chronology—arrangement by time, list of events by date. *The book included a chronology of the poet's life against the background of the major political events of his age.* The Greek *chronos* (time) likewise gives us *chronic* (occurring over a long time), *chronicle* (a history written in time order), and *chronometer* (a time-measuring device—a highly accurate clock).

quorum—minimum number of members that must be present for an assembly to conduct business. *No votes may be taken until there are enough representatives present to constitute a quorum.*

bibliography—a list of sources of information on a particular subject. *She assembled a bibliography of major works on early American history published since 1960.* Although the Greek root *biblion* means "book," a bibliography may include other sources besides books—articles on microfiche, for instance.

archives—historic records. *A separate building houses the United States archives in Washington.*

dichotomy—division of one thing into two parts, often opposed. *The dichotomy of his position—half instructor, half administrator—made efficient work in either field impossible.*

schism—a split, break-up, especially over a difference in doctrine and usually within a church. *The Great Schism split medieval Christianity into two branches, now called Eastern Orthodox and Roman Catholic.*

hegemony—predominance, exclusive leadership, especially among nations. *Hitler's aim was German hegemony over the world.*

epitome—a summary, an abstract, an individual part taken to represent the whole or class. *He prepared an epitome of his work to show the editor. Epitome* comes from a Greek word meaning "to cut short." The verb form is *epitomize*.

referendum—the holding of a vote in which the entire electorate instead of its representatives decides on a public issue. *A state referendum can override the decision of the legislature. Referendum* comes from the same Latin root as *refer*, which literally means "to carry back." In a referendum, a public issue is referred or carried back to the ultimate public authority, the voters.

Answers to the following exercises are on page 202.

EXERCISE I Choose the best word to complete each sentence. Write it in the blank.

1. Although the regime was able to subvert the judicial process within its own border, it was convicted in the _____ of world opinion.
    precedent   tribunal
    referendum   chronology

2. Logical thought recognizes a _____ between a thing and its negation, as for instance between *true* and *untrue*.
    referendum   hegemony
    schism   dichotomy

3. At its height, Roman _____ extended across Europe as far north as Scotland.
    hegemony   archives
    bibliography   tribunals

4. A(n) _____ treatment of historical material makes clear the sequence of specific events but does little to clarify the long-term causes of social upheavals.
    archival   bibliographical
    schismatic   chronological

5. The student consulted a _____ to discover what criticism had been written about the novelist's works.
    bibliography   chronology
    dichotomy   quorum

6. The Constitution of the Student Council specifies that two-thirds of the membership shall constitute a(n) _____.
    hegemony   archives
    quorum   epitome

7. The voters of the state endorsed the tax reform by a _____.
    referendum   schism
    precedent   quorum

8. In a(n) _____ over basic philosophy, the party split into two rival factions.
    quorum   dichotomy
    schism   epitome

9. Anthologies attempt to present a(n) _____ of an author's work.
    referedum   precedent
    bibliography   epitome

10. The uncatalogued _____ of the historical society could be a gold mine for anyone researching the early settlement of the territory.
    dichotomy   hegemony
    tribunal   archives

11. There is no _____ for this event: nothing like it has ever happened before.
    chronology   precedent
    hegemony   epitome

EXERCISE II Circle the letter of the best choice to complete each sentence.

1. Quorum refers to   a) trials   b) number of convictions   c) number of members   d) type of legislature

2. A precedent is   a) an earlier instance   b) something present   c) something forgotten   d) an outcome

3. An epitome   a) indexes   b) infers   c) links   d) summarizes

4. Hegemony is a kind of   a) power   b) resistance   c) business   d) plant

5. A dichotomy involves   a) opposed halves   b) churches   c) training   d) holders of public office

6. Bibliographies list   a) historical events   b) sources of information   c) court cases   d) addresses

7. Archives are most likely to interest   a) voters   b) politicians   c) historians   d) the aged

8. A tribunal is a place of   a) historical interest   b) worship   c) judgment   d) research

9. A referendum is a kind of   a) recall   b) list   c) resource   d) vote

10. A schism usually involves a conflict of   a) beliefs   b) facts   c) schedules   d) tastes

11. Chronological order is   a) sequential   b) ahistorical   c) short   d) alphabetical

EXERCISE III From memory, try to complete the following sentences with words from this lesson. The first letter of each answer is given before the blank. Write your answers in the blanks.

1. An earlier case in which the same law was interpreted by the court may serve as a [p] _____.

2. In the Hollywood films of the thirties, Marlene Dietrich was the [e] _____ of the sultry, sophisticated temptress.

3. Records of geological expeditions spanning several decades are stored in the museum's [a] _____.

4. The Monroe Doctrine declared United States [h] _____ over the western hemisphere.

5. The proposition will appear as a [r] _____ on the ballot in November.

6. The book included a [b] _____ listing all the works that the author had cited.

7. The Reformation at the end of the Middle Ages marked a permanent [s] _____ between the Catholic and Protestant churches.

8. A head count of the assembly determined that there was a
   [q] _____ present.

9. I know in general what happened, but I'm uncertain about the
   [c] _____ of events.

10. If a President is impeached, he must be tried in the [t] _____ of
    the Senate.

11. Analyses of the human condition in the West frequently rest on a
    [d] _____, such as body and soul or matter and spirit.

LESSON 23

This lesson and the next one are comprised of verbs.

satiate—gratify completely, surfeit. *Employees at candy factories soon get so satiated that they never eat the stuff.* The state of complete gratification in which desire is extinguished is *satiety*.

ensconce—place in a comfortable or secure position. *Ensconced in an easy chair, he spent the evening reading his favorite Hardy novel.* Ensconce etymologically means "to place in a small fortification"; it still suggests a position of snug safety.

disparage—speak slightingly of, belittle. *A teacher who disparages the efforts of beginners in a subject is not helping them.*

commiserate—feel or express sympathy or pity for. *It is natural to commiserate with the innocent victim of an accident.*

belie—lie about, misrepresent, show to be false, fail to fulfill. *Her laughing face belied her pretense of annoyance.* In this sentence *belied* means "showed to be false." In the sentence, *Her words belied her thoughts, belied* means "disguised or lied about." With *belie*, you must determine from the context which meaning is appropriate.

reminisce—recall past events, remember, especially to talk about the past in a fond or nostalgic way. *When old college chums get together they like to reminisce about their undergraduate adventures.*

vacillate—fluctuate, change back and forth, be inconsistent. *The employer's manner vacillated between oppressive friendliness and peremptory command.*

inundate—flood, overwhelm. *When the craze was at its height, the police were inundated daily with reports of UFO sightings.* Based on a Latin word *unda* (wave), *inundate* literally means "to flood or cover in waves." A river overflows its banks and inundates the fields. But the word is very often used figuratively, as in: *The company was inundated with orders.*

metamorphose—transform, change radically in form or character. *Two months abroad metamorphosed him from a naive youth into a man of the world.* The noun meaning transformation is *metamorphosis*, plural *metamorphoses*.

allude—refer indirectly or by suggestion, refer to without naming explicitly. *The book alludes to an earlier document that we have been unable to locate or even identify.* An act of alluding is *allusion.* Don't confuse this word with *elude,* "escape."

Answers to the following exercises are on page 202.

EXERCISE I Synonyms. Circle the letter of the word or phrase closest in meaning to the given word.

1. commiserate: a) be instrumental   b) sympathize   c) earn a commission   d) be miserable

2. belie: a) reveal as false   b) underlie   c) resemble   d) lie to

3. allude to: a) be shy   b) mention indirectly   c) harp on   d) condemn

4. reminisce: a) send back   b) reduce in size   c) talk about the past   d) nag

5. vacillate: a) be devoid of interest   b) tremble   c) be unswerving   d) go back and forth

6. satiate: a) spill over   b) satisfy to the limit   c) weaken   d) relax

7. metamorphose: a) change form   b) change one's mind   c) overdose   d) mythologize

8. inundate: a) vibrate   b) flood   c) sink   d) move like a wave

9. ensconce: a) position snugly   b) sink   c) kindle   d) defend vigorously

10. disparage: a) discard   b) cancel   c) put down   d) bombard

EXERCISE II Choose the best word to complete each sentence. Write it in the blank.

1. A parent who is alternately too strict and too indulgent is one who

_____.

    vacillates   reminisces

    satiates   belies

2. Because they are periodically _____ by the Nile, the fields are productive.

    satiated   alluded to

    ensconced   inundated

3. The transformation of an ugly duckling into a graceful swan is a(n)

_____.

    metamorphosis   inundation

    vacillation   disparagement

4. His disparaging comments about television _____ his own fascination with the medium.

    ensconce   belie

    vacillate   commiserate

5. The author's adoption of the name Ishmael is a(n) _____ to the Biblical Ishmael, an outcast and a wanderer.

    allusion   satiety

    vacillation   metamorphosis

6. Having comfortably _____ the invalid on the couch, the nurse went into the kitchen to make tea.

    belied   ensconced

    reminisced   alluded to

7. We had eaten Italian pastries to the point of _____. We couldn't even think about supper.

    metamorphosis   inundation

    satiety   commiseration

8. Joanne's _____ of those days were bathed in a nostalgic glow: they were not at all the way Bill remembered things.

    commiserations   disparagements

    reminiscences   vacillations

9. Anyone who suffers such misfortunes deserves some _____.

    disparagement   allusion

    ensconcing   commiseration

EXERCISE III From memory, try to complete the following sentences with words from this lesson. The first letter of each answer is given before the blank. Write your answers in the blanks.

1. The professor mystified most of the class by [a] _____ to economic theories they had no acquaintance with.

2. The outbreak of renewed hostilities [b] _____ our hopes for an early ceasefire.

3. We met at a coffee shop to [c] _____ over the difficulty of the assignments.

4. Jealousy caused her to [d] _____ the appearance of her rival.

5. Having received the appointment as a political payoff, he spent many years [e] _____ at public expense in a job that paid well and demanded little.

6. Every year at this time the department is [i] _____ with requests for extensions: it seems everyone needs more time to finish his paper.

7. Wrapped in its cocoon, the caterpillar will [m] _____ into a butterfly.

8. Most people learn about their family histories by listening to older members [r] _____.

9. Three movies and a concert in a single week can [s] _____ anyone's desire for entertainment.

10. Some people who [v] _____ endlessly over trivial matters can nevertheless make momentous decisions quickly and decisively.

Metamorphoses

A metamorphosis is a radical change. Biologists use the word to label the transformation certain animals undergo—pupa into adult insect, tadpole into frog. At about the time of Christ, the Latin poet Ovid used it to refer to shape changes in Greek and Roman myths. His long poem called the *Metamorphoses* is an encyclopedia of transformations. Men and women are turned into trees, birds, snakes, flowers; gods disguise their shapes to meddle in human affairs; heroes are raised to the heavens as stars. The world itself, as an orderly cosmos, has metamorphosed from primeval chaos and remains in constant flux. Although everything is threatened with transformation, though everything passes away, the poet hopes by his work to make his name immortal.

LESSON 24

traverse—cross and recross, go back and forth over. *For days the ship traversed the area, searching for the lost whaling boat.*

emanate—derive, issue forth. *American law emanates largely from English common law.*

corroborate—provided added proof. *Laws of evidence require that testimony on a crime be corroborated by other circumstances.*

dissemble—conceal or misrepresent the true nature of something. *He dissembled his real motives under a pretense of unselfish concern.*

stultify—make appear or feel stupid, absurd, or useless. *The hot, smoky atmosphere of the room was stultifying: no one could concentrate on the work.*

ossify—become bone, become rigidly set in a pattern, habit, or custom. *The flexible limbs of the infant were not yet completely ossified.*

proscribe—outlaw, forbid by law. *Theft is proscribed for the most part by state law.*

ascribe—attribute, assign as a cause or source. *His death was ascribed to poison.* *Ascribe* and *proscribe* are both derived from the Latin verb *scribere*, "to write." Among the many other descendants of *scribere* are *script, describe, inscribe, subscribe,* and *scribble.*

vilify—defame, attempt to degrade by slander. *The man was sued for attempting to vilify the physician.*

inure—harden or accustom to difficulty or pain. *A life of hard physical labor has inured them to petty discomforts.*

Answers to the following exercises are on page 203.

EXERCISE I Synonyms. Circle the word or phrase closest in meaning to the given word.

  1. traverse: a) double-cross b) crisscross c) crosshatch d) crossbreed

2. corroborate: a) support b) corrode c) fabricate d) testify

3. dissemble: a) forget b) adjourn a meeting c) feign d) differ

4. inure: a) eschew b) calcify c) deplete d) accustom

5. vilify: a) brag b) premeditate c) attack a reputation d) supplant

6. proscribe: a) make illegal b) write an order for c) eradicate
     d) underwrite

7. stultify: a) intrigue b) make stupid c) deprecate d) enliven

8. emanate: a) allude b) derive c) retrogress d) mimic

9. ossify: a) terrify b) melt c) harden d) decay

10. ascribe: a) attribute b) authorize c) substitute d) cause

EXERCISE II Fill in the blanks from the list of words below.

stultified	proscribed
ascribed	ossified
traversed	corroborated
dissembled	inured
emanated	vilified

1. We have _____ this terrain many times in our discussions but so far have been unable to reach a satisfactory compromise.

2. The possession of an unlicensed handgun is _____ by statute in this city.

3. Early feminists were frequently _____ in the press as comical and unnatural harridans.

4. The candidate's letter only _____ the opinion I had already formed of him: I was more convinced than ever that his election would be disastrous for the state.

5. He was not a handsome man; his great attractiveness _____ from a forceful and exuberant personality rather than physical appearance.

6. She soon felt _____ by the turgid and lackluster prose: after twenty minutes of studying she put the textbook down and dropped off to sleep.

7. Envious rivals _____ her success to sheer ruthlessness.

8. Discovered in the moonlit courtyard by the murderer, the heroine _____ her real reason for being out so late by pretending that she had heard a crash.

9. I am so _____ to her complaints that I don't even hear them anymore.

10. The rules of the game had become so _____ by custom that no one even considered whether they could be improved.

EXERCISE III Antonyms. Draw a line connecting each word with the word or phrase most nearly its *opposite*.

1. vilify	go back to a source
2. inure	soften
3. dissemble	require legally
4. stultify	dispute
5. corroborate	make brilliant
6. proscribe	be forthright
7. ossify	sensitize
8. emanate	exalt

EXERCISE IV From memory, try to complete the following sentences with words from this lesson. The first letter of each answer is given before the blank. Write your answers in the blanks.

1. His happiness can be [a] _____ to his forthcoming wedding.

2. An impartial eyewitness came forward to [c] _____ the victim's version of the accident.

3. Although she tried out of shyness to [d] _____ her feelings, love was obvious in the way she gazed at the older boy.

4. We could not locate the source of the alarm in our building; it seemed to [e] _____ from the store across the street.

5. Working in an emergency room must [i] _____ people to grisly sights.

6. Over the years, doctrines that begin as flexible and responsive attempts to serve present needs tend to [o] _____ into rigid prescription.

7. The drugs scheduled by the FDA are [p] _____ for sale except by a doctor's prescription.

8. The tedious lecture had so [s] _____ the class that they couldn't come up with a single question.

9. The hunters knew every foot of the river, having [t] _____ it many times in pursuit of game.

10. She had [v] _____ her former colleague by spreading rumors of his avarice and incompetence.

The *ify* ending of many verbs means "to make." It is from the same Latin *facere* (to make) that gives us *factory* and *munificent* (see Lesson 11).
Since *stultus* means "foolish," *stultify* means _____.
Since *os* means "bone," *ossify* means _____.
Since *vilis* means "vile," *vilify* means _____.
Without looking them up, you can easily analyze the roots of

beautify _____

glorify _____

solidify _____

falsify _____

signify _____

Now try to guess the root meanings of the following words. Use your dictionary to check your answers. In each case, does the etymological (root) meaning reflect the way we really use the word?

mortify _____

sanctify _____

deify _____

reify _____

petrify _____

rectify _____

calcify _____

LESSON 25

The adjectives in this lesson all describe sense experiences—sight, hearing, touch, smell, and taste.

impervious—not able to be permeated or penetrated, therefore not open to influence or able to be affected. *Wood is often treated with a finish, such as wax or polyurethane, to make it impervious to water.*

luminous—bright, shining, bathed in light or giving off light. *The night was clear and luminous from the full moon.*

torrid—uncomfortably hot, scorching, parched by heat. *Death Valley is reputed to have the most torrid temperatures of any place in the United States.*

dulcet—sweet-sounding, soft and soothing to hear. *It was pleasant to wake to the dulcet chiming of the bells.*

resonant—echoing, full-sounding, vibrating to a sound and thereby amplifying it. *The cello, like other stringed instruments, consists of a resonant box over which strings are stretched to different pitches.*

palatable—tasty, pleasing to the taste. *The water was slightly greenish but still palatable.*

effervescent—bubbling, foaming, therefore vivacious, lively. *Carbonated beverages are effervescent.*

malleable—able to be shaped, adaptable. *Gold, a soft metal, is highly malleable.*

fetid—evil-smelling, stinking. *The fetid smell of rotting garbage permeated the alley.*

gossamer—filmy, very soft and light, thin. *The gossamer fabric felt as light as a cobweb.*

verdant—green with vegetation, fresh with plant life. *The verdant lawn made the old house look beautiful.*

Answers to the following exercises are on page 203.

EXERCISE I Antonyms. Circle the letter of the word or phrase most *opposite* in meaning to the given word.

1. effervescent: a) flat b) tepid c) boiling d) sublime

2. gossamer: a) semitransparent b) resilient c) wintry d) thick

3. resonant: a) parched b) sound-deadening c) stiff d) audible

4. impervious: a) rocklike b) lifelike c) spongelike d) wet

5. verdant: a) summery b) sere and brown c) tried and true d) blooming

6. malleable: a) rotten b) unbending c) nonmetallic d) liquid

7. dulcet: a) sour-tasting b) bitter c) strident d) restless

8. luminous: a) darkened b) unpleasant c) harsh-sounding d) horrific

9. torrid: a) unrestrained b) untwisted c) clean d) frigid

10. palatable: a) in poor taste b) evil-smelling c) inedible d) flowery

11. fetid: a) icy b) fragrant c) postnatal d) nervous

EXERCISE II Choose the best word to complete each sentence. Write it in the blank.

1. Since it had been left uncovered, the clay had dried and was no
   longer _____.

fetid	palatable
malleable	verdant

2. The novel was advertised as a _____ romance of unbridled passions and burning desire.

gossamer	dulcet
torrid	palatable

3. When the child saw his mother returning, his face became _____ with joy.

impervious	luminous
fetid	resonant

4. Wastes drained into a(n) _____ sewer that ran down the middle of the street.

torrid	luminous
effervescent	fetid

5. The cave was so _____ that even the slightest whisper echoed loudly.

resonant	impervious
dulcet	luminous

6. The meal, though not fancy, was _____ and the salad was especially delicious.

palatable	luminous
verdant	effervescent

7. Worn and cracked with age, the tarp was no longer _____ to rain.

      effervescent   resonant

      impervious   malleable

8. The dancers were dressed in long, _____ skirts that floated as they moved.

      resonant   malleable

      dulcet   gossamer

9. _____ mixers such as tonic or soda water make alcohol enter the bloodstream faster.

      Gossamer   Effervescent

      Palatable   Impervious

10. In May the fields are _____ with the young crops.

      fetid   torrid

      gossamer   verdant

11. The harpsichord has a tinkling, _____ sound best suited to small chamber performances.

      malleable   torrid

      dulcet   palatable

EXERCISE III From memory, try to complete the following sentences with words from this lesson. The first letter of each answer is given before the blank. Write your answers in the blanks.

1. Children are more [m] _____ than adults and adapt to new environments more readily.

2. In his dream the man was approached by a [l] _____ figure, blindingly bright, whom he took to be an angel.

3. She is [i] _____ to criticism because she doesn't care what other people think.

4. During the rainy season the landscape becomes [v] _____, burgeoning with fresh life.

5. He did not, for the most part, find German Romanticism [p] _____, and the music of Wagner positively turned his stomach.

6. The evangelist denounced the city as a new Babylon, a [f] _____ sink of corruption and vice.

7. The [d] _____, melodious entrance of the English horn contrasted with the brassy sound of the trumpets.

8. At the party we were in an [e] _____ mood, bubbling with excitement and eager to dance.

9. By ten o'clock the highway was [t] _____, the heat rising visibly from the asphalt.

10. The gown was of silky, [g] _____ material, so fine as to be almost weightless.

11. A well-trained, [r] _____ voice can fill a concert hall without electronic amplification.

EXERCISE IV Circle the letter of the best choice to complete each sentence.

1. A resonant concert hall is a) luxuriously accoutred b) acoustically live c) commodious d) impervious to extraneous noise

2. A palatable dish is a) baked b) unique c) highly spiced d) savory

3. If the figures in a painting appear on a verdant background, the scene is probably a) outdoors b) northern European c) stylized d) impressionistic

4. A fetid odor is a) inexorable b) vernal c) exotic d) repulsive

5. An example of a gossamer fabric is a) chiffon b) serge c) twill d) linen

6. An effervescent personality tends not to be a) malleable b) imperviously calm c) adaptive d) excitable

7. The pleasing babble of a stream sounds a) torrid b) resonant c) dulcet d) luminous

LESSON 26

This lesson and the next introduce a variety of adjectives.

execrable—extremely bad, hateful, detestable. *Although her acting was execrable, all her relatives in the audience applauded.*

inveterate—long and firmly established, entrenched. *The distrust of foreigners was inveterate among the native inhabitants.*

palpable—able to be felt, touched, or perceived distinctly, clear to the senses or the mind. *A drop in temperature was palpable five minutes after they turned on the air conditioning.* The Latin verb *palpare* means "to touch," so strictly speaking *palpable* means "able to be touched," though it is often used more loosely for anything that can be unquestionably perceived. The related word *palpate* is used by medical professionals to mean "examine by touching."

sable—black, dark. *The gentleman's servants were dressed in sable livery as a sign of mourning.* The *sable* is a small mammal valued for its dark fur. Its name, used by extension to mean "dark" or "black," is applied especially to things like fabric, hair, or fur.

pristine—untouched, unspoiled, in a state of original perfection or purity. *The wilderness looked pristine, as if they were the first people ever to set foot there.*

endemic—peculiar to or prevalent in an area or group. *Severe lung disease is endemic in coal-mining regions.*

pandemic—universal, found everywhere or over an entire large region, especially epidemic over a large area. *Malaria used to be pandemic in the tropical regions of the earth.* The three words *epidemic, endemic,* and *pandemic* are all used to describe conditions—often diseases—among populations (Greek *demos,* "people"). *Epidemic* connotes a prevalent condition that spreads rapidly. An epidemic may affect a large number of people but be over quickly. *Endemic* describes a persistent, long-term condition found in a limited area. If a condition is found over a very large area, it is *pandemic.*

multitudinous—very numerous. *The main design has been agreed upon, but there are multitudinous details still to be worked out. Multitudinous* is derived from the noun *multitude,* "great number."

sentient—able to feel or perceive, having sense perception or consciousness. *All sentient creatures respond to their environments.*

sonorous—resonant, having a rich, deep, full sound. *His sonorous voice helped make him a famous orator.*

succulent—juicy. *Plums ought to be sweet and succulent.* In botany, plants with juicy flesh, such as cacti, are called *succulents.*

Answers to the following exercises are on page 203.

EXERCISE I Antonyms. Circle the letter of the word or phrase most *opposite* in meaning to the given word.

1. endemic: a) free from disease   b) firmly established   c) unknown in a given area   d) extroverted

2. multitudinous: a) facile   b) united   c) unitarian   d) few

3. sonorous: a) tinny   b) loud   c) tawny   d) lewd

4. pristine: a) populated   b) sullied   c) austere   d) decorated

5. palpable: a) without merit   b) imperceptible   c) uncomfortable   d) imperturbable

6. pandemic: a) tranquil   b) resistant   c) autocratic   d) limited in scope

7. inveterate: a) venerable   b) well founded   c) newly introduced   d) reasonable

8. succulent: a) desiccated   b) malleable   c) preserved   d) cooked

9. sable: a) hairless   b) well lit   c) light in color   d) altering rapidly

10. execrable: a) immaculately clean   b) astonishing   c) justly despised   d) admirable

11. sentient: a) unconscionable   b) silly   c) without sensation   d) rarely found

EXERCISE II Choose the best word to complete each sentence. Write it in the blank.

1. He traced his _____ hatred of arbitrary discipline to the traumas he suffered as a child in an old-fashioned boarding school.
   sentient   pandemic
   endemic   inveterate

2. The _____ leaves of the aloe plant are soothing for minor burns.
   sonorous   sable
   succulent   execrable

3. _____ things are often compared to the grains of sand on a beach or the stars in the sky.
   Inveterate   Palpable
   Execrable   Multitudinous

4. Since researchers have detected pollutants in the atmosphere over the most sparsely inhabited southwestern deserts, they have concluded that air pollution is _____ in the United States.
   pandemic   execrable
   endemic   multitudinous

5. Although their intelligence is minimal, even fish are _____ creatures.
   multitudinous   inveterate
   sentient   succulent

6. The acoustic qualities of the cathedral made even reedy voices seem _____.
   sable   sonorous
   sentient   multitudinous

7. Wrapped in a _____ cloak, the woman was almost invisible in the darkness.
   succulent   pristine
   sable   palpable

8. As the star emerged suddenly onto the stage, the excitement in the crowd was almost _____, like a shock of electricity.
   pandemic   palpable
   execrable   pristine

9. The sight of a _____ sheet of paper waiting in the typewriter first thing in the morning has driven many writers to drink.
   pristine   sable
   sentient   sonorous

10. By professional standards the snapshots were _____: they were poorly framed and not a single one was in focus.
   succulent   endemic
   palpable   execrable

11. For many years hepatitis has been _____ to the southern shore of Lake Atitlan.
   endemic   pandemic
   pristine   sonorous

EXERCISE III Synonyms. Draw a line connecting each word with the word or phrase that means most nearly the same.

1. succulent	very bad
2. palpable	conscious
3. sonorous	long prevalent in one place
4. endemic	full sounding
5. sentient	touchable
6. pandemic	full of juice
7. execrable	black
8. multitudinous	deeply ingrained
9. pristine	unspotted
10. inveterate	of great number
11. sable	prevalent over a large area

LESSON 27

dilatory—slow, delaying, especially for the purpose of gaining time or postponing action. *A filibuster is one type of dilatory tactic that can delay action on a bill.*

culpable—faulty, deserving of blame. *The culpable shall not escape punishment. Culpable* comes from the Latin noun *culpa,* meaning "guilt" or "crime."

laudable—praiseworthy. *The girl listened to the old man's endless and repetitive stories with laudable patience.* The Latin root *laud* means "praise," so *laudable* literally means "able to be praised." Another word built on the same root is

laudatory—expressing praise. *Gracious in victory, the candidate made laudatory comments about the opposition.*

archaic—no longer in use, of an earlier period. *Some words like* thou, *once a common form of address, are now archaic.*

fallible—capable of erring or of being deceived in judgment. *All humans are fallible, although some are mistaken more often than others.*

reticent—reserved, unwilling to speak. *He was a shy boy, too reticent to participate in the class discussion.*

laconic—terse, pithy. *His laconic replies conveyed much in few words. Reticent* and *laconic* both describe a habit of not talking much, but they connote different things. A reticent woman is one who stays silent because she doesn't want to communicate certain information, for whatever reason. *Laconic* suggests packing a lot of significance into a few words. The laconic speaker communicates briefly but effectively.

voluble—very talkative, characterized by an easy flow of words. *He was a voluble speaker, never at a loss for words.*

tacit—silent, unspoken, implied rather than stated. *They had a tacit agreement never to mention the problem in front of the children.* Unlike the previous three entries, *tacit* is not used to describe people. It applies only to things—promises, alliances, ideas—that are understood by the people involved without being put into words.

obdurate—hard, unyielding, hardhearted. *The rancher was obdurate in resisting the pleading of his friends. Obdurate* may just mean very stubborn, but it frequently carries a negative connotation: an obdurate person is likely to be stubborn in a bad cause or unyielding to compassion or pity. The *dur* root from Latin, meaning "hard or lasting," is the same root that gives us *durable.*

tractable—easily led, directed, or controlled. *A tractable worker is a boon to the supervisor but is not usually a good leader.* The Latin root *tract* means "draw" or "pull." A tractable person is easy to pull along.

Answers to the following exercises are on page 203.

EXERCISE I Synonyms. Circle the letter of the word or phrase closest in meaning to the given word.

1. tacit: a) silent b) polite c) tactful d) palpable

2. obdurate: a) argumentative b) unbending c) ill-advised d) irrational

3. laudable: a) noisy b) ancient c) deserving praise d) speechless

4. fallible: a) marred b) criminal c) capable of error d) stumbling

5. reticent: a) reserved b) deceptive c) slow-moving d) refined

6. tractable: a) able to be traced b) deceptive c) slow-moving d) docile

7. laconic: a) verbose b) terse c) unspoken d) lazy

8. culpable: a) impeached b) guilty c) doubtful d) charged with negligence

9. laudatory: a) full of praise b) servile c) long-winded d) concerning hearing

10. voluble: a) gossiping b) enormous c) talkative d) taciturn

11. dilatory: a) widening b) stalling c) collapsing d) political

12. archaic: a) newfangled b) rounded c) useless d) obsolete

EXERCISE II Fill in the blanks from the list of words below.

voluble	tacit
obdurate	laconic
reticent	tractable
laudable	dilatory
archaic	laudatory
fallible	culpable

1. Although the President's proposal doesn't go as far as we would like, it is a _____ beginning and deserves our support.

2. Many older respondents especially are _____ about answering questions concerning their personal lives on questionnaires.

3. John Wayne was famous for his _____ drawl: in some films he seems hardly to speak at all.

4. The crowd at the Fourth of July celebration was pleased and flattered by the governor's _____ speech about the people of her state.

5. The more Anne drinks, the more _____ she becomes, until it's impossible for anyone else to slip a word in edgewise.

6. Although no one had actually said so, there was a _____ understanding that the meeting had to end by midnight.

7. The government was _____ in its refusal even to consider the just demands of the strikers.

8. Even a computer is _____ in that, if its initial data is wrong, its conclusions will be wrong.

9. His _____ behavior was unconsciously aimed at postponing his departure.

10. Everyone who exacerbated the situation is _____ to some extent for the tragedy that ensued.

11. The poems of the elderly Drayton were in the _____ style of an earlier age.

12. Despite their bulk, oxen are _____ animals, obedient and relatively easy to control.

EXERCISE III Antonyms. Draw a line connecting each word with the word or phrase most nearly its *opposite*.

1. fallible   frank
2. dilatory   contemporary
3. reticent   tractable
4. tacit   invariably correct
5. laudatory   laudable
6. laconic   condemning
7. culpable   expeditious
8. archaic   spelled out
9. obdurate   voluble

The Latin *tract* (draw or pull) is at the root of many familiar English words. A *tractor,* for instance, is literally a machine for pulling. To *contract* is to pull together, in other words, to *shrink*. Try to guess the literal or etymological meaning of each of the verbs *italicized* below. Use your dictionary to check your answers.

The sloppiness of her syntax *detracts* from the power of her writing.

_____

I was *distracted* from my work by the yelling in the street.

_____

Travelers are *attracted* to the picturesque beauty of the region.

_____

The dentist had to *extract* the tooth.

_____

The hearings were *protracted* by the oratorical performances of individual committee members.

_____

The newspaper *retracted* the story and printed an apology.

_____

LESSON 28

The twelve adjectives below describe the qualities and behavior of people.

blasé—jaded, bored, too accustomed to something, such as pleasure or excitement, to show any interest. *Having seen innumerable horror films, they were too blasé to be frightened by old-fashioned ghost stories. Blasé* comes from a French word meaning "sated."

ascetic—practicing self-denial, austere. *In accordance with their beliefs, the community lived an ascetic life of hard physical labor, frugal meals, and no stimulants. Ascetic* implies a deliberate self-denial of physical pleasures. A person who goes hungry on purpose is ascetic; a person who goes hungry because he or she can't afford food is poor.

ebullient—very lively, bubbling over with energy or high spirits. *The children, ebullient at the prospect of a picnic, tumbled out of the bus the moment it stopped.* Since the Latin root *ebullire* means "to boil up," *ebullient* expresses the same figurative meaning as the English word *bubbly.*

gauche—without social grace, tactless. *They consider it gauche to ask acquaintances how much they earn or how much they paid for something.*

proficient—capable, skilled, expert. *Only someone entirely proficient in both languages can do simultaneous translation.*

suave—smoothly polite, very polished or sophisticated in social relations. *His suave manners reflected great confidence and poise.*

insolent—openly disrespectful, impertinent. *The teacher, who refused to tolerate insolent behavior, sent the pupil to the principal's office for talking back in class.*

obsequious—servile, overly willing to obey. *His obsequious obedience to the conquerors turned our stomachs.*

choleric—quick to anger, short-tempered. *The coach had a choleric personality and was frequently ejected from games for insulting the referees.*

phlegmatic—unexcitable, slow to act, sluggish. *On hearing that he had won two million dollars in the lottery, the phlegmatic man looked mildly pleased.*

melancholy—habitually sad, depressed, gloomy, brooding. *Abraham Lincoln was a melancholy figure, somberly dressed and rarely seen to smile.* An alternative form is *melancholic.*

sanguine—ardent, confident, optimistic. *The spokesperson was sanguine about the movement's chances for success.*

Answers to the following exercises are on pages 203 and 204.

EXERCISE I Fill in the blanks from the list of words below.

insolent	obsequious
blasé	ebullient
sanguine	proficient
melancholy	gauche
suave	phlegmatic
choleric	ascetic

1. Someone who always finds something to be depressed about is by nature _____.

2. A person who expects things to improve is _____ about the future.

3. A(n) _____ host knows how to put people at ease and how to smooth over awkward moments.

4. Anyone who can type eighty words a minute is a(n) _____ typist.

5. A young man who jeers at authority in general and insults his parents in particular is _____.

6. A woman who flies into a rage over trifles is _____.

7. A person who disapproves of physical indulgence is _____.

8. A guest who embarrasses people at a party by saying all the wrong things and criticizing the food is _____.

9. A person who by nature never seems to get worked up over anything is _____.

10. Many people feel that it is a sign of sophistication to act _____ about sex.

11. A(n) _____ employee flatters the ego of an insecure boss.

12. A cheerleader appears _____ when her team is winning.

EXERCISE II Antonyms. Circle the letter of the word or phrase most *opposite* in meaning to the given word.

1. suave: a) foolish b) mentally unbalanced c) gauche d) decorous

2. melancholy: a) adept b) ominous c) slow-paced d) cheerful

3. blasé: a) excited b) passé c) demented d) ridiculous

4. obsequious: a) ebullient b) insolent c) joyous d) submissive

5. proficient: a) tired b) lazy c) inept d) poker-faced

6. choleric: a) serviceable b) phlegmatic c) monotone d) insufferable

7. ebullient: a) placid b) repetitious c) peaceable d) exhaustive

8. ascetic: a) sympathetic b) uncritical c) ugly d) self-indulgent

9. sanguine: a) pessimistic b) resentful c) diffident d) haughty

EXERCISE III Choose the best word to complete each sentence. Write it in the blank.

1. Though they could afford it, they were too _____ to install a hot tub.

    melancholy   proficient
    ascetic   gauche

2. Though she had pretended to be blasé about the match, she became _____ when she defeated her rival.

    ebullient   choleric
    sanguine   phlegmatic

3. Long experience had made the physician _____ at quick diagnoses.

    ascetic   sanguine
    insolent   proficient

4. The _____ old storekeeper continually became enraged at the insolent manners of his customers.

    choleric   gauche
    blasé   phlegmatic

5. In his long movie career, Cary Grant epitomized _____ sophistication.

    choleric   ascetic
    melancholy   suave

6. While I take a(n) _____ view of our financial prospects, I don't think we can afford to go to Europe this year.

    sanguine   obsequious
    blasé   insolent

7. Pierre became increasingly _____ as, one by one, his illusions were shattered.

    suave   melancholy
    sanguine   ebullient

8. Carole was deferential to her superiors without being _____.

    proficient   ascetic
    obsequious   ebullient

9. It was _____ of them to try to drag other people into their private squabble.

    suave   gauche
    blasē   phlegmatic

10. The judge was a calm, _____ sort, though I did see him lose his temper once.

<blockquote>
obsequious   insolent
choleric   phlegmatic
</blockquote>

Words from Medieval Medicine

Until modern times, medical theory in Europe held that four bodily fluids, called humors, determined each person's physical and emotional health. The humors were thought to be blood (Latin *sanguis*), choler (also called yellow bile), black bile (Greek *melancholia*), and phlegm. Certain personality traits were said to be caused by an imbalance among the humors. In a *sanguine* person, blood was dominant; a quick-tempered person was *choleric*; a sluggish, *phlegmatic* individual had too much clammy phlegm; and the *melancholy* man suffered from an excess of black bile.

Since in the medieval view each human being was a microcosm, or world in miniature, the four humors were analogous to the four elements (earth, water, fire, and air) that together made up the universe as a whole.

LESSON 29

The following terms are all Latin words and phrases that have been borrowed unchanged into English. If you are not sure how to pronounce any of them, check your dictionary. The literal meanings in Latin are given in parentheses.

alter ego—(other I) other self, person who represents another aspect of one's own personality, a close friend or companion. *As a child I was so attached to my sister that she seemed like my alter ego.*

bona fide—(in good faith) genuine, honest, without deceit or fraud. *Many people who saw the house expressed interest, but theirs was the first bona fide offer.*

moratorium—(a delaying) the lawful delaying of a payment, as in an emergency, any formally declared period of delay. *Students declared a moratorium on classes for the week of the national strike.*

de jure—(according to right) according to law, legal though not necessarily actual. *Although in power, the regime was not considered a government de jure by the neighboring countries.*

de facto—(according to fact) actual as opposed to legal, in fact. *Despite having no government title, he was the de facto head of state.*

ad hoc—(to this) for a special purpose or occasion only. *The ad hoc constitution committee will be dissolved as soon as its job is accomplished.*

modus vivendi—(way of living) a way of living, an arrangement conflicting parties work out for getting along despite their differences. *People who work in the same office usually have a modus vivendi by which they can work together even if they don't like one another.*

modus operandi—(way of operating) way of operating, the way something or someone works. *Police refer to the particular method or style of a criminal as his modus operandi, or m. o.*

per annum—(by the year) every year, by the year. *The membership fee is payable per annum.*

per diem—(by the day) every day, by the day. *A private investigator is often hired on a per diem basis.*

sine die—(without a day) without a day being set, usually, without a date for reconvening appointed. *Congress adjourned sine die.*

alumnus—(foster child) a pupil or student, usually a former student who has graduated. *We sent invitations to the class reunion to every alumnus for whom we have an address. Alumnus is the masculine form; its plural is alumni. The feminine form is alumna, plural alumnae.*

Answers to the following exercises are on page 204.

EXERCISE I Synonyms. Circle the letter of the word or phrase closest in meaning to the given term.

1. de jure: a) by legal right b) permanent c) former d) by jury

2. per diem: a) once b) for each person c) not nocturnal d) daily

3. de facto: a) facetious b) manufactured c) factitious d) actual

4. sine die: a) deathless b) timeless c) without setting a date d) tireless

5. bona fide: a) fraudulent b) done in good faith c) promised d) loyal

6. modus operandi: a) real circumstances b) how something works
    c) conflict of opinion d) glamorous business

7. alumnus: a) graduate b) recruit c) professor d) professional

8. moratorium: a) concert hall b) death c) suspension of activity d) lack
    of provision

9. alter ego: a) repressed anger b) second self c) radical alteration
    d) self-conceit

10. ad hoc: a) entrenched b) temporizing c) extemporaneous d) temporary

11. per annum: a) each day b) on salary c) yearly d) on commission

12. modus vivendi: a) criminal method b) means of smoothing over
    differences c) cooperative apartment d) cooperative venture

EXERCISE II Circle the letter of the best choice to complete each sentence.

1. A group is most likely to adjourn sine die a) when there is a deadlock
    b) just before a long recess c) on principle d) when it is meeting
    regularly

2. An ad hoc group is formed a) for a limited purpose b) by lot c) by
    secret ballot d) for subversive purposes

3. A modus vivendi is required when parties are a) in love b) in a meeting
    c) in potential conflict d) at war

4. A bona fide first edition of a book is   a) leatherbound   b) old   c) in poor condition   d) a real first edition

5. One might describe as an alter ego a person who is   a) an alien   b) a soulmate   c) schizophrenic   d) notorious

6. A person's modus operandi includes his or her   a) wardrobe   b) birth certificate   c) habitual conduct   d) assets

7. The graduates of a women's college are   a) alumna   b) alumnae c) alumnus   d) alumnuses

8. If one rents a machine per diem, one has it   a) on a day-to-day basis b) for a month   c) for an indefinite period of time   d) for a year

9. The opposite of de jure is   a) defunct   b) per annum   c) in default   d) de facto

10. One declares a moratorium in order to   a) posit something   b) flush out a culprit   c) postpone something   d) test something

EXERCISE III From the following list of terms, pick the one most appropriate to each of the sentences below. Write the terms in the blanks.

alumnus	ad hoc
moratorium	de facto
per diem	per annum
de jure	sine die
alter ego	bona fide
modus vivendi	modus operandi

1. Though we do not approve of their ideology or believe that they hold office legally, we must recognize that they do in fact have firm control of the nation's political institutions.   _____

2. Mr. Hyde is the expression of the savage side of Dr. Jekyll's nature.   _____

3. As a graduate of the college he contributes to the scholarship fund.   _____

4. The interest on the loan amounts to ninety dollars for one year.   _____

5. He works nights and she works days, so they manage to share the apartment without too much conflict.   _____

6. When the meeting broke up, no date was set for the first fall session.   _____

7. The council appointed a committee for the purpose of greeting the incoming president.   _____

8. Police suspect that the same person committed all the burglaries because in every case the means of entry was the same.   _____

9. On the verge of bankruptcy, the city government obtained legal authority to postpone repaying its loans.   _____

10. Once suspected of being a forgery, the portrait is now known to be genuine. _____

11. Although he has no power, many of his fellow exiles recognize him as the rightful leader of their country. _____

LESSON 30

The following are twelve more Latin terms that have been adopted without change into English. The literal meaning of each word or phrase in Latin is given in parentheses. Once again, check your dictionary if you are unsure of pronunciation.

placebo—(I shall please) a sugar pill, a remedy without medical value given usually for psychological effect. *Believing the placebo to be a sedative, the anxious patient soon began to relax.*

mores—(customs) customs, principles of conduct within a culture. *The mores of any group are enforced by indoctrination and social pressure to conform.*

pro forma—(for form's sake) as a matter of form or propriety. *The confirmation vote is purely pro forma, since there is no opposition to this nominee.*

non sequitur—(it does not follow) a conclusion that does not follow from the premises or evidence, a logically unjustified conclusion or inference. *The supposedly logical argument was nothing but a tissue of non sequiturs.*

gratis—(as favors) free of charge, without payment. *When I had selected a large purchase of fruits and vegetables, the grocer added a couple of ripe tomatoes gratis.*

quid pro quo—(this for that) a fair exchange of one thing for another. *The rent is a quid pro quo not only for the use of the space but for certain services that the landlord is obligated to provide.*

tabula rasa—(scraped tablet) a blank slate, a writing table scraped clean to receive fresh impressions. *Philosophers formerly compared the mind of a newborn to a tabula rasa on which sensory experiences were impressed.*

status quo—(the state in which) the way things are, the present state of affairs. *The name conservative implies a desire to maintain the status quo, to keep things the way they are.*

sine qua non—(without which not) an essential condition or prerequisite for something. *The knack for knowing what people want is the sine qua non of successful public relations.*

emeritus—(having served out one's time) retired but still holding one's professional title. *He no longer teaches but is listed in the catalogue as a professor emeritus.*

erratum—(an error) a mistake in printing or writing. *The proofreader marked the erratum for correction by the printer.* The plural is *errata*.

sic—(thus) this way in the original. *Sic* in English has very specialized use. If in writing you quote a source that contains a mistake, you should put *sic* in brackets [ ] after the mistake to indicate to your reader that the passage appears thus in the original.

Answers to the following exercises are on page 204.

EXERCISE I Synonyms. Circle the letter of the word or phrase closest in meaning to the given word.

1. tabula rasa: a) razor's edge   b) clean table   c) graph   d) blank slate

2. mores: a) regulations   b) customs   c) avarice   d) affections

3. gratis: a) without recompense   b) as a suggestion   c) grateful   d) scraped

4. errata: a) illogical conclusions   b) grammatical errors   c) typographical errors   d) misdemeanors

5. quid pro quo: a) tender offer   b) tit for tat   c) gift   d) payment for professional services

6. emeritus: a) having completed service   b) experienced   c) enrolled as a student   d) planning retirement

7. placebo: a) pleasantry   b) worthless effort   c) sugar pill   d) locality

8. pro forma: a) formless   b) as a formality   c) formalist   d) computed by a formula

9. sic: a) interesting   b) bogus   c) not in the original   d) thus in the original

10. status quo: a) existing state of things   b) flux   c) high social standing   d) economic crisis

11. non sequitur: a) argumentation   b) untrue premise   c) illogical inference   d) guesswork

12. sine qua non: a) conundrum   b) frill   c) fine point   d) necessary precondition

EXERCISE II From the following list of terms, pick the one most appropriate to each of the sentences below. Write the terms in the blanks.

quid pro quo	gratis
non sequitur	mores
status quo	emeritus
placebo	errata
tabula rasa	sine qua non
pro forma	

1. I had to pay for the repairs, but he gave me the advice free of charge.

   _____

2. Having been bit by one dog, he concluded that all dogs were dangerous.

   _____

3. As a matter of respect, she is addressed by her title even though she has been retired for many years.

   _____

4. Fresh ingredients are the basis of excellent cuisine; you must start with good food to make good food. _____

5. After the book had been printed, the publisher inserted a slip in the front listing several printer's errors that hadn't been corrected.

   _____

6. In the experiment, one group was given the drug while a control group was given a sugar pill that looked identical. _____

7. Since you have already been paid, submitting a bill is merely a formality; the company requires a bill for its records. _____

8. They wished to wipe out the past and start over, as if they were facing the issue for the first time, without preconceived notions. _____

9. Those who benefit most from the present state of affairs have a vested interest in seeing that power is not redistributed. _____

10. Society operates according to a huge system of rules, only a small portion of which are actually codified in laws. _____

11. The president promised the representative a federal work project in his district in exchange for support on the tax bill. _____

EXERCISE III Circle the letter of the best choice to complete each sentence.

1. "John Kennedy, elected in 1956 [sic], was felled by an assassin's bullet in 1963." *Sic* in this sentence means that   a) Kennedy's election was regrettable   b) the outcome of the 1956 election was highly unexpected   c) the author of the sentence is incorrect about the date of Kennedy's election   d) the person quoting the passage has added this date

2. A non sequitur is a kind of   a) prejudice   b) gratuity   c) fallacious conclusion   d) error in writing

3. The sine qua non of college acceptance is almost always   a) a high school diploma   b) emeritus standing   c) an average above B   d) an academic record that is a tabula rasa

4. In learning the mores of a society, one learns   a) how to dance   b) private secrets   c) how to behave with decorum   d) occult knowledge

5. A quid pro quo is a kind of   a) status quo   b) swap   c) false remedy   d) formality

REVIEW TEST 3

1.   *Anything to equal the determined reticence of Mr. Jaggers under that roof I never saw elsewhere, even in him.*

                                                            —*Charles Dickens*

The writer implies that Mr. Jaggers was normally   a) not voluble   b) a raconteur   c) effervescent   d) not phlegmatic

2.   *A sullen darkness now hovered above us—but from out of the milky depths of the ocean a luminous glare arose and stole up along the bulwarks of the boat.*

                                                            —*Edgar Allan Poe*

Luminous here means   a) brightly shining   b) phosphorescent   c) artificial   d) white

3.   *I shall satiate my ardent curiosity with the sight of a part of the world never before visited, and may tread a land never before imprinted by the foot of man.*

                                                            —*Mary Shelley*

The speaker expects his curiosity to be   a) aroused   b) satisfied to the limit   c) boundless   d) dampened

4.   *The Act of 1833 cautiously added that such wares must be* bona fide *articles of Mediterranean trade, that is, must not have come into that sea by way of the Atlantic.*

                                                            —*J. H. Clapham*

Bona fide means   a) valuable   b) laudable   c) genuine   d) ethnic

Questions 5 and 6.

        He seemed part of the mute melancholy landscape, an incarnation of its frozen woe, with all that was warm and sentient in him fast bound below the surface. . . .

                                                            —*Edith Wharton*

5. The landscape seems   a) torrid   b) gloomy   c) alien   d) verdant

6. Sentient here means   a) capable of feeling   b) angry   c) intelligent   d) jubilant

Questions 7 and 8.

        Had she been ensconced here under other and more pleasant conditions

98

she would have become alarmed; but, outside humanity, she had at
present no fear.

—*Thomas Hardy*

7. The woman described is a) a gamin b) obdurate c) an interloper in
   society d) estranged from her fellow beings

8. Ensconced means a) introduced b) snugly situated c) discovered
      b) threatened

9.   *The day is an epitome of the year.*

—*Henry David Thoreau*

Thoreau means that a day a) summarizes the year b) is a significant part of a
      year c) seems very long d) is a de facto year

Questions 10–12.
      By this time the company began to hold their noses; but the doctor, with-
      out taking the least notice of this signal, proceeded to show that many
      fetid substances were not only agreeable but salutary. . . .

—*Tobias Smollett*

10. The doctor was a) describing mores b) impervious to signals c) dis-
      sembling d) commiserating with the ill

11. A fetid substance a) stinks b) is swollen c) bubbles d) is a placebo

12. As a learned fool, the doctor may be called a a) vilifier b) nemesis
      c) wiseacre d) doctor emeritus

13.   *He was one of a class . . . who, from cultivating within their bosom a*
      certain tendency toward suspicion, have come to think that all Govern-
      ment servants are idle, dilatory, supercilious, and incompetent.

—*Anthony Trollope*

The character described suspects public servants of a) overzealousness
      b) deliberately causing delays c) errata d) corroborating each
      other's stories

14.   *Now a free nation must have liberty to bring forward schemes for the*
      public accommodation, and to have them decided by some public tri-
      bunal after full investigation, and hearing all parties.

—*R. D. Baxter*

A tribunal is a) a place of judgment b) an investigation of facts c) an
      election d) an impeachment

15.   *So now, as an infallible way of making little ease great ease, I began to*
      contract a quantity of debt.

—*Charles Dickens*

If a way is infallible, it a) is private b) is highly ordered c) always
      works d) is without precedent

Questions 16 and 17.

> *Some of them are unmannered, rough, intractable, as well as ignorant; but others are docile, have a wish to learn, and evince a disposition that pleases me.*
>
> —*Charlotte Brontë*

16. An intractable person   a) resists being taught   b) is dull   c) disparages the efforts of others   d) is confused

17. To evince a disposition is to   a) modify behavior   b) criticize a decision   c) hint at a possibility   d) display a character

18.
> *I sat at a table where were rich food and wine in abundance, an obsequious attendance, but sincerity and truth were not; and I went away hungry from the inhospitable board.*
>
> —*Henry David Thoreau*

Obsequious attendance refers to   a) execrable service   b) a gaudy setting   c) fawning servants   d) a meticulous attention to detail

19.
> *This is by no means a truism, but on the contrary a palpable falsehood.*
>
> —*Bertrand Russell*

Palpable in this sentence means   a) obvious   b) able to be touched   c) emotionally charged   d) disgraceful

20.
> *I tasted them out of compliment to Nature, though they were scarcely palatable.*
>
> —*Henry David Thoreau*

The author found the food   a) unripe   b) bad-tasting   c) evil-smelling   d) succulent

Answers to the above questions are on page 204.

LESSON 31

The following ten nouns name kinds of places.

bastion—stronghold, fortified place, bulwark. *She was a bastion of common sense in a time of widespread hysteria.* Originally, a *bastion* was a projecting part of a fortified wall. It is now usually used figuratively to describe any strong defense.

enclave—small territory surrounded on all sides by an entity of which it is not a part. *West Berlin survives as an enclave in communist East Germany. Enclave* is similar in meaning to *bastion* but refers more to territorial isolation and political separateness. *Bastion* is less geographical and emphasizes the idea of strength and defense.

terra incognita—unknown land, territory yet unexplored. *They steamed up the river, past the last outpost, into a terra incognita of lush green jungle.* In Latin, *terra incognita* means literally "earth unknown." It is often used figuratively for anything unexplored, such as an area of research.

pantheon—originally, an ancient Roman temple to all of the gods, now used figuratively for any building or imagined place where the gods or the great heroes of a people are enshrined. *Andrew Sarris, in his seminal book,* The American Cinema, *proposed a pantheon of the greatest Hollywood directors.* In Greek, *pantheon* means "all the gods."

firmament—the sky, especially conceived as a vault arching over the earth. *As night fell, stars appeared in the firmament. Firmament* comes from the Latin *firmus* (steadfast), the same root that gives us the English *firm*. It was formerly believed that the earth stood motionless at the center of the universe. Beyond the sun and moon and the moving planets was a great celestial sphere of "fixed" stars which were thought to be unchanging, hence the term *firmament*.

sepulcher—tomb, burial vault. *The remains of the king were placed in a rich and ornate sepulcher.* Also spelled *sepulchre*. The adjective *sepulchral* means "gloomy, tomblike, suggestive of the grave."

repository—any place where things are put for safekeeping or are stored securely. *She rented a safe-deposit box as a repository for her jewelry and bonds.*

kiosk—small, open-sided structure, such as a newsstand. *Tickets are sold at the kiosk at the entrance to the amusement park. Kiosk* comes from a Turkish word for an open-air pavilion.

vestibule—small entranceway. *The vestibule was just large enough for a coatrack and an umbrella stand.*

midden—a refuse heap marking the site of a prehistoric settlement. *Excavating the midden, they uncovered piles of broken shells. Midden,* often *kitchen midden,* is a term used by archeologists.

Answers to the following exercises are on page 204.

EXERCISE I Synonyms. Draw a line connecting each word with the word or phrase that means most nearly the same.

1. pantheon
2. kiosk
3. sepulcher
4. bastion
5. firmament
6. midden
7. terra incognita
8. enclave
9. vestibule
10. repository

unexplored land
place for safekeeping
fortress
foyer
vault of heaven
burial vault
area isolated within a larger one
newsstand
temple to all the gods
ancient trash heap

EXERCISE II Circle the letter of the best choice to complete each sentence.

1. A bastion is a place of   a) garbage   b) reverence   c) burial   d) protection

2. Terra incognita is likely to attract·   a) explorers   b) astronomers   c) people with valuables to protect   d) vacationers

3. A vestibule is generally   a) surrounded by hostile neighbors   b) a passageway to a larger space   c) spacious   d) uncharted

4. At a kiosk one is likely to find   a) verdure   b) armaments   c) magazines   d) lawn furniture

5. A midden is of interest to   a) archeologists   b) thieves   c) hoboes   d) architects

6. A repository is a place where property is   a) likely to be stolen   b) held securely   c) liquidated   d) catalogued

7. In the firmament one can observe   a) statues of the gods   b) the relics of the past   c) current events   d) the constellations

8. The original Pantheon was a place of   a) internment   b) barter   c) worship   d) sacrilege

9. As a region, an enclave is usually   a) indistinguishable from its environs   b) politically encircled   c) politically radical   d) walled

10. A sepulcher is a resting place for   a) the dead   b) weary travelers   c) valuables   d) the ambulatory

EXERCISE III From memory, try to complete the following sentences with words from this lesson. The first letter of each answer is given before the blank. Write your answers in the blanks.

1. The front door opened into a [v] _____ from which another door led into a much larger waiting room.

2. The empty house stood gloomy and silent, like a [s] _____ in which all his hopes had been buried.

3. We walked down to the corner to a [k] _____ on the sidewalk where one could buy newspapers and maps of the city.

4. People invest in insurance as a [b] _____ against the economic ruin that can follow from major disasters like prolonged illness.

5. The pottery shards found in the [m] _____ do not seem to have been made locally; they may have been carried there by a migrating tribe.

6. One wing of the portrait gallery was a [p] _____ of America's great inventors.

7. Cabinets in the museum's basement served as a [r] _____ for valuable nineteenth-century photographs.

8. The community of orthodox Amish is an [e] _____ set apart from mainstream American culture by different customs and beliefs.

9. Antarctica, that vast unknown expanse of ice, is the last great [t] _____ on the surface of this planet.

10. As the earth rotates, the signs of the zodiac seem to move across the [f] _____.

EXERCISE IV Circle the letter of the best choice to complete each sentence.

1. To one who has never studied it, the history of China is   a) a midden   b) a terra incognita   c) a repository of learning   d) a pantheon of emperors

2. A bell with a sepulchral tone sounds   a) an alarm   b) like wind chimes   c) like a death knell   d) cracked

3. At night in the fields shepherds studied the   a) pantheon   b) enclave   c) firmament   d) kiosk

4. A politically distinct enclave may also be   a) a bastion of resistance   b) a national repository   c) a vestibule   d) a midden of great archeological interest

5. A vestibule is   a) part of a firmament   b) dedicated to the gods   c) part of a larger architectural structure   d) not a palpable entity

Gods and Demons

In the epic poem *Paradise Lost*, the metropolis in Hell where Satan sits enthroned is called Pandemonium, the place of "all demons." It is in the great hall in Pandemonium that Satan proclaims to his followers that he has corrupted mankind, only to be answered by a universal hiss as all the fallen angels metamorphose into serpents. Milton coined the name by analogy with *pantheon*, and like the broadening of *pantheon*'s meaning, the definition of *pandemonium* over the years has widened. *Pandemonium* can now refer to any scene of wild and deafening confusion.

LESSON 32

The nouns below name kinds of workers.

emissary—one sent to influence opponents politically. *The rebels sent an emissary to propose a truce.*

diva—prima donna, a leading female singer in opera. *The diva received a standing ovation at the close of her aria.*

lapidary—worker or dealer in precious stones. *We took the emerald pendant to a lapidary for appraisal.*

curator—person who takes care of or supervises something such as a museum, a collection, or a library. *The curator supervised the installation of the paintings for the exhibit.* Curator comes from the Latin verb *curare,* "to care for."

steward—one who manages or supervises household affairs, finances, or property for others, especially, a person employed to oversee food and drink. *The wine steward made sure that the guests were well supplied with champagne.* Steward has many shades of meaning in different contexts. In labor unions, for instance, a *shop steward* is a member elected to represent the workers of his or her department.

choreographer—person who creates dances, one who plans the movements of a dance, especially a ballet. *Nijinsky was a choreographer as well as one of ballet's great dancers.*

pedagogue—teacher, often a pedantic or narrow-minded one. *A pedagogue was hired to tutor the children in music and math.*

philologist—scholar who studies the structure and evolution of languages as preserved in texts. *The philologist described the transmutation of Latin into the various Romance languages.* Etymologically, *philologist* means "word-lover." The word has been shifting in meaning over the last two centuries; at the moment it usually refers to a specialist in ancient Greek and Latin.

milliner—maker or seller of ladies' hats. *Reduced to poverty, Lily finds employment at a milliner's, trimming hats.*

ombudsman—public official charged with overseeing the activities of government agencies in order to protect the rights and interests of citizens. *Believing that the state office of education was acting irresponsibly, the couple appealed to a state ombudsman to intervene.* We have borrowed both the concept and the word *ombudsman* from the Swedish. The plural is *ombudsmen.*

thespian—actor. *Twenty would-be thespians auditioned for the leading role in the school play.* Thespis is said to be the first Greek to stage tragedies. The word *thespian* usually has a somewhat pretentious or comical tone.

entrepreneur—one who assumes the risks and the profits of a business. *He became an entrepreneur when he inherited a small import business.*

Answers to the following exercises are on page 204.

EXERCISE I Synonyms. Circle the letter of the word or phrase closest in meaning to the given word.

1. pedagogue: a) negotiator   b) political organizer   c) archivist
   d) dogmatic instructor

2. curator: a) faith healer   b) dealer in gems   c) museum caretaker
   d) janitor

3. ombudsman: a) police officer   b) outlander   c) citizen's advocate
   d) plaintiff

4. lapidary: a) stamp collector   b) lover of books   c) dog trainer
   d) diamond cutter

5. entrepreneur: a) practicing physician   b) owner of a business
   c) pensioner   d) employee

6. diva: a) ballerina   b) actress   c) star singer   d) female diver

7. choreographer: a) dance arranger   b) business manager of a dance troupe
   c) music critic   d) choral director

8. milliner: a) men's tailor   b) hat maker   c) flour producer   d) shoe
   salesperson

9. thespian: a) Greek scholar   b) student of theology   c) tragedian
   d) ballet master

10. emissary: a) actuary   b) representative to an enemy   c) teacher of
    languages   d) minister

11. philologist: a) troubleshooter   b) writer of romances   c) speech therapist
    d) language specialist

12. steward: a) manager of provisions   b) owner of an estate   c) arbiter of
    taste   d) Scottish noble

EXERCISE II Circle the letter of the best choice to complete each sentence.

1. Typically, a curator is trained to evaluate   a) art works   b) wines
   c) literary merit   d) industrial capacity

2. A lapidary must be a good judge of   a) cuisine   b) character   c) horses
   d) gems

3. An emissary is sent out to   a) sabotage factories   b) foster confusion
   c) influence political decisions   d) overthrow a government

4. One would go to a milliner to buy   a) a necklace   b) coins   c) yard goods
   d) a hat

5. An entrepreneur is generally   a) wealthy   b) a union member
   c) self-employed   d) an artist

6. A choreographer is concerned with   a) economic indicators   b) coordinated
   movement   c) preserving paintings   d) semantics

7. An ombudsman represents a) the people's interests b) paying clients c) national security interests d) a museum

8. A diva must have a highly disciplined a) following b) color sense c) voice d) routine of physical exercise

9. On a large estate, a steward is likely to be in charge of a) the education of the young b) domestic arrangements c) marital disputes d) washing the dishes

10. A philologist must have a firm grasp of a) tax law b) architectural principles c) paleontology d) grammatical structure

11. A thespian needs to be able to a) follow a conductor b) read music c) memorize easily d) evaluate a prospectus

12. A pedagogue is expected to a) educate others b) keep a household running smoothly c) move gracefully d) follow fashions

EXERCISE III From the following list of names, pick a term to match the description given in each of the sentences below. Write the names in the blanks.

choreographer	steward
emissary	thespian
milliner	diva
curator	philologist
lapidary	entrepreneur
ombudsman	pedagogue

1. From the form of some of the words, the professor concluded that the lyric was not from the classical period but earlier, from the Homeric period.

_____

2. For many years Beverly Sills was one of the foremost figures in American opera.

_____

3. On her income taxes she deducted part of her rent because she operated a mail-order business out of her apartment. _____

4. Besides being a dancer and a dance teacher, Martha Graham created numerous modern dance compositions, including *Frontier* and *Errands into the Maze.*

_____

5. Although a government employee herself, her job is to defend the public against the abuse of power by government. _____

6. The agent lobbied government leaders for an end to the embargo on arms sales to his country.

_____

7. Spreading the stones out on a velvet tray, she explained how the value of a diamond is determined.

_____

8. His job was to plan the menus and supervise the cooks and waiters.

_____

9. She worked in a boutique that sold everything in fashionable headgear from tiaras to turbans to sunshades. _____

10. Over the next year, the director is planning to expand the dinosaur exhibit and open a children's wing devoted to showing the experience of childhood in other cultures. _____

11. He strode across the stage, declaiming in stentorian tones that the question was "to be or not to be." _____

12. He drilled his young pupils over and over until they could recite the capitals of Europe in their sleep. _____

LESSON 33

The nouns in this lesson name people.

heretic—one who believes contrary to his or her church or established belief. *The Church condemned Galileo as a heretic for claiming that the earth moved around the sun.* The thing the heretic believes is called *heresy.*

tyro—novice, inexperienced beginner, especially an aggressive or overconfident one. *As a tyro in finance, he learned from his mistakes.*

zealot—one who is excessively dedicated to or zealous for a cause, a fanatic. *Zealots for reform, they had no patience for anyone who counseled conservatism.* Both *zealot* and *heretic* are frequently used in a religious context but both can be used more generally of other kinds of beliefs.

altruist—a person who acts unselfishly in the interests of others. *She proved herself an altruist by volunteering to help the flood victims when there was no hope of recompense.* The adjective to describe such a person is *altruistic.*

dilettante—a dabbler, a person who follows an interest, especially in the arts, only superficially or as an amusement. *She could afford to be a dilettante as a musican, since she did not depend on her playing for an income.*

charlatan—one who pretends to have skill or to know more than he does, especially in order to take advantage of others. *Charlatans who pretend they can cure cancer have been responsible for many deaths.*

ingrate—an ungrateful person. *After all they had done to help, only an ingrate would have failed to thank them.*

mendicant—a beggar. *Visitors to impoverished countries are often shocked at the number of mendicants in the streets. Mendicant* can also be used as an adjective, as in *mendicant friars.*

sycophant—a self-serving flatterer, one who flatters those in power for his or her own advantage. *Among the hangers-on at court were many sycophants prepared to tell the king anything he wanted to hear.*

paragon—a model of excellence, a person perfect in some way. *Odysseus, the deviser of the Trojan Horse, is a paragon of craftiness.*

nonagenarian—a person between ninety and one hundred years old. *Although he must have been a nonagenarian, he was still vigorous and his mind was lucid.*

Answers to the following exercises are on page 205.

EXERCISE I Synonyms. Circle the letter of the word or phrase closest in meaning to the given word.

1. mendicant: a) one who lies for personal gain b) would-be artist c) one who asks for alms d) generous person

2. paragon: a) wretch b) mimicker c) autocrat d) perfect model

3. ingrate: a) beggar b) unthankful person c) nervous person d) person with no family

4. nonagenarian: a) very old person b) legislator c) bad-tempered man d) parent

5. zealot: a) overenthusiastic proponent b) moving orator c) underpaid hireling d) talented organizer

6. heretic: a) conformist b) simpleton c) person who praises others d) person who rejects a common faith

7. sycophant: a) mindreader b) monarchist c) flatterer d) true believer

8. dilettante: a) gourmet d) mere amateur c) professional d) successful painter

9. tyro: a) beginner b) instructor c) sports fan d) veteran

10. altruist: a) irascible person b) worker c) kind of doctor d) self-sacrificing individual

11. charlatan: a) fool b) mature person c) knowledgeable person d) imposter

EXERCISE II Fill in the blanks from the list of words below.

nonagenarian	paragons
sycophants	mendicants
heretic	tyro
ingrate	charlatan
dilettante	altruist
zealots	

1. Rose had cause to resent her two older siblings who had always been held up by their parents as _____ of virtue.

2. The _____ for moral reform confiscated objects of worldly vanity—mirrors, portraits, wigs, finery, books—and made a bonfire of them in the town square.

3. She was a(n) _____ who ridiculed the very people whose kindness she had once depended on.

4. Part of the monarch's household budget was allocated for alms to be given daily to the _____ who gathered at the gates.

5. Anyone who dared to question the community's beliefs publicly was likely to be driven out of the settlement as a dangerous _____.

6. The letter-writer was a(n) _____ who pretended to know of their daughter's whereabouts in order to extract money from the distraught parents.

7. Five generations of the family were present, including one great-great-grand-mother, a frail _____.

8. He was a(n) _____ who worked tirelessly for others and gave little thought to his own comfort.

9. Visitors to the great director were disgusted by the fawning _____ with which he had surrounded himself.

10. The young man was a _____ with a smattering of knowledge in many fields but no real competence in any.

11. She had joined the firm as an ambitious _____ when she was just out of college.

EXERCISE III Circle the letter of the best choice to complete each sentence.

1. An ingrate never says _____.
    a) he's sorry   b) please   c) thank you   d) he doesn't know

2. An altruist acts for _____.
    a) her own good   b) irrational reasons   c) other people's welfare   d) the good of the state

3. A sycophant always _____ people in power.
    a) contradicts   b) flatters   c) plots against   d) emulates

4. A mendicant is likely to be _____.
    a) fastidious   b) neatly dressed   c) a paragon   d) a pauper

5. Someone with _____ is a tyro.
    a) a good appetite   b) a lot to learn   c) many advantages   d) great expertise

6. You can expect a nonagenarian to appear _____.
    a) aged   b) interested in politics   c) nonchalant   d) foreign

7. A dilettante _____ the arts.
    a) is zealous for   b) despises   c) teaches   d) dabbles in

8. A(n) _____ is one kind of charlatan.
    a) voluable talker   b) quack   c) ancestor   d) altruist

9. Heresy is a denial of _____.
    a) the existence of God   b) what those in power believe   c) individual rights   d) one's own identity

10. A zealot is _____ in devotion to a cause.
    a) ambivalent   b) lackadaisical   c) fanatical   d) treacherous

11. A paragon is someone to be _____.
    a) imitated   b) expunged   c) questioned   d) taught

Nonagenarian comes from a Latin word *nonaginta,* meaning "ninety." A non-agenarian is a person in his or her nineties. The same *non* stem can be seen in our word *nonagon,* a figure with nine sides and nine angles. Other words for people's ages have been constructed on number stems. See if you can guess how old the following people are. Check your answers in the dictionary.

a sexagenarian _____

a septuagenarian _____

an octogenarian _____

a centenarian _____

LESSON 34

This lesson and the next two present adjectives.

dormant—sleeping, inactive. *Perennial flowers such as irises remain dormant in the winter and bloom in the spring.* Latin *dormire* literally means "to sleep"; the same root gives us *dormitory,* a place for sleeping.

sedentary—spending a lot of time sitting, requiring sitting. *Office workers for the most part have sedentary jobs.*

somatic—bodily, physical. *Psychological disturbances often manifest themselves indirectly as somatic symptoms.*

palliative—easing the severity of, mitigating, alleviating, extenuating. *The guard's apology had a palliative effect on the angry visitor.*

egregious—flagrantly bad, outstanding in a negative way. *He paid dearly for his egregious mistake.* Like *gregarious* (see Lesson 14), *egregious* is built on the Latin root *gregis,* "of the herd." The prefix *e* means "out," so in Latin *egregius* means "standing out from the herd, superior, eminent." In English the word has gradually taken on a negative connotation so that it now is applied only to things that stand out for being unusually bad.

deciduous—shedding leaves every year. *Deciduous trees, unlike evergreens, lose their foliage in autumn.*

vernal—pertaining to spring, springlike. *The vernal influence was everywhere apparent, especially in the park, where young couples strolled hand in hand among the roses.*

diurnal—relating to a day, daily, happening in a day or during daylight. *Nocturnal animals sleep during the diurnal hours.*

sidereal—starry, relating to a star or the stars. *Sidereal time is measured by the apparent motion of the stars.*

internecine—very destructive of life, deadly to both sides of a conflict. *The First World War was an internecine struggle that blighted a whole generation of European youth.*

mundane—of this world, commonplace, humdrum, unexciting. *The film was undistinguished, a mundane exercise in horror movie clichés.* The Latin term for the world is *mundus; mundane* was originally opposed to *spiritual* or *celestial.* It now is generally used to mean "dully ordinary," the opposite of "out of this world."

littoral—having to do with the shore of an ocean or large body of water. *The area on a beach between the highwater mark and the low-water mark is called the littoral zone.*

feral—untamed and brutal, savage, like a wild beast. *Undomesticated carnivores are feral animals. Feral* is often applied to animals descended from domesticated beasts that have at some point reverted to a wild state. It is often used figuratively to compare people to savage creatures.

Answers to the following exercises are on page 205.

EXERCISE I Synonyms. Circle the letter of the word or phrase closest in meaning to the given word.

1. mundane: a) opaque b) obsolete c) weekly d) ordinary

2. diurnal: a) pertaining to the stars b) inactive c) recurring every twenty-four hours d) cloudy

3. egregious: a) extremely undesirable b) select c) imprecise d) unpalatable

4. somatic: a) sitting b) pertaining to the body c) lying down d) psychogenic

5. dormant: a) impotent b) impassive c) sleeping d) defunct

6. feral: a) hairy b) satiated c) savagely wild d) rust-colored

7. internecine: a) fraternal b) predictable c) heavenly d) highly destructive

8. vernal: a) of the spring b) thawed c) gelid d) of the earth

9. littoral: a) of the planets b) of the coast c) of the body d) autumnal

10. palliative: a) preemptive b) exacerbating c) consolidated d) soothing

11. sidereal: a) ghostly b) of secondary importance c) astral d) daily

12. deciduous: a) not evergreen b) perennial c) hibernating d) deadly

13. sedentary: a) sedate b) migratory c) seated d) unhealthy

EXERCISE II Fill in the blanks from the list of words below.

diurnal littoral
vernal dormant
internecine deciduous
egregious palliative
mundane sedentary
feral somatic
sidereal

1. The prehistoric inhabitants of the area had been a(n) _____ people, living around the shore of the inland sea.

2. The Indians chewed coca leaves as a(n) _____ drug to ease exhaustion and altitude sickness.

3. The seeds may remain _____ for long periods until favorable conditions trigger their growth.

4. The _____ equinox is so named because it occurs at that point in the spring when day and night are of equal duration.

5. Arab astronomers of the Middle Ages used the astrolabe to precisely chart _____ movements.

6. She felt the _____ effects of the shock as her breath grew short and her hands became clammy.

7. Maples are among the _____ trees whose dying leaves take on spectacular colors.

8. A(n) _____ series of errors in navigation left us a hundred miles off course in waters for which we had no chart.

9. The book told a plodding, _____ story of everyday people and their typical problems.

10. Abandoned by their owners, the dogs turn _____, running loose in the woods and hunting deer in packs.

11. It was a(n) _____ battle; there were so many casualties neither side could claim a victory.

12. He isn't interested in a(n) _____ job; he would rather be out in a blizzard than be chained to a desk all day.

13. A day is measured by the _____ rotation of the earth on its axis.

EXERCISE III Circle the letter of the best choice to complete each sentence.

1. Deciduous describes a type of   a) topography   b) climate   c) person   d) vegetation

2. If a passion is dormant, it may yet be   a) rekindled   b) reciprocated   c) obsessive   d) out of control

3. An internecine conflict is   a) a skirmish   b) a spat   c) very bloody   d) unilateral

4. An egregious decision is   a) one that is postponed   b) a serious misstep   c) the right choice   d) anticipatory

5. The vernal season is marked by   a) withered leaves   b) high tides   c) fresh foliage   d) torrid weather

6. Sidereal light is   a) stronger than moonlight   b) reflected sunlight   c) fluorescent   d) fainter than moonlight

7. A somatic effect occurs   a) in an organic body   b) on a spectroscope   c) in the heavens   d) in the spring

8. A feral smile makes a person appear   a) concilatory   b) brutal   c) craven
   d) crabby

9. A palliative circumstance may   a) increase a penalty   b) result in shock
   c) exonerate a suspect   d) extenuate a fault

10. A mundane course is   a) fascinatingly different   b) run-of-the-mill   c) a
    course in geology   d) always an elective

11. A diurnal cycle is completed   a) in a day   b) only once   c) in a year
    d) in a human lifetime

12. A person in a sedentary position is   a) sitting down   b) uncomfortable
    c) pensive   d) likely to tire quickly

13. A littoral environment is likely to offer   a) alpine vegetation   b) a desert
    c) deep-sea fishing   d) salt marshes

LESSON 35

redolent—fragrant, smelling like and therefore strongly suggestive of something. *In the spring the dining room, its windows open to the garden, is redolent of lilacs.*

unctuous—greasy, oily, too smooth or hypocritically suave in manner. *He had the unctuous manner of a used-car salesman trying to unload a lemon on an unsuspecting grandmother.*

ostensible—professed, apparent. *Their ostensible purpose in leaving the party was to pick up some groceries, but really they just wanted to be alone. Ostensible* is similar in meaning to *putative* (Lesson 8) but has a slightly different focus. *Putative,* from the Latin verb for "suppose," emphasizes the observer—what an observer thinks or supposes about something. *Ostensible*, from a verb meaning "show," emphasizes the deliberate creating of a false impression—what a person wants to make others believe or suppose.

hallowed—made or considered sacred, consecrated, venerated as holy. *Many of England's illustrious men and women are buried within the hallowed precincts of Westminster Abbey.*

circumspect—watchful in all directions, wary. *A public official must be circumspect in all his actions to avoid even the appearance of impropriety.*

somnolent—sleepy. *The somnolent child dropped off to sleep as soon as the train started moving.*

limpid—transparent, perfectly clear, not muddied. *You can see the fish easily in the limpid water of the lake.*

turbid—muddied, roiled, cloudy, full of sediment and therefore unclear or confused. *The stream was turbid where the cattle had just forded.*

baleful—fatal, harmful, evil. *A baleful glance from the professor silenced the obstreperous student. Baleful* is used most frequently for people's looks or expressions.

incendiary—using fire for willful destruction, tending to arouse or inflame to violence or revolt. *The general's limousine was destroyed by an incendiary bomb.* Also, a person who instigates political violence can be called an *incendiary*.

propitious—favorable, predicting future good, kindly disposed. *With clear skies and propitious winds, the craft reached the coast in only three days.*

exemplary—serving as a pattern or example, deserving imitation. *The leader's exemplary behavior in both her public and private life made her a model for all to follow.*

Answers to the following exercises are on page 205.

EXERCISE I Synonyms. Circle the letter of the word or phrase closest in meaning to the given word.

1. circumspect: a) odorous b) amorous c) reticent d) careful

2. unctuous: a) overly smooth b) liquid c) balmy d) sinuous

3. hallowed: a) empty b) eerie c) sanctified d) saluted

4. exemplary: a) abominable b) admirable c) authentic d) actual

5. baleful: a) medicinal b) wheat-filled c) wailing d) malign

6. turbid: a) stirred up b) sorted c) swollen d) pernicious

7. incendiary: a) ardent b) insulting c) incipient d) fiery

8. redolent: a) odious b) sweet-sounding c) resinous d) aromatic

9. propitious: a) preternatural b) auspicious c) owned outright d) too sudden

10. limpid: a) flaccid b) adamant c) shining d) crystalline

11. ostensible: a) seeming b) ostentatious c) pulled taut d) veritable

12. somnolent: a) flowery b) neurotic c) drowsy d) battle-fatigued

EXERCISE II Choose the best word to complete each sentence. Write it in the blank.

1. The basilisk is a mythical serpent whose _____ glance and breath can kill.

      exemplary   circumspect
      baleful   propitious

2. After the rains the river was swollen and so _____ that the water appeared brown.

      somnolent   baleful
      limpid   turbid

3. The opposition charged that while the _____ purpose of the bill was to ease inflation, it would in fact give a windfall to the largest corporations at the expense of the consumer.

      propitious   redolent
      ostensible   incendiary

4. He tried to lead a(n) _____ life, believing that his children would pay more attention to what he did than to what he preached.

           hallowed   exemplary

           ostensible   baleful

5. The royal astrologers were commanded to determine the most _____ date for the king's coronation.

           unctuous   limpid

           incendiary   propitious

6. The poem by the great satirist was dripping with venom and was _____ with scorn.

           redolent   somnolent

           circumspect   exemplary

7. Although her smooth flattery won over my partner, I thought her too _____ to be trusted.

           ostensible   hallowed

           turbid   unctuous

8. The village was an out-of-the-way, _____ place where chickens wandered the alleys and a lost pig was considered big news.

           baleful   incendiary

           somnolent   ostensible

9. The more complex an argument, the more it requires a _____ prose style.

           redolent   turbid

           hallowed   limpid

10. The attorney was extremely _____ in not giving professional advice until she had all the facts.

           circumspect   redolent

           turbid   unctuous

11. At the funeral of the martyred protestors, a(n) _____ speech by a comrade sparked further violence.

           exemplary   limpid

           incendiary   circumspect

12. Valley Forge and Gettysburg are _____ places in American history.

           hallowed   somnolent

           propitious   unctuous

EXERCISE III Circle the letter of the best choice to complete each sentence.

1. An incendiary may also be called a) maniacal b) a firebrand c) a plebeian d) a pacifist

2. A baleful influence cannot be a) perceived b) undesirable c) counteracted d) propitious

3. Exemplary work deserves to be a) shunned b) imitated c) hallowed d) picked apart

4. A person ostensibly employed   a) is underpaid   b) does gainful work   c) is likely to be unctuous   d) may in fact be unemployed

5. A somnolent mood is suggested by   a) a costume party   b) a clenched fist   c) a breathtaking view   d) a rocking cradle

6. A turbid stream cannot be   a) limpid   b) swum   c) redolent of rotting vegetation   d) charted

7. Someone too circumspect is   a) frequently beguiled   b) afraid to take a reasonable risk   c) always disconsolate   d) too forward

8. Burn ointments are generally   a) limpid   b) unctuous   c) baleful   d) somnolent

9. An example of a hallowed place is   a) a backyard   b) the ocean   c) a church   d) a freeway

LESSON 36

magnanimous—noble-minded, extremely generous, especially in overlooking injury. *The painter was magnanimous enough to praise the work of a man he detested.* The Latin roots *magnus* and *animus* mean "great spirit." Magnus also gives us *magnify* (make great), *magnificent* (doing great things), and *magnitude* (size).

eclectic—drawing from diverse sources or systems. *His eclectic record collection included everything from Bach cantatas to the latest rock imports.*

noxious—harmful, injurious, unwholesome. *The noxious fumes from the refinery poisoned the air.*

detrimental—causing damage or harm. *The support of fringe groups can be detrimental to the image of an office-seeker.* Noxious is the stronger and more limited term. It describes something damaging to health—usually physical, but sometimes mental or moral. *Detrimental* is a milder and more general term applied to any kind of harm.

sinister—evil, especially in a secret or mysterious way, predicting harm or misfortune. *The actor's sinister appearance made him perfect for the role of Dracula.*

cynical—tending to doubt the virtue or sincerity of people's actions, inclined to believe the worst about motives and behavior. *A cynical person would say that he was acting out of self-interest.*

impetuous—sudden, rash, not thinking beforehand. *The rescue was an impetuous act of heroism; if they had stopped to discuss it, they would have been too late.*

garrulous—talkative, loquacious. *She was so garrulous she said everything three times.*

punctilious—very exact in the fine points of conduct, scrupulously observant of proper procedure or ceremony. *Punctilious in his social relations, he always responded to invitations immediately.*

astute—difficult to deceive, shrewd. *It takes an astute player to know when someone is bluffing. Shrewd* and *cunning* are very close in meaning to *astute* but sometimes have negative connotations that *astute* lacks. To be cunning is often unattractive, but there's never anything wrong with being astute.

tangible—capable of being touched, having objective reality and value. *The new position offered an opportunity for creativity as well as the more tangible reward of increased pay.*

Answers to the following exercises are on page 205.

EXERCISE I Circle the letter of the best choice to complete each sentence.

1. Actions detrimental to your own best interests ought to be
   _____ .
   a) pursued   b) elucidated   c) enumerated   d) avoided

2. An astute observer of human behavior is not likely to be
   _____ .
   a) insightful   b) patient   c) fooled   d) reliable

3. A sinister omen predicts _____ .
   a) the weather   b) misfortune   c) winning the lottery   d) the future

4. A person with eclectic tastes likes _____ .
   a) lots of different things   b) to travel   c) spicy foods   d) music

5. A noxious substance is likely to be _____ .
   a) dangerous if swallowed   b) hard to find   c) ubiquitous   d) aromatic

6. _____ can make a person cynical.
   a) Too much noise   b) Bitter experiences   c) Good news   d) Staying out late

7. Garrulous people tend to _____ .
   a) borrow money   b) exaggerate their own virtues   c) impress others
   d) monopolize conversations

8. It takes a magnanimous person to _____ .
   a) analyze an essay   b) achieve a difficult goal   c) forgive an enemy
   d) admit failure

9. A tangible offer is _____ .
   a) specific and concrete   b) contingent on a loan   c) already accepted
   d) vague or tentative

10. A person who observes social conventions punctiliously probably has
    _____ .
    a) a learning disability   b) a high income   c) formal and gracious manners   d) a poor attitude

11. Impetuous people tend to make decisions _____ .
    a) frequently   b) cautiously   c) reluctantly   d) on impluse

EXERCISE II Antonyms. Draw a line connecting each word with the word or phrase most nearly its *opposite*.

1. punctilious   beneficial
2. noxious   auguring good fortune
3. garrulous   like a Pollyanna
4. detrimental   sloppy in social matters
5. astute   invisible
6. tangible   cautious
7. sinister   health-giving
8. magnanimous   petty
9. impetuous   gullible
10. cynical   taciturn
11. eclectic   from a single source

EXERCISE III From memory, try to complete the following sentences with words from this lesson. The first letter of each answer is given before the blank. Write your answers in the blanks.

1. In picking a jury, an attorney needs to be an [a] _____ judge of character.

2. Having been divorced three times, she was somewhat [c] _____ about the joys of wedlock.

3. Moving frequently and changing schools can be [d] _____ to a child's educational progress.

4. A public library must be [e] _____ in its acquisitions so as to serve all kinds of readers.

5. In Jane Austen's novel *Emma*, Miss Bates is an extremely [g] _____ talker, a harmless and good-natured character but very tiresome to listen to.

6. "Look before you leap" is a proverb aimed at [i] _____ individuals.

7. I had stupidly offended my aunt, but she was [m] _____ in forgiving me and forgetting the incident.

8. [N] _____ household products should be kept safely locked out of the reach of children.

9. A [p] _____ woman makes a conscientious effort to arrive punctually for her appointments.

10. The dilapidated house, with its broken shutters and overgrown hedges, looked so [s] _____ by moonlight that I could almost believe it was haunted.

11. I think their reading has improved, though I have no [t] _____ evidence.

Right and Left
As all left-handed people know from trying to use scissors and school chairs with attached writing arms, our culture favors right-handed people. As often happens

with minority traits, the right-handed culture has traditionally regarded left-handedness as an undesirable, inferior, and even wicked preference. Like the metaphors of black and white, the metaphors of left and right are deeply ingrained in our language. The double meaning of *right* is no accident. Right is right and left is wrong.

Our word *sinister* is borrowed from the Latin word for left hand. *Right* in Latin is *dexter,* the source of our words *dexterity* and *dexterous* (see Lesson 14). Even the term *ambidextrous* shows a right-handed bias. The word literally means "having both hands right hands," as if right hands are always the more skilled.

LESSON 37

The words in this lesson and the next are all verbs.

expunge—erase, blot out, delete, obliterate. *The military censors expunged any passages in the letters that they thought might jeopardize security.*

accrue—be added as a natural or expected growth or advantage. *Interest accrues to a savings account at a fixed rate.*

slough—shed a skin or covering, cast off as no longer wanted or needed. *The snake sloughed its dead skin. Slough* in this sense is pronounced *sluf.* The same spelling can mean "a deep mire or swamp," in which case it is pronounced *slew.*

obtrude—enter where not invited or welcome. *It is impolite to obtrude upon their privacy.*

acquiesce—comply, accept, accede, often reluctantly. *Employees are expected to acquiesce in a boss's decisions even when they disagree.*

bifurcate—divide into two branches or offshoots, split into two parts. *Where the road bifurcates, take the left fork.*

recoup—get back, make up for a loss. *When he sells the building, he will recoup all his losses.*

behoove—be necessary, required, or fitting. *It behooves you to inform the school of your plans if you wish to take a leave of absence.* This word is very limited in its use. It always appears in the construction "it behooves (someone) to (do something)."

predispose—dispose in advance, create a likelihood, make susceptible. *Poor nutrition may predispose one to colds.*

eradicate—eliminate thoroughly, wipe out, root out, destroy the roots of. *The practice of inoculation has virtually eradicated smallpox.* Latin *radix* means "root"; etymologically, the Latinate *eradicate* means exactly the same as the English *root out.* As gardeners know, to destroy a weed completely you must pull it out by its roots. The same radix gives us *radish* and *radical.* A radical solution is one that attacks the roots of a problem, not just its temporary or superficial manifestations—its branches, so to speak. *Radix* is also the source of

deracinate—uproot, pull up by the roots, destroy totally. *Deracinated peoples suffer great emotional stress to the extent that they are cut off from their native culture.* Though it has been borrowed from French, *deracinate,* too, goes back to the Latin *radix;* etymologically, it means the same as *eradicate.* It can mean "destroy totally," but it is usually used in reference to people or things cut off from their origins but not annihilated. To be deracinated is to be uprooted from your home or out of touch with your "roots." Another word based on the same metaphor is

extirpate—pull up by the roots, root out, destroy utterly, annihilate. *The Inquisitor vowed to extirpate heresy.* In Latin, *stirps* is the base or root of a tree. Like the previous two entries, *extirpate* etymologically means "root out." Perhaps because uprooting a tree is a much more violent act than pulling a weed, *extirpate* is the most destructive of the three in its connotation. It always suggests utter destruction.

Answers to the following exercises are on page 205.

EXERCISE I Synonyms. Circle the letter of the word or phrase closest in meaning to the given word.

1. recoup: a) rescind b) recover a loss c) renege d) demean

2. extirpate: a) reduce b) emulate c) carry out d) eradicate

3. accrue: a) be added as a benefit b) allege c) charge d) depreciate

4. predispose: a) make responsible for b) throw out c) make subject to d) promise

5. bifurcate: a) fork b) adhere c) conflate d) swerve

6. expunge: a) defray b) erase c) soak out d) sever

7. deracinate: a) derange b) ponder c) rationalize d) uproot

8. slough: a) sink b) discard as useless c) muddy d) smite down

9. behoove: a) be a responsibility b) prevail c) hinder d) be inevitable

10. acquiesce: a) concur with reservations b) applaud c) charge with wrongdoing d) find innocent

11. obtrude: a) instigate b) display c) annihilate d) interrupt

EXERCISE II Choose the best word to complete each sentence. Write it in the blank.

1. The radical right-wing party was committed to _____ communism.
   recouping   extirpating
   behooving   sloughing off

2. The chances are that you will not _____ your roulette losses by playing blackjack.
   bifurcate   accrue
   recoup   deracinate

3. Standing in front of the fire, they _____ their wet coats.

       sloughed off   expunged

       deracinated   obtruded

4. There is evidence that there is a genetic _____ to certain diseases, for instance heart disease.

       acquiescence   extirpation

       predisposition   accruing

5. Conscientious voters are _____ to keep themselves informed on public issues.

       obtruded   behooved

       eradicatcd   acquiesced

6. I was trying to concentrate, but unwanted thoughts kept _____.

       obtruding   predisposing

       behooving   acquiescing

7. Separated from their homes and families, the youngsters felt _____.

       expunged   behooved

       predisposed   deracinated

8. We _____ the proposal because we believed it was the lesser of two evils.

       expunged   eradicated

       acquiesced in   recouped

9. After his fall from power, his name was _____ from the history books by the new regime.

       expunged   recouped

       bifurcated   deracinated

10. Islam _____ into two main branches.

       obtruded   extirpated

       bifurcated   sloughed

11. Profits from the sales will _____ the estates of the former owners.

       slough   accrue to

       extirpate   eradicate

12. Food stamps were proposed as a means of _____ hunger in America.

       accruing   predisposing

       eradicating   bifurcating

EXERCISE III Circle the letter of the best choice to complete each sentence.

1. To eradicate by violent means is to   a) modify   b) bifurcate   c) extirpate   d) annul

2. One sloughs something that is   a) no longer needed   b) accrued   c) bifurcated   d) highly valued

3. Deracinated immigrants are   a) obtrusive   b) predisposed to illness caused by anxiety   c) immune to normal stress   d) tradition-bound

4. An expunged passage has been   a) highlighted   b) misunderstood   c) explicated   d) crossed out

5. An acquiescent person   a) meddles in other people's affairs   b) is agreeable to something   c) is silent   d) protests something

6. When you have borrowed money and lost it, it behooves you to   a) eradicate the loan   b) accrue the funds   c) recoup the amount   d) slough off your obligation

LESSON 38

requite—give in return, repay. *The man's sympathy and good humor were requited by the enthusiastic affection of the children.*

envisage—imagine, call up in the mind as a picture, visualize. *I could not envisage what the house might look like when the renovation was complete. Envisage* means virtually the same as *envision.*

gallivant—gad about in search of fun and excitement, especially with members of the opposite sex. *She resented his gallivanting about town having a good time while she worked the night shift.*

placate—soothe the anger of, pacify. *A quick temper is often easily placated.* The adjective meaning "not able to be placated" is *implacable.*

insinuate—suggest subtly, especially something negative. *By asking so pointedly if I had seen her book, she insinuated that I had something to do with its disappearance.*

append—attach as a supplement. *Exhibits should be appended to the report.*

maunder—talk at length in a pointless, incoherent fashion. *After a three-hour ride we were thoroughly bored with his maundering about the good old days.*

curtail—reduce, shorten, cut back. *Classes were reduced to curtail teaching costs.*

transgress—commit a sin, break a law, step over a boundary or limit. *The child felt guilty knowing she was transgressing her parents' command.* Meaning literally *overstep, transgress* is the Latin equivalent of the English expressions *cross the line, step over the line,* or *step out of line.*

obfuscate—make obscure, cloud, confuse. *Dredging up past quarrels will only obfuscate the present issues.*

divulge—reveal, make public. *Newspaper reporters have long fought the courts for the right not to divulge their sources of information.*

stipulate—make an express demand or agreement, set a formal condition. *The lawyers stipulated that the contract would not go into effect for thirty days.*

Answers to the following exercises are on page 206.

EXERCISE I Synonyms. Circle the letter of the word or phrase closest in meaning to the given word.

1. maunder: a) wander off course b) talk aimlessly c) stagger under a burden d) weep copiously

2. insinuate: a) accuse publicly b) sneak away c) suggest indirectly d) slither

3. stipulate: a) get an injunction b) propose a solution c) variegate d) set a requirement

4. envisage: a) draw a sketch of b) grimace c) inhabit d) picture to oneself

5. requite: a) be sufficient b) recompense c) fight back d) adore

6. divulge: a) revile b) publicly reveal c) libel d) confess to a sin

7. gallivant: a) go out on the town b) seclude oneself c) teetotal d) have a respite

8. obfuscate: a) succor b) precipitate c) lose one's temper d) make more confused

9. placate: a) melt b) bend c) mollify d) mortify

10. append: a) set down in writing b) affix c) excise d) turn sideways

11. transgress: a) break a commandment b) have a breakdown c) exhume d) imprecate

12. curtail: a) promulgate b) deactivate c) reduce d) simplify

EXERCISE II Circle the letter of the best choice to complete each sentence.

1. Once divulged, information is no longer a) dangerous b) pertinent c) secret d) useful

2. If service on a bus line is curtailed, probably a) passengers will have to wait longer for a bus b) ridership will increase c) the fare will increase d) riders will be more comfortable

3. The law requires that transgressions be a) reported b) filed with the county clerk c) equitable d) punished

4. An appendage is something a) unattractive b) attached to something larger c) no longer used d) isolated and self-contained

5. A person who gallivants is looking for a) trouble b) a good time c) clues d) a father figure

6. A stipulation a) undermines a relationship b) nullifies a contract c) makes an agreement conditional d) enforces a rule

7. One envisages a person's face by a) imagining it b) painting it c) aspiring to it d) touching it

8. An implacable resentment is difficult to a) resist b) condemn c) elucidate d) overcome

9. A maundering account of an incident cannot be   a) repeated   b) credible   c) germane   d) succinct

10. An unrequited lover is   a) not loved in return   b) just a gigolo   c) too different   d) easily confounded

11. An insinuation   a) is generally welcome   b) is charitable   c) hints at wrongdoing   d) is an incontrovertible proof

12. A person is likely to obfuscate a quarrel when he feels that   a) a quick resolution is essential   b) his cause is just   c) his case is weak   d) clarity is a virtue

EXERCISE III Antonyms. Draw a line connecting each word with the word or phrase most nearly its *opposite*.

1. maunder		accuse directly
2. divulge		clarify
3. insinuate		speak to the point
4. transgress		abide by the law
5. placate		expand
6. curtail		enrage
7. obfuscate		conceal

EXERCISE IV From memory, try to complete the following sentences with words from this lesson. The first letter of each answer is given before the blank. Write your answers in the blanks.

1. At the last minute a rider was [a] _____ to the bill to facilitate its passage.

2. Installing insulation in the attic allowed residents to [c] _____ their use of space heaters.

3. By not claiming hardship, the owners avoided having to [d] _____ their profits during the contract negotiations.

4. If we fail to ameliorate conditions now, economists [e] _____ still greater problems down the road.

5. Nick and Nora spent a dissipated week in New York, throwing parties and [g] _____ to all the famous nightspots.

6. The attorney attempted to discredit the witness in the eyes of the jury by [i] _____ that she was a liar.

7. The drunken man [m] _____ on for some time about his dog without ever reaching the point of the story.

8. It took the examiner an hour to unravel the tenant's original complaint, which had been [o] _____ by harassment and recriminations on both sides.

9. The frustrated toddler was quickly [p] _____ by a lollipop.

10. A grateful guest had [r] _____ their hospitality with a lovely bouquet.

11. The agreement [s] _____ that an acceptable manuscript must be delivered no later than June 30.

12. The person who commits wanton murder [t] _____ the most fundamental principle of civilized behavior.

LESSON 39

The words and phrases in this chapter have all been borrowed unchanged from French. They should be pronounced more or less as they are in French; check your dictionary if you are not sure how to say them. The literal meaning in French is given in parentheses for each entry.

bête noire—(black beast) a pet hatred, bugbear, something or someone especially disliked or feared. *Since he teaches logic, it is natural that sloppy thinking is his bête noire.*

canaille—(pack of dogs) mob, rabble. *The aristocrat despised tradespeople as part of the canaille. Canaille* is a derogatory term for the common people; like *rabble* or the phrase *filthy rich,* it carries heavy ideological baggage. French *canaille* derives from the Latin *canis* (dog), the same root that gives us *canine.*

savoir-faire—(to know how to do) a knowing what to do in any circumstances, a knack for always doing the right thing. *Her savoir-faire made her at home in the most extraordinary places.*

raison d'être—(reason for being) reason for existence, justification. *Serving the needs of the people is the whole raison d'être of social programs.*

coup—(blow, stroke) a sudden and successful action, a quick and brilliant maneuver or triumph. *Wooing a major account away from the competition was his first coup as a salesman.*

coup d'état—(a blow of the state) a sudden overthrow or change of a government, especially by force. *The government was toppled overnight in a coup d'état.*

coup de grâce—(a blow of mercy) a final blow, the finishing stroke to kill a victim and so put him out of his misery. *With his sword, the matador delivered the coup de grâce.*

laissez-faire—(let do, that is, let people do as they please) noninterference, especially a public policy of economic nonregulation. *A laissez-faire policy allows producers to run business without government control.*

dénouement—(an untying) the unraveling of a plot, the end or outcome of a story. *In the dénouement of traditional comedy, the impediments to a happy ending are removed.*

contretemps—(against the time) a mildly unfortunate event, a mishap, a minor embarrassment or misunderstanding. *We had a brief contretemps when we thought we had mislaid the tickets.* Originally, *contretemps* was a fencing term for a poorly timed thrust.

idée fixe—(fixed idea) an obsession, a fixed idea, a single notion which dominates a person's thinking. *The opposition of good and evil was for him an idée fixe; he saw all of life as a moral battlefield.*

canard—(a duck) a false story, an absurd lie or rumor, a hoax. *She denied the story as a ludicrous canard invented to sell newspapers.* Why a false rumor should be called a "duck" is a mystery.

en masse—(in a mass) all together, as one, in a body. *The demonstrators were arrested en masse.*

Answers to the following exercises are on page 206.

EXERCISE I Synonyms. Draw a line connecting each word with the word or phrase that means most nearly the same.

1. savoir-faire	hands-off policy
2. coup d'état	mortal stroke
3. en masse	obsessive idea
4. idée fixe	as a body
5. coup de grâce	government overthrow
6. canaille	social know-how
7. raison d'être	stunning success
8. coup	rationale
9. bête noire	rabble
10. canard	slight upset
11. contretemps	pet dislike
12. dénouement	untrue story
13. laissez-faire	end of a story

EXERCISE II Using the words and phrases in this lesson, fill in the blanks. Be very careful to write your answers correctly, including the diacritical (accent) marks.

1. The legend about Washington was an old _____, repeated because it was a good story, though untrue.

2. Conservatives, opposed to what they termed government meddling, advocated a _____ economic policy.

3. Thousands of citizens marched _____ to Versailles to escort the royal family back to Paris.

4. She detests all kinds of sports; gym class has been her _____ since the second grade.

5. Getting accepted at that college is a real _____. You must have done impressively well at the interview.

6. Opposition leaders were conspiring to take over the reins of leadership in a bloodless _____.

7. Their ragged clothes marked them as part of the penniless _____.

8. One of the violinists broke a string, but aside from that slight _____ the concert went off very smoothly.

9. His _____ is remarkable; unembarrassed himself, he puts everyone else at ease no matter how awkward the situation.

10. The car's whole _____ was to make things more convenient for us; if it's more trouble than it's worth, let's get rid of it.

11. The program was already moribund; this last cutback merely gave it the _____.

12. In the _____ of Shakespearean tragedy, the hero dies.

13. Nutrition is her _____: she thinks everything from a hangnail to a heart attack can be prevented by the proper diet.

EXERCISE III Circle the letter of the best choice to complete each sentence.

1. The _____ of the laboratory sessions is to teach students empirically.
   a) bête noire b) savoir-faire c) raison d'être d) coup de grâce

2. A contretemps is often _____.
   a) tragic b) mildly annoying c) untrue d) planned

3. A canard may be a _____.
   a) deliberate hoax b) verfiable c) ineffable d) accomplished with violence

4. A person with savoir-faire has reason to be _____.
   a) nervous b) timorous c) rambunctious d) self-confident

5. A _____ may result in a coup.
   a) sudden illness b) brilliant strategy c) cliché d) feeling of hindsight

6. In implementing a laissez-faire policy, a government _____.
   a) eases restrictions on businesses b) raises taxes c) fixes prices
   d) puts a ceiling on profits

7. The old regime was _____ by a coup de'état.
   a) controlled b) preserved c) voted in d) terminated

8. An idée fixe _____ to the person who cherishes it.
   a) is ephermeral b) constantly recurs c) is unconscious d) reverts

9. A bête noire is something _____.
   a) universally hated b) terrifying c) particularly disliked by an individual d) amiable

10. A creature is _____ in a coup de grâce.
    a) petted b) finished off c) cajoled d) nourished

11. The opposite of a dénouement is _____.
    a) a favorite thing b) an initial situation c) a true story d) a cycle of tales

12. When animals move en masse, they _____.
    a) scatter b) keep together c) swim d) make little headway

13. *Canaille* is a derogatory term because it _____.
    a) refers to the populace b) is French c) compares people to cattle
    d) compares people to dogs

LESSON 40

Here are twelve more terms borrowed unchanged from French. Be sure to consult your dictionary if you are not sure how to pronounce them. The literal meaning in French of each term is given in parentheses.

ingénue—(ingenuous woman) in plays or films, an innocent young woman, an actress who plays naive young women. *Many screen actresses who began their careers as ingénues have made a successful switch to playing older women.*

ambiance—(atmosphere) atmosphere, mood. *Spotless tablecloths and fresh flowers gave the modest restaurant a pleasant ambiance.* In English, ambiance is only used to mean atmosphere in the figurative sense of "mood."

faux pas—(false step) a mistake in social manners, a tactless blunder. *To forget a dinner engagement is a serious faux pas because it both insults and inconveniences other people.*

précis—(summary) summary, outline, abbreviated version. *The novelist submitted to the publisher one complete chapter and a précis of the rest of the book.*

manqué—(failed, lacking) would-be, unsuccessful or defective, not fulfilling potential. *I guessed from the way he told stories for the children that he was an actor manqué.*

au courant—(in the current) with it, up-to-date, in the know, well-informed. *She browsed through fashion magazines to keep au courant with the latest styles.*

soupçon—(suspicion) hint, tiny amount, trace. *The chef seasoned the dish with a soupçon of cayenne.*

rapprochement—(a drawing closer) a reconciliation, a reestablishing of friendly relations. *The couple became estranged with no hope of rapprochement.*

sobriquet—(nickname) nickname, pseudonym. *His name was Edgar, but he wrestled professionally under the sobriquet Tiny.*

coterie—(social set) group of people who frequently socialize together, a clique, especially a socially or intellectually exclusive group. *She held a salon frequented by a coterie of painters, writers, and intellectuals.*

élan—(spirit) ardor, energy, active drive. *The boy threw himself into the game with such élan that what he lacked in skill he made up for in enthusiasm.*

éclat—(a sudden burst) dazzling brilliance, success that brings wide acclaim. *The newly discovered actor burst upon the social scene with such éclat that his name and picture were soon a regular feature of the gossip columns.*

Answers to the following exercises are on page 206.

EXERCISE I Synonyms. Circle the letter of the word or phrase closest in meaning to the given word.

1. coterie: a) partnership   b) scintillating brilliance   c) group that meets socially   d) mob

2. manqué: a) unfulfilled b) shy c) of minor status d) employed as a model

3. précis: a) harmonious proportion b) an abridgement c) exact copy d) valuable item

4. ambiance: a) elation b) mood c) uncertainty d) sophistication

5. soupçon: a) slight insult b) misnomer c) slight trace d) slip of the tongue

6. faux pas: a) gauche error b) dance step c) fatal accident d) miscalculation

7. ingénue: a) ingenuous boy b) imposter c) ingenious solution d) naive girl

8. rapprochement: a) return to harmonious accord b) repast c) an upbraiding d) intimate conversation

9. au courant: a) knowledgeable of history b) studious c) aware of current happenings d) adrift

10. élan: a) energetic spirit b) perplexity c) wide acclaim d) sense of humor

11. éclat: a) obscurity b) security c) apex d) conspicuous success

12. sobriquet: a) epitaph b) name-calling c) assumed name d) anonymity

EXERCISE II Fill in the blanks from the list of words below. Be sure to write your answers correctly, including the diacritical marks.

soupçon	au courant
manqué	ambiance
rapprochement	faux pas
ingénue	sobriquet
éclat	précis
coterie	élan

1. The field of economic theory is changing rapidly; a student must read the current journals in order to stay _____.

2. In his grandmother's eyes, the boy had committed an embarrassing _____ in failing to stand when a lady entered the room.

3. The _____ of her debut made her the toast of the fashionable set.

4. Class notes can serve as a(n) _____ of what was said in a lecture or discussion.

5. A person's _____ is often a short version of his or her given name, such as *Mike* for *Michael*.

6. I detected in her tone the faintest _____ of reproach.

7. Their youthful _____ was such that no setbacks could dampen it.

8. The music, smoke, and dim lights gave the room the _____ of a nightclub.

9. The friends formed a(n) _____ that met at least once a week to discuss their work and to exchange ideas.

10. In old-fashioned melodrama, the heroine is a sweet _____ menaced by a black-hearted villain and rescued by a dashing young hero.

11. At heart she was a teacher _____. Although she had a successful career in business, she regretted that she hadn't gone into education.

12. The resumption of diplomatic relations is the necessary first step in the _____ of the two former allies.

EXERCISE III Circle the letter of the best choice to complete each sentence.

1. A faux pas is a failure   a) in the theater   b) to observe proper manners   c) to walk a straight line   d) of nerve

2. An ingénue must be   a) highly experienced   b) renowned   c) young   d) in films

3. A sobriquet may be used   a) to stop the flow of blood   b) as a stopgap measure   c) as a refreshment   d) as an endearment

4. The quantity suggested by *soupçon* is   a) prodigious   b) minuscule   c) penultimate   d) moderate

5. The opposite of élan is   a) ennui   b) cruelty   c) old age   d) depletion

6. The object of a précis is to   a) hone   b) whet   c) summarize   d) proselytize

7. An ambiance is created by   a) a combination of gases   b) all the elements of a particular setting   c) smoke and fog   d) chefs

8. A movie director manqué is   a) a scriptwriter   b) still a student   c) world famous   d) not a successful filmmaker

9. The opposite of a rapprochement is a   a) falling out   b) consonance   c) consequence   d) vaunting

10. To be au courant, a person must   a) pursue a career   b) keep up with the latest developments   c) work out regularly   d) isolate himself

11. An éclat is a success   a) slow in coming   b) that dazzles with its brilliance   c) that goes unnoticed   d) in the political arena

12. A more negative term for a coterie is a   a) blunder   b) rag   c) nincompoop   d) clique

REVIEW TEST 4

1.   *That animals of different geological periods differ specially,* en masse,
        *from those of preceding or following formations, is a fact satisfactorily
        ascertained.*

                                                                —*Louis Agassiz*

According to Agassiz, the animals of each period differ   a) radically
        b) minutely   c) as a group   d) as individuals

Questions 2 and 3.
        *The objection is that the doctrine requires a ridiculous amount of erudi-
        tion (pedantry), a claim which can be rejected by appeal to the lives of
        the poets in any pantheon. It will even be affirmed that much learning
        deadens or perverts poetic sensibility.*

                                                                —*T. S. Eliot*

2. Pantheon in this case means   a) university   b) imaginary assembly of great
        poets   c) poetic enclave   d) bibliography

3. According to Eliot, some people will claim that learning   a) is detrimental to
        poetry   b) is for poetic charlatans   c) makes artists out of dilettantes
        d) is somatic

4.   *For a moment a livid sun shot horizontally the last rays of sinister light
        between the hills of steep, rolling waves.*

                                                                —*Joseph Conrad*

We are told that the light appears   a) vernal   b) specious   c) malign
        d) sidereal

Questions 5 and 6.
        *In spite of her sedentary habits such abrupt decisions were not without
        precedent in Zeena's history.*

                                                                —*Edith Wharton*

5. Zeena does not   a) talk much   b) think of herself   c) work   d) move
        around a great deal

6. We know that Zeena   a) has trouble making up her mind   b) has made
        abrupt decisions before   c) is somnolent   d) lacks intelligence

Questions 7 and 8.
        The events of the day. . . pleased him; but the accompaniments of that

event, the glad tumult, the garrulous glee of reception, irked him: I saw he wished the quieter morrow was come.

—*Charlotte Brontë*

7. The happiness of the reception was expressed in   a) lively chatter   b) endless questions   c) tears of joy   d) baleful glances

8. The man described feels   a) unctuous   b) ambivalent about the event
   c) cynical about happiness   d) placated by noise

9.   *When Swift invites us to consider the race of Struldbugs who never die, we are able to acquiesce in imagination. But a world where two and two make five seems quite on a different level.*

—*Bertrand Russell*

To acquiesce in a fantasy is to   a) tolerate it   b) obfuscate its premises
   c) divulge it   d) willingly envisage it as a reality

Questions 10 and 11.
    She was ashamed of herself for her gloom of the night, based on nothing more tangible than a sense of condemnation under an arbitrary law of society which had no foundation in Nature.

—*Thomas Hardy*

10. The character's gloom was based on   a) a stipulation   b) something not concrete   c) a bête noire   d) superstitious fears

11. In the "arbitrary law of society" Hardy refers to   a) an ambiance   b) a coup   c) mores   d) the canaille

12.   *Roland's life was not exemplary. The "Chanson" had taken pains to show that the disaster at Roncesvalles was due to Roland's headstrong folly and temper.*

—*Henry Adams*

According to Adams, Roland   a) was not a paragon of wisdom   b) was execrable   c) lacked temerity   d) lacked élan

Questions 13 and 14.
    For Daisy was young and her artificial world was redolent of orchids and pleasant, cheerful snobbery and orchestras which set the rhythm of the year, summing up the sadness and suggestiveness of life in new tunes.

—*F. Scott Fitzgerald*

13. Fitzgerald describes Daisy's world as figuratively   a) snobbish   b) a terra incognita   c) degenerate   d) suffused with fragrance

14. In keeping with her surroundings, one would expect Daisy to be   a) an ingrate   b) complacent   c) a mendicant   d) dormant

15.   *We need to witness our own limits transgressed, and some life pasturing freely where we never wander.*

—*Henry David Thoreau*

Transgressed literally means   a) overlooked   b) foreseen   c) drawn
     d) overstepped

16.   *It was the only battle which I have ever witnessed, the only battle-field I ever trod while the battle was raging; internecine war; the red republicans on the one hand, and the black imperialists on the other.*

                                                      —Henry David Thoreau

Thoreau describes the battle—between two armies of ants—as   a) costly to both sides   b) racially motivated   c) ludicrous   d) fraternal

17.   *Having dwelt thus long on the subjects and aim of these poems, I shall request the reader's permission to apprise him of a few circumstances relating to their style . . . .*

                                                      —William Wordsworth

Apprise means   a) convince   b) inform   c) expunge   d) remind

18.   *The dew fell, but with propitious softness; no breeze whispered. Nature seemed to me benign and good. . . .*

                                                      —Charlotte Brontë

The falling of the dew is described as   a) miraculous   b) mundane   c) a requital   d) boding well

Answers to the above questions are on page 206.

LESSON 41

The nouns in this lesson all name people.

egotist—person completely preoccupied with himself, a selfish and conceited person, especially one who expresses this self-concern in speaking or writing. *Peter is a complete egotist; if you're willing to talk about him all the time, the two of you will get along splendidly.*

necromancer—person who practices black magic, a sorcerer, especially one who claims to communicate with the dead. *A necromancer told her that her late husband did not approve of her remarrying.*

miscreant—villain, criminal, wicked person. *In the end the miscreant was given a life sentence.*

neophyte—new convert, a beginner or novice, especially in a belief or religious order. *Neophytes are often the most zealous proselytizers for their beliefs.*

virtuoso—person with great skill, an accomplished performer, a master. *It takes natural aptitude as well as immense dedication to become a musical virtuoso.* The term *virtuoso* is borrowed from Italian and is usually used in connection with the arts, especially music. The plural can be either *virtuosos* or *virtuosi*.

epicure—person with fastidious or highly cultivated tastes in food or drink. *The epicure sniffed the cork before tasting the wine.*

arbiter—person having power to determine a dispute, a judge. *The arbiter ruled in favor of the union.*

demagogue—leader who exploits mob passions, one who stirs up passions and prejudices to gain power. *Hitler was a demagogue who built his power on national pride and hatred of outsiders.* The Greek *demos* means "the people" and *agogos* means "a leader." Originally, a *demagogue* was a leader of the common people. Since over the centuries those in power have for the most part distrusted the common people as an irrational and unstable rabble, the word has taken on a negative connotation.

kleptomaniac—person who steals compulsively. *A kleptomaniac will often steal items of very small value.*

dipsomaniac—person with an uncontrollable desire for alcohol. *A dipsomaniac cannot resist drinking if liquor is available.*

philistine—person without genuine aesthetic appreciation or who denigrates high culture, person with narrowly conventional views on art. *She regards anyone who doesn't run to the premiere of every art exhibit as a philistine.*

Answers to the following exercises are on page 206.

EXERCISE I Circle the letter of the best choice to complete each sentence.

1. A demagogue seeks _____ .
   a) friendship b) security c) political power d) anonymity

2. People with _____ are kleptomaniacs.
   a) an uncontrollable desire to steal   b) illicit gains   c) delusions of grandeur   d) morbid fears about health

3. A neophyte is a kind of _____ .
   a) thief   b) connoisseur   c) tyro   d) tyrant

4. One who practices _____ is a necromancer.
   a) a wind instrument   b) black magic   c) astrology   d) law

5. Someone who _____ the fine arts is sometimes called a philistine.
   a) underwrites   b) practices   c) venerates   d) is indifferent to

6. An epicure _____ food.
   a) prefers drink to   b) is very particular about   c) loves any kind of   d) eats enormous amounts of

7. An arbiter _____ conflicts.
   a) foments   b) avoids   c) judges   d) suffers from

8. The egotist always thinks about _____ .
   a) himself   b) pleasure   c) obligations   d) getting ahead

9. One who deserves _____ is a miscreant.
   a) approbation   b) consternation   c) opprobrium   d) recidivism

10. You can expect _____ from a virtuoso.
    a) a polished performance   b) unsophisticated taste   c) antisocial acts   d) an obsession with food

11. A dipsomaniac suffers from a powerful urge to _____ .
    a) sleep   b) drink   c) steal   d) convert others

EXERCISE II From the following list of names, pick a term to match the description given in each of the sentences below. Write the names in the blanks.

philistine   kleptomaniac
demagogue   arbiter
virtuoso   epicure
neophyte   necromancer
miscreant   egotist
dipsomaniac

1. The referee decided the round in favor of the challenger. _____

2. Faust used incantations to call up the infernal powers. _____

3. The man was referred to a psychiatrist for help because he couldn't control his drinking. _____

4. The criminal seemed to feel no compunction for crimes that had shocked the whole nation. _____

5. His speeches inflamed the audience with a self-righteous hatred of all who did not subscribe to his political program. _____

6. She found herself pilfering things she didn't even want or need. _____

7. This pianist is deservedly one of the best-known artists on the concert circuit today. _____

8. For years the writer kept a journal in which she recorded every transitory thought and every nuance of feeling. _____

9. The nun was preparing to take her final vows. _____

10. The man discouraged his son from reading poetry by saying that it was for sissies. _____

11. She does not demand that the decor be elegant, only that the fare be consistently fresh and impeccably prepared. _____

EXERCISE III Circle the letter of the best choice to complete each sentence.

1. According to legend, Merlin's rival Morgan le Fay practiced   a) epicurism   b) arbitration   c) necromancy   d) virtuosity

2. A person frequently charged with petty larceny may well suffer from   a) demagoguery   b) kleptomania   c) dipsomania   d) philistinism

3. The opposite of a virtuoso is   a) an arbiter   b) an American   c) a sculptor   d) a dilettante

4. A neophyte probably needs   a) a greater egotism   b) further indoctrination   c) rehabilitation   d) lengthy incarceration

5. A miscreant performs   a) evil actions   b) altruistic deeds   c) classical music   d) rabble-rousing entertainments

The History of a Label
The etymology of *philistine* goes back through Latin, through Greek, to the Hebrew *p'lishtim*. *Philistine* was long familiar to English readers as the name of the tribe in the Old Testament with whom the Israelites waged war. In 1867 the English critic Matthew Arnold coined a new meaning, labelling as Philistines his middle-class contemporaries. Philistines were those who "believe most that our greatness and welfare are proved by our being very rich, and who most give their lives and thoughts to becoming rich." They are at war with culture and blind to aesthetic and intellectual values. Thanks to Arnold, we now use *philistine* in this sense.

Hebrew *p'lishtim* is today also translated *Palestinian*. To call a smugly conventional person a philistine is in a sense an ethnic slur against Palestinians, though using the word in two different forms disguises the fact.

LESSON 42

The nouns in this lesson name human behavior, feelings, and qualities.

derision—mockery, scorn, ridicule. *Darwin's theory that people were descended from ape-like ancestors was greeted in many circles by derision.* The noun *derision* is based on the verb *deride*, "to laugh at, mock, or ridicule."

ennui—boredom, lack of interest or enthusiasm, feeling of weary dissatisfaction. *Suffering from ennui, he found neither work nor pleasure could engage his interest. Ennui,* borrowed unchanged from French, is related etymologically to the older English word *annoy*.

histrionics—an overacting, melodramatic behavior, a theatrical or affected display of feeling. *The toddler's rolling on the floor was pure histrionics; she hadn't been hurt in the slightest.*

chagrin—disappointment, embarrassment or vexation caused by a failure or disappointment. *The failure of the play filled its backers with chagrin.*

levity—lightness of spirit, frivolity, playfulness. *The party toys and silly costumes epitomized the levity of the occasion.*

foible—a small, harmless weakness or eccentricity of character. *One of the man's foibles was always to count his change and stack it neatly on the dresser just before retiring.*

mendacity—lying, a lie, falsehood. *The mendacity of the report lay in its deliberate distortion of the congresswoman's views.* The adjective is *mendacious*.

vertigo—dizziness, giddiness, a sense of apparent rotary movement of the body. *The physician explained that the vertigo was due to a chronic disease of the heart.*

audacity—daring, boldness, personal courage amounting even to recklessness or impudence. *The general was known for his audacity and personal charisma; no one disputed his courage, though many questioned his judgment.* The adjective is *audacious*.

rancor—malice, ill will, bitter or deep anger. *In spite of the insults of his opponent, the man remained calm and answered without rancor.*

sagacity—wisdom, discernment, keen judgment. *Among all the characters of the Hebrew Scriptures. Solomon is most famed for his sagacity.*

Answers to the following exercises are on page 207.

EXERCISE I Circle the letter of the best choice to complete each sentence.

1. Mendacity is a) courageous b) innocent of guile c) keenly intelligent d) untruthful

2. Vertigo involves a) public mockery b) a sincere affection c) a loss of equilibrium d) fine judgment

3. An object of derision is the target of a) jealousy b) extradition c) benevolence d) contempt

4. A person who indulges in histrionics   a) hams it up   b) deceives others
   c) hones his talents   d) is subtly persuasive

5. Chagrin results from   a) justified pride   b) humiliating disappointment
   c) circumspection   d) boredom

6. Audacity is an extreme form of   a) bravery   b) falsehood   c) humor
   d) phobia

7. Levity suggests a   a) citation for heroism   b) solemn rite   c) frivolous
   mood   d) theatrical performance

8. A foible is a   a) quirk   b) query   c) quibble   d) quick temper

9. A person known for sagacity is   a) tenacious   b) keenly perceptive
   c) pedantic   d) courteous

10. Rancor is a feeling of   a) reciprocity   b) remorse   c) nostalgic loss
    d) bitter hostility

11. Ennui can result from   a) protracted tedium   b) heartfelt sorrow   c) a
    stunning victory   d) a lively interest in others

EXERCISE II From the following list of nouns, pick a term to match each
description given in the sentences below. Write the nouns in the blanks.

rancor	vertigo
sagacity	derision
levity	audacity
ennui	histrionics
mendacity	chagrin
foible	

1. Having boasted to everyone that the famous director would attend, the host
   was annoyed and embarrassed when his guest of honor failed to show up.
   _____

2. The amateur thespian gave a ludicrous performance, gaping and howling
   with laughter when the script called for mild amusement.
   _____

3. Dizzy from exhaustion and loss of blood, the woman felt the world spinning
   around her.   _____

4. Not only is she brilliant; she is able to look at situations objectively and
   see through people's pretensions to their true motives.   _____

5. I wasted the whole day feeling vaguely tired and depressed, unable to decide
   what to do.   _____

6. They took a huge risk, mortgaging their futures to back the film, but their
   daring paid off.   _____

7. For nearly twenty years the old man harbored a bitter hatred for the man
   who had cheated him.   _____

8. Her dislike of the telephone inconvenienced no one but herself; although
   she would answer it when it rang, she would happily walk blocks to
   avoid calling someone herself.   _____

9. Every word out of their mouths was a lie.   _____

10. Before his steamboat proved successful, Fulton was the laughingstock of
people who called his vessel "Fulton's Folly."   _____

11. Giggling at their own jokes, the kids were much too giddy to listen seriously.

                                                _____

EXERCISE III Antonyms. Draw a line connecting each word with the word or
phrase most nearly its *opposite*.

1. rancor   triumph
2. audacity   normal sense of balance
3. chagrin   good will
4. sagacity   understand manner
5. histrionics   timidity
6. mendacity   truthfulness
7. vertigo   seriousness
8. levity   enthusiasm
9. ennui   foolishness

EXERCISE IV From memory, try to complete the following sentences with words
from this lesson. The first letter of each answer is given before the blank. Write your
answers in the blanks.

1. A mild eccentricity that hurts no one is a [f] _____.

2. The guru's reputation for [s] _____ was borne out by the
soundness of his advice.

3. An infection of the inner ear resulted in [v] _____; the patient
was advised not to drive.

4. Morale reached its nadir as forced inactivity led to widespread
[e] _____. The whole company was listless and bored.

5. [M] _____ is a habit with him: he lies just for practice.

6. The fans expressed their [r] _____ by writing angry letters to the
local newspapers and by picketing the games.

7. [H] _____ are a way of overreacting to a situation, of
dramatizing one's emotions in an exaggerated way.

8. A person expresses [d] _____ by making jokes at another's
expense.

9. The girl felt [c] _____ when her attempt to make friends was
rudely rebuffed.

10. The last day of school was a day of sheer [l] _____ in which no
work was accomplished and all sorts of goofy pranks were tolerated.

11. The [a] _____ of the plan was its best guarantee of success; the
enemy did not anticipate such a recklessly bold attempt.

LESSON 43

More nouns:

austerity—quality of being strict, rigorous, very simple, or unadorned. *To save money they went on an austerity program in which they cut down on their driving and on nonessential purchases.* The adjective is *austere.*

dilemma—choice of two undesirable alternatives, any awkward choice, a problem. *She was faced with a dilemma: if she went back for the book she needed, she would be late for the class.*

enigma—a riddle, anything that defies explanation. *The origin of the statues on Easter Island is an enigma.* The adjective is *enigmatic.*

euphemism—the substitution of an inoffensive or mild expression for a more straightforward one. *Like many other people, he used "gone" and "passed away" as euphemisms for "dead."*

euphoria—extreme feeling of physical well-being or happiness. *Their euphoria at being the first ever to climb the mountain was heightened by their narrow escape from death.* Both *euphemism* and *euphoria* include the Greek prefix *eu,* meaning "good, well." *Euphemism* is a kind of speaking well—using a good or lucky word in place of an evil one—and *euphoria* is a sense of well-being. The same root gives us a name meaning "well-born," *Eugene.*

oblivion—a complete forgetting, state of being utterly forgotten. *The names of the clerks who wrote the chronicles have been lost in oblivion: no one today knows who they were.* The adjective *oblivious* means forgetful or utterly unaware, as in: *Absorbed in his work, he was oblivious of the time.*

empathy—a sense of identification with another person. *Her empathy with her brother was very strong; she generally knew what he was feeling without his having to explain.* Both *empathy* and *sympathy* are built on the Greek root *pathos,* "feeling." They are close in meaning, but sympathy allows for greater detachment. With *empathy,* you not only feel something in common with another person, but you put yourself in the other's place so that you seem to feel what he or she is feeling. The same *path* root gives us:

pathology—the study of disease or the symptoms, course, and effects of a particular disease. *A high temperature is part of the pathology of scarlet fever.*

idiosyncrasy—peculiar tendency of an individual, an unsual, odd, or individual habit of behavior. *His idiosyncrasies were sufficient to label him eccentric but not sufficient to classify him as insane.*

longevity—lifespan, long life. *The Bible credits the first generations of men with a longevity unheard of today.*

brevity—briefness, conciseness, terseness. *Brevity is the essence of journalism.*

Answers to the following exercises are on page 207.

EXERCISE I Antonyms. Circle the letter of the word or phrase most *opposite* in meaning to the given word.

1. empathy: a) lack of judgment b) subjectivity c) freedom from disease
   d) detachment

2. euphoria: a) depression b) great daring c) harmony d) sense of
   balance

3. longevity: a) low stature b) shortness of life c) decrepitude d) dismay

4. idiosyncrasy: a) universal idiom b) predilection c) universal trait
   d) prognostication

5. euphemisms: a) condolences b) pronouncements c) earthy language
   d) bad influences

6. austere: a) pecuniary b) obese c) scandalous d) luxurious

7. enigmatic: a) clear and obvious b) plentiful c) hard and fast
   d) insoluble

8. brevity: a) solemnity b) length c) height d) insufficiency

9. dilemma: a) no-win situation b) indecision c) solution
   d) narrow-minded attitude

10. oblivious: a) trendy b) fully aware c) durable d) commiserating

EXERCISE II Fill in the blanks from the list of words below.

enigma	oblivion
euphemism	idiosyncrasy
longevity	austerity
euphoria	dilemma
brevity	pathology
empathy	

1. An intuitive _____ with the child allowed the woman to
   understand his anger.

2. Having seen many cases of hepatitis before, the rescue worker immediately
   recognized its _____ .

3. Observers were struck by the _____ of the great man's style of
   living. His home was very sparsely furnished and except for a few books,
   he owned little of value.

4. The one-act play was embarrassingly bad: _____ was its only
   virtue.

5. Michael had either to lie to his parents or hurt their feelings; there was no
   other way out of his _____ .

6. Cocaine can induce a sense of _____ in which the user feels
   tremendously energetic.

7. Much of the increase in average _____ over the past couple of
   centuries is due to a drastic reduction in infant mortality.

8. Since certain common words describing sexual activity are banned from the airwaves, the announcer used a polite _____ .

9. Although her novels were popular in their own day, they have since sunk into _____ .

10. His personality is a(n) _____ , full of mysteries and apparent contradictions.

11. A(n) _____ harmless in itself—humming to oneself, always sleeping with the windows shut—can annoy a sensitive roommate.

EXERCISE III Synonyms. Draw a line connecting each word with the word or phrase that means most nearly the same.

1. brevity	emotional identification
2. pathological	substitute word
3. empathy	quirk
4. idiosyncrasy	emotional high
5. dilemma	puzzle
6. euphemism	forgetfulness
7. austerity	strictness
8. oblivion	length of life
9. longevity	unpleasant choice
10. euphoria	typical of a disease
11. enigma	shortness

EXERCISE IV Circle the letter of the best choice to complete each sentence.

1. If the longevity of sharks is a matter of dispute, scientists are not certain _____ .

    a) how long they live   b) where they breed   c) how large they can grow
    d) whether they are social animals

2. The adage "Brevity is the soul of wit" means that effective witticisms are _____ .

    a) funny b) elaborate c) personal d) pointed

3. An enigma usually _____ people.
    a) isolates b) intrigues c) nauseates d) corrodes

4. Euphoria is most likely to result from _____ .
    a) careful planning b) a debilitating illness c) mental composure
    d) sudden good fortune

5. A person who empathizes feels _____ .
    a) always in the right b) what someone else feels c) incensed
    d) oblivious to others

6. An idiosyncrasy is a habit or preference _____ —like putting hot sauce on watermelon.
    a) deserving censure b) worth trying c) that society considers taboo
    d) not shared by most people

7. In a dilemma, one generally has _____ .
   a) two alternatives b) not enough information c) a second chance
   d) emotional outbursts

8. _____ is a common euphemism for the taboo word *damn*.
   a) *Save* b) *Hell* c) *Darn* d) *Damnation*

9. As part of her work, the pathologist analyzes _____ .
   a) tissue specimens b) dreams c) patients d) expenditures

LESSON 44

The words in this lesson and the next one are all verbs.

decimate—destroy a large part of. *The Black Death decimated the population of Europe in the mid-fourteenth century.* Built on the Latin root *dec*, "ten," *decimate* literally means "destroy one-tenth of" a population, but it is used more loosely to mean "destroy a large part of." It is allowable to use it of the Black Death, for instance, even though the plague killed much more than a tenth of Europe's population.

encumber—weigh down, hinder, burden, prevent from moving quickly or freely. *Encumbered by our baggage, we almost missed the bus.* A thing that encumbers is an *emcumbrance*; the adjective to describe it is *cumbersome*.

mollify—soothe, placate, calm the temper of. *The irate customer was mollified by the manager's apology and prompt action.*

temporize—evade immediate action, delay in order to gain time. *He sought to temporize while the sun was in his eyes.* The Latin *tempus* (time) is also at the root of *temporary* (for a time only) and *contemporaneous* (happening at the same time).

discern—perceive, identify. *The fog was so thick we could barely discern the other cars.*

fester—grow worse, become infected, produce pus. *Left untreated, the sore will fester. Fester,* from the Latin word *fistula* (ulcer), refers literally to what happens to sores as they ulcerate and form pus. Figuratively, it can describe any ugly, messy sort of decaying or embittering.

vitiate—weaken, debase, corrupt, make invalid or ineffective. *My trust in him was vitiated by the rumors I had heard of his underhanded methods.*

conjecture—guess, speculate. *We are certain that Shakespeare and Ben Jonson knew each other, but we can only conjecture what they might have said to each other over drinks at the Mermaid Tavern.* The noun is the same, *conjecture.*

deviate—stray, turn aside from. *Under cross-examination, the witness did not deviate from his story one iota.*

simulate—pretend, feign, give a false appearance of. *Although she had guessed what the gift would be, she simulated surprise when she unwrapped the package.*

abominate—loathe, hate, feel disgust for. *I abominate all laws that deprive people of their rights.* Something that deserves to be abominated is *abominable*.

sequester—seize by authority, set apart in seclusion. *The jury was sequestered until the members could reach a verdict.*

Answers to the following exercises are on page 207.

EXERCISE I Antonyms. Circle the letter of the word or phrase most *opposite* in meaning to the given word.

1. vitiated: a) placated b) strengthened c) devitalized d) demoralized

2. encumbered: a) free of impediment b) well organized c) sluggish d) ascetic

3. conjecture: a) convince b) make probable c) puzzle over d) know with certainty

4. sequestered: a) unidentified b) arrested c) not set apart d) not sought after

5. decimated: a) in extreme penury b) pushed to the limit c) restored to full number d) happy

6. temporize: a) make excuses b) rush into action c) pray d) procrastinate

7. abominate: a) adore b) waste away c) console d) ingratiate

8. mollified: a) confused b) unchanged c) outraged d) unkempt

9. discernible: a) incognito b) foggy c) imperceptible d) not able to be learned

10. fester: a) cure an ulcer b) stall c) be somber d) heal

11. deviate: a) look ahead b) stick to a straight course c) march in time d) err on the side of safety

12. stimulated: a) autonomous b) realistic c) bored d) genuine

EXERCISE II Choose the best word to complete each sentence. Write it in the blank.

1. The authorities _____ certain documents and held them as evidence.

                    decimated   mollified
                    conjectured   sequestered

2. Despite pressure to compromise, the representative stood on principle, refusing to _____ from her original position.

                    deviate   discern
                    vitiate   fester

3. The twins looked eerily identical; from a short distance I could not
_____ the slightest difference between them.

    deviate   sequester

    conjecture   discern

4. The contract was _____ by the fact that the seller did not have a
legal right to dispose of the property.

    festered   sequestered

    vitiated   temporized

5. We know only that the ship never reached port. What actually happened to it
is pure _____.

    abomination   conjecture

    encumbrance   simulation

6. Small-scale automata were constructed and filmed to _____
dinosaurs.

    vitiate   mollify

    simulate   deviate

7. If the package is too _____ to carry, we can have it delivered.

    decimated   cumbersome

    conjectural   mollified

8. As unemployment worsened and services declined, the neighborhood
_____ with anger and despair.

    temporized   festered

    deviated   simulated

9. Wildlife preservationists _____ the slaughtering of endangered
species for their pelts.

    discern   vitiate

    abominate   sequester

10. The press secretary attempted to _____ the offended parties by
explaining away the President's remarks.

    abominate   temporize

    mollify   decimate

11. Scheherazade _____ by telling the Sultan stories, thus postponing
her execution night after night.

    encumbers   festers

    simulates   temporizes

12. The fruit trees were _____ by an infestation of flies.

    encumbered   discerned

    abominated   decimated

EXERCISE III Circle the letter of the best choice to complete each sentence.

1. An abominable practice is one that ought to be a) disseminated
b) stopped c) protected d) reiterated

2. One way a speaker can temporize is to   a) ask for the question to be repeated   b) cut her remarks short   c) try to please everyone   d) take an unpopular stand

3. To vitiate a good intention is to   a) follow it   b) counterfeit it   c) corrupt it   d) endorse it

4. A sequestered witness is kept   a) on the witness stand   b) in a hospital   c) on call   d) in isolation

5. If a situation is festering, it is   a) deteriorating   b) ameliorating   c) resolving itself   d) changing rapidly

6. A conjecture is similar to   a) evidence   b) a hypothesis   c) a clue   d) a statement

7. A simulated action is   a) not legal   b) pretended   c) pretentious   d) not provable

8. To deviate from a path is to   a) cease progress   b) stop and wait   c) forge a coalition   d) turn aside

9. If a person discerns something, he or she is able to   a) define it   b) see it   c) measure it   d) spend it

10. One needs to mollify a person who has been   a) soothed   b) intimidated   c) pampered and petted   d) angered and upset

11. A decimated community has been   a) segregated   b) severely reduced   c) quarantined   d) plagued by problems

12. A person may feel encumbered by   a) lack of restraint   b) a sense of elation   c) too many commitments   d) a vacation

LESSON 45

abdicate—give up a power or function. *The father abdicated his responsibility by not setting a good example for the boy.*

gesticulate—use the hands and face to convey meaning or supplement speech; gesture, especially in a lively way. *Since they understood little Spanish, she gesticulated to communicate the directions.*

importune—ask, urge, or plead repeatedly; pester with demands or requests. *Importuned by her family, the woman finally agreed to sell the farm.*

intercede—intervene on behalf of, request or plead for someone else's benefit. *The parolee asked his preacher to intercede with the judge.*

peruse—read carefully, study. *She perused the text, absorbing as much of the information as she could.*

interpolate—change a text by inserting new material. *The editor interpolated the latest news into the proofs just before the book was printed.*

censure—disapprove, blame, condemn as wrong. *The unprofessional conduct of several of its members has been officially censured by the organization.*

designate—name, appoint, indicate, point out or mark. *We will rendezvous at the time and place designated on the sheet.*

relegate—transfer to get rid of, assign to an inferior position. *He relegated the policeman to a suburban beat.*

exhort—urge strongly to a proper or necessary action, admonish to do what is right. *We exhorted him to repair the damage he had done.*

incite—urge to action, rouse, inspire. *The presence of his idol in the balcony incited him to an extraordinary performance.* While *exhort* always implies a desirable action, one can *incite* to both good and bad actions. Also, one must use words to exhort, but almost anything—language, an idea, a spectacle—can incite a person to act.

Answers to the following exercises are on page 207.

EXERCISE I Circle the letter of the best choice to complete each sentence.

1. To censure is to   a) express sorrow   b) restrict use   c) express disapproval   d) exterminate

2. A worker may be relegated to a new job if his superior   a) trusts him   b) has little confidence in him   c) promotes him   d) rewards him for outstanding work

3. A person who intercedes wants to gain   a) recognition for himself   b) a benefit for someone else   c) a position of power   d) inside knowledge

4. An exhortation is an attempt to   a) persuade   b) reject compromise   c) undermine confidence   d) provoke a quarrel

5. A designated route is one that has been   a) proposed   b) put off limits   c) marked out   d) disputed

6. An interpolation will make a text   a) more legible   b) more enjoyable   c) shorter   d) longer

7. Perusing a text requires   a) less time than reading it   b) fluency in more than one language   c) a blue pencil   d) concentration

8. A person who is being importuned is harassed by   a) incessant demands   b) groundless complaints   c) public derision   d) vandalism

9. A person gesticulates in order to   a) breathe   b) write   c) communicate   d) digest

10. By abdicating, an individual   a) abandons a function   b) abandons a child   c) shoulders a burden   d) gains status

EXERCISE II Choose the best word to complete each sentence. Write it in the blank.

1. The panhandler pursued Steve down the block, _____ him for bus fare.

inciting	censuring
importuning	interceding with

2. A careful _____ of the manuscript revealed nothing more serious than a couple of typographical errors.

relegation	gesticulation
perusal	interpolation

3. An elected official who puts special interests above the public good deserves to be _____.

incited	abdicated
importuned	censured

4. The pathos and irony of Antony's speech, culminating in the spectacle of Caesar's bloody corpse, _____ the crowd to violence.

incites	designates
exhorts	importunes

5. Disgusted with her efforts at revision, the writer _____ the half-finished story to the back of the files where she wouldn't have to look at it.

designated	abdicated
perused	relegated

6. We _____ Mark to be team captain, since he seemed to know the rules.

censured	designated
relegated	interceded with

7. It is thought that *Beowulf* as we know it is not all by the same poet; some lines are probably later _____ designed to give the poem a more Christian character.

interpolations	perusals
gesticulations	exhortations

8. The ghost of his royal father _____ the young Hamlet to avenge his unnatural murder.

exhorts	abdicates
interpolates	relegates

9. The instructor, who had faith in the student's integrity, offered to _____ the administration.

peruse	intercede with
interpolate	incite

10. Edward VIII of England _____ his throne in order to marry an American divorcée.

designated	censured
gesticulated	abdicated

11. Since he could not be heard in the gale wind, the sailor _____ wildly to signal for help.

gesticulated	importuned
interceded	exhorted

EXERCISE III Antonyms. Draw a line connecting each word with the word or phrase most nearly its *opposite*.

1. interpolate   promote
2. censure   commend
3. peruse   dissuade
4. abdicate   take on responsibility
5. relegate   refuse to speak up for
6. intercede   skim rapidly
7. exhort   edit out

EXERCISE IV Circle the letter of the best choice to complete each sentence.

1. To put a problem "on the back burner" is to   a) focus on it   b) relegate it   c) designate it   d) importune it

2. To incite to heroism is to   a) aspire to it   b) peruse it   c) inspire it   d) interpolate it

3. One who importunes is   a) persistent in pleading   b) exhorted by circumstances   c) abdicating his proper role   d) always gesticulating

4. People who intercede, importune, and exhort are all trying in various ways to   a) help a third party   b) censure misconduct   c) arbitrate a dispute   d) influence another person's actions

5. Effective preachers punctuate their exhortations with appropriate   a) intercessions   b) gesticulations   c) relegations of sin   d) censures of virtue

LESSON 46

The items in this lesson and the next are all adjectives.

salient—conspicuous, very noticeable, important, prominent. *The salient points of the speech could not be forgotten by the audience. Salient* comes from the Latin verb *salire,* participle *saliens,* "leaping." A salient feature, say of a landscape or a building, is one that figuratively leaps out at you and grabs your attention.

banal—commonplace, trite. *The novel was competently written but so banal that I could predict the entire plot by the time I had finished the first chapter.*

deleterious—injurious, harmful. *DDT, taken internally, has a deleterious effect on the body.*

arcane—secret, mysterious, hidden. *Once researchers had deciphered the ancient script, the arcane science of the priest cult was revealed. Arcane* is usually used not to refer to physical objects but to knowledge or practices. A cave is hidden, but the significance of something may be arcane.

esoteric—limited to a few, secret. *The esoteric rites of the fraternity were held sacred by the members and were never divulged to outsiders.* Like *arcane, esoteric* is not used to describe things physically hidden but things hidden from the understanding of most people, often because they are too sacred, difficult, or specialized for common knowledge.

clandestine—secret, furtive. *The conspirators held a clandestine meeting. Clandestine* describes something deliberately kept secret because it is wrong, illegal, contrary to the wishes of those in power, or liable to be prevented or punished if known.

nascent—in the process of being born, just beginning. *By pouring money into building public roads, the government indirectly subsidized the nascent automobile industry in the early days of this century. Nascent* is used figuratively for anything that is very new and has yet to establish itself firmly.

ludicrous—apt to raise laughter, ridiculous. *The scene was so ludicrous that the audience roared with laughter.*

nebulous—hazy, indistinct. *He had a nebulous theory about memorizing key words as an aid to study, but he was so vague about the details we could never figure out how to apply it. Nebulous* comes from the Latin noun *nebula,* "mist." A nebulous idea is ill-defined or vague, like an object seen in a fog.

adept—skilled, well versed. *A journalist is adept at the use of words.*

spurious—false, counterfeit, phony. *The junta's promise of free elections was spurious, calculated solely to disarm world opinon.*

ersatz—substitute, imitation, usually of inferior quality. *The burger was of ersatz beef made from soybeans. Spurious* and *ersatz* both mean "not genuine," but in different senses. *Spurious* is more general and usually implies an evil motive. *Ersatz* most often describes a product designed to serve as a substitute for another, as margarine is ersatz butter.

Answers to the following exercises are on pages 207 and 208.

EXERCISE I Choose the best word to complete each sentence. Write it in the blank.

1. It has been proved that smoking has _____ consequences to the heart and lungs.

arcane	ludicrous
deleterious	banal

2. The toddler's _____ understanding of numbers was not adequate for counting the coins she had found.

banal	spurious
salient	nascent

3. Through long practice, Sheila has become _____ at ping pong.

ersatz	deleterious
adept	ludicrous

4. To take useful notes, a student must be able to pick out the _____ points of a lecture.

salient	arcane
adept	nebulous

5. Nylon became popular as a kind of _____ silk, cheaper and easier to produce than the real thing.

      spurious   banal
      nascent   ersatz

6. The questions on the teacher's exam were so general and the answers so _____ that we couldn't tell whether the students had learned anything in the course or not.

      nebulous   clandestine
      esoteric   ludicrous

7. The middle-aged woman was shocked and deeply hurt when she discovered that her husband had been carrying on a(n) _____ affair for over a year.

      esoteric   adept
      nascent   clandestine

8. Once the document had been exposed as a forgery, the plaintiff's _____ claim to the property was dismissed.

      spurious   banal
      arcane   salient

9. To avoid fighting every time we meet, my brother and I stick to _____ and harmless topics like the weather.

      ersatz   deleterious
      banal   arcane

10. The topic of the economist's talk—the economic reorganization of Poland between 1945 and 1955—was too _____ to engage the interest of the nonspecialist.

      clandestine   nebulous
      ludicrous   esoteric

EXERCISE II Antonyms. Circle the letter of the word or phrase most *opposite* in meaning to the given word.

1. ludicrous: a) awe-inspiring b) riotous c) public d) carefully rehearsed

2. clandestine: a) ordinary b) above board c) illicit d) forceful

3. ersatz: a) mutant b) elegant c) genuine d) complicated

4. arcane: a) sedate b) barely perceptible c) legible d) commonly known

5. nebulous: a) cloudy b) specific c) well documented d) smooth

6. adept: a) unchanging b) clumsy c) common d) rife

7. salient: a) sleepy b) unsalted c) sharp d) inconsequential

8. deleterious: a) calm b) savory c) fantastic d) beneficial

9. esoteric: a) easy to understand b) native c) realistic d) sensible

10. nascent: a) flourishing b) modern c) dying d) solemn

11. banal: a) extraordinary b) surreptitious c) permitted d) extraneous

12. spurious: a) unadulterated b) legitimate c) fraudulent d) incipient

EXERCISE III Fill in the blanks from the list of words below.

arcane   ludicrous
adept   nascent
nebulous   salient

1. An association which has been created and so far has few members may be described as _____ .

2. A person who mounts a publicity campaign needs to be _____ at public relations.

3. The spectacle of pigs dancing in tutus may best be called _____ .

4. A symbol understood only by a few initiates and mysterious to everyone else is _____ .

5. In New York City, the twin towers of the World Trade Center are a(n) _____ feature of the skyline.

6. A social movement which has ill-defined goals and no effective leadership may be described as _____ .

LESSON 47

mordant—biting, caustic, cutting, sarcastic. *Her mordant wit could make anything appear ridiculous.* Derived from the Latin verb *mordere, mordant* literally means "biting."

indigenous—native to a country or region, occurring naturally in a given place. *The indigenous trees of the Rockies are mostly evergreens.*

contingent—dependent upon something happening, conditional. *His plans were contingent on the arrival of the check on time.*

resilient—able to spring back, bouncing back to a former state or position. *The spring was still resilient after years of use. Resilient* applies literally to physical objects like springs, and figuratively to things like health and temperaments.

asinine—stupid, silly. *The heckler's comments were too asinine to deserve a serious answer. Asinine* is descended from *asinus,* the Latin word for "ass" or "donkey," a proverbially stupid animal. The English word *ass* is a cousin of the Latin.

subliminal—below the threshold of awareness, too quick or subtle to be perceived. *A subliminal stimulus is too minor for the conscious mind to notice but it may make an impression on the unconscious mind.* In Latin, *sub limine* means, literally, "below the threshold."

tenable—capable of being held or defended. *The club had no tenable reasons for the exclusion; it was purely a case of prejudice.* The Latin root *tenere* means "to hold"; it is the same root that gives us *tenacious* (holding firmly) and *tenant* (one who holds or has use of a property). The adjective frequently appears in its negative form, *untenable.*

viable—able to live, capable of surviving without extraordinary aid. *Only the viable seeds will sprout. Viable* is used especially to describe a fetus or premature infant developed enough to survive outside the uterus. It may also be used loosely to mean "possible" or "practical," as in: *Our only viable alternative is to sell the house.*

portentous—foreshadowing future events, especially somber ones. *The thunderstorm that broke as we were leaving seemed portentous, but in fact the weather was lovely for the rest of the vacation.* A *portent* is an evil omen. The verb *portend* means "to foreshadow, especially to warn of coming evil or disaster." Only things, not people, portend. People predict or foretell future events; natural occurrences portend them, at least to superstitious minds.

frenetic—frenzied, frantic. *Frenetic activity is evident in the dormitory just before exams.* Like *frenzy, frenetic* comes from a Greek word, *phrenitis,* meaning "inflammation of the brain, madness." *Frenetic* indicates a crazy, disorganized, excited kind of activity.

Answers to the following exercises are on page 208.

EXERCISE I Fill in the blanks from the list of words below.

contingent	asinine
untenable	frenetic
viable	portentous
indigenous	subliminal
resilient	mordant

1. The flash of light was so quick it was almost _____ : we couldn't be sure if we had seen it or only imagined it.

2. The applicant's acceptance by the college is _____ on his completion of high school successfully.

3. Although they seemed so tiny and weak at first, all the pups in the litter were _____ and grew up to be healthy beagles.

4. Her date's _____ wisecracks about the program made the girl feel ashamed that she had taken it so seriously.

5. In Shakespeare's play, _____ happenings—lions in the streets and night birds screeching at noon in the marketplace—augur the murder of Caesar.

6. Since his major support has evaporated, his position in the company is _____ . He will probably resign very soon.

7. Even for a farce the play was unusually _____ . I heard a twelve-year-old describe it as "dumb."

8. The reporter was pounding the typewriter in a _____ , last-minute effort to get the story in under the deadline for the morning edition.

9. After a good night's sleep, his _____ enthusiasm reasserted itself and he looked forward to resuming work.

10. The gypsy moth is not _____ to New England but was brought there originally as part of an ill-fated scheme to produce silk.

EXERCISE II Antonyms. Draw a line connecting each word with the word or phrase most nearly its *opposite*.

1. asinine	without bite
2. mordant	auspicious
3. viable	obvious to the senses
4. frenetic	unconditional
5. portentous	intelligent
6. contingent	imported
7. subliminal	indefensible
8. resilient	not springy
9. tenable	calm
10. indigenous	doomed

EXERCISE III Circle the letter of the best choice to complete each sentence.

1. A _____ must be resilient.
   a) mirror b) floor c) trampoline d) pool

2. A contingency plan is one to be followed only if _____ .
   a) certain circumstances arise b) everyone agrees c) it is guaranteed d) war is declared

3. Someone who is packing frenetically is probably _____ .
   a) moving lethargically b) folding clothes neatly c) stuffing things in a suitcase d) ahead of schedule

4. A viable business is one that is likely to _____ .
   a) make outstanding profits b) survive c) be sold for back taxes d) change location

5. Some rare natural occurrences, such as a brilliant comet or the appearance of a nova, may be interpreted as a portent by _____ .
   a) optimists b) astrologers c) astrophysicists d) amateurs

6. A subliminal message is not _____ .
   a) written b) truthful c) consciously received d) dependent on context

7. An indigenous species occurs _____ in a particular country.
   a) in zoos b) everywhere c) ominously d) naturally

8. A tenable proposition is one that can be reasonably _____ .
   a) refuted with certainty b) proved by examples c) defended d) outlined

9. A mordant editorial is one that probably _____ .
   a) exhorts to action b) attacks with wit c) is obscene d) doesn't get printed

10. An asinine suggestion probably _____ .
    a) won't work b) registers unconsciously c) bodes ill d) is insightful

Adjectives from Animals

Lots of proverbial expressions, or clichés, compare people to animals. A person can wolf down a sandwich, chicken out, eat like a bird, and feel as happy as a hog in slops. Less familiar versions of such comparisons, or metaphors, often come from Latin roots. As we have seen, *asinine* literally means "donkey-like." Check your dictionary for the literal meaning of:

bovine   _____

porcine   _____

aquiline   _____

leonine   _____

Such adjectives are a small manifestation of the universal impulse to connect human society with animal life. In ancient mythologies all over the world, gods and heroes are associated with certain creatures. The Egyptian Horus, for instance, has the head of a hawk, and the Greek Hercules wears a lion's skin. Families in Native American tribes had totem animals with whom they claimed blood kinship. Nor is our animal imagery only something left over from more primitive days. Manufacturers use names like Mustang and Rabbit to sell cars and also today many places in America have their totem animals—Razorbacks in Arkansas, for example, and Dolphins in Miami.

LESSON 48

Throughout the medieval period and into the modern era, medical knowledge in Europe was based on the theory and practice of medicine among the ancient Greeks. Most of our medical, including psychological, terminology comes from Greek roots, although the actual words may have been coined quite recently. Even today researchers will use Greek words to invent a "scientific" name for a condition. The following words are all from Greek roots.

phobia—abnormal and persistent fear. *The patient has such a phobia of cats that she feels uncomfortable even seeing pictures of them. Phobia* is often combined with other roots to describe specific kinds of fear, as in:

agoraphobia—unreasoning fear of open places. *A person suffering from agoraphobia may be unable to go outdoors without experiencing panic.* The word in Greek literally means "fear of the marketplace."

xenophobia—unreasoning fear and hatred of strangers or foreigners. *The xenophobia of the candidate expressed itself in an extreme and unrealistic isolationism.*

megalomania—mental state marked by delusions of grandeur or an extreme passion for greatness, power, or glory. *People who conceive a desire to rule the world suffer from megalomania. Mania* is Greek for "madness." *Megalo* is a combining form from *megas* (great, large), and is also at the root of *megaphone* and *megaton.*

hypochondria—morbid and unrealistic anxiety about one's health. *Obsessive fear of germs can be a symptom of hypochondria.* In Greek the word means "under the cartilage below the chest," where the condition was once thought to originate. The *hypo* form, meaning "under," gives us many terms, including *hypothermia* (lowered body temperature) and *hypodermic* (under the skin).

telekinesis—the movement of a physical object without being touched, supposedly by spiritual or psychic force. *Researchers in psychic phenomena tested subjects for telepathy and telekinesis. Tele* is the combining form meaning "distance" (as in *telephone* and *television*) and *kinesis* means "movement." *Telekinesis* is an example of a modern coinage that derives from Greek, although the Greeks never invented it.

phenomenon—perceptible occurrence, any event that can be observed and described scientifically. *Tropical hurricanes are a common phenomenon on the East Coast in the late summer and early fall. Phenomenon* can be confusing because it is also sometimes used to mean "an extraordinary event," as when we say that a play was a phenomenal success at the box office. Avoid this use in formal prose. The plural is *phenomena.*

criterion—standard of judging. *The answer was used as a criterion for grading the test papers.* The plural is *criteria.*

plethora—excess, superabundance, too great quantity. *The garden by mid-August was producing a plethora of tomatoes, more than we could possibly use.*

synopsis—summary, condensed version, brief review. *Each chapter of* Tom Jones *begins with a synopsis of the main events of that chapter.*

Answers to the following exercises are on page 208.

EXERCISE I Synonyms. Draw a line connecting each word with the word or phrase that means most nearly the same.

1. megalomania	movement of bodies at a distance
2. agoraphobia	abnormal sense of power
3. hypochondria	summary
4. criterion	abnormal fear of illness
5. phenomenon	observable occurrence
6. xenophobia	fear of open space
7. telekinesis	fear of strangers
8. synopsis	overabundance
9. plethora	unreasoning fear
10. phobia	standard for judgment

EXERCISE II Choose the best word to complete each sentence. Write it in the blank.

1. The office received such a _____ of applicants that we were not able to interview even all of the highly qualified candidates.

    phobia   hypochondria
    plethora   synopsis

2. The medium claimed that he could lift objects and bend spoons by _____.

    xenophobia   megalomania
    hypochondria   telekinesis

3. The _____ was in the doctor's office every week complaining of
   ills that were mostly imaginary.

         agoraphobic   megalomaniac
         telekinetic   hypochondriac

4. Psychiatrists attempt to cure _____ by uncovering their origins in
   early traumatic experiences.

         synopses   phobias
         phenomena   criteria

5. The woman was _____ in her suspicions of anyone who looked
   different.

         xenophobic   phenomenal
         megalomaniacal   agoraphobic

6. As the comet approached, astronomers prepared to photograph the
   _____.

         phenomenon   plethora
         phobia   telekinesis

7. His _____ was such that the idea of the open ocean or an empty
   plain was a nightmare to him.

         xenophobia   criterion
         agoraphobia   plethora

8. In the grip of a _____, she began to believe that she was a special messenger of God.

         agoraphobia   megalomania
         hypochondria   telekinesis

9. Since the interest of the book does not lie in its plot, a mere
   _____ of the incidents cannot convey its true flavor.

         plethora   criterion
         xenophobia   synopsis

10. To practice science is to conform to certain _____ of evidence.

          phobias   synopses
          criteria   phenomena

EXERCISE III Circle the letter of the best choice to complete each sentence.

1. A woman who is a hypochondriac is likely to   a) panic easily   b) be afraid
   of heights   c) get a great deal of exercise   d) medicate herself

2. The phenomena of science are   a) the result of childhood traumas
   b) impossible events   c) rare occurrences   d) natural events that can be
   perceived and analyzed

3. A phobia differs from a normal fear in that it   a) is without cause   b) is
   irrational   c) passes quickly   d) is unconscious

4. A synopsis of a man's biography can be expected to give   a) a psychological
   analysis   b) a brief account of his life   c) harangues   d) an impression
   of fearfulness

5. The opposite of a plethora is   a) a dearth   b) a superfluity   c) a normal
   condition   d) an anxiety

6. A set of criteria allows one to   a) evaluate things relative to each other
b) have an abundance of something   c) exorcise fears   d) produce
formulae

7. As often portrayed in popular books and films, telekinesis is supposed to
operate by   a) nescience   b) potential energy   c) parental introjects
d) psychic energy

8. An agoraphobic can be expected to feel uneasy   a) in an enclosed space
b) meeting strangers   c) in a large, bare room   d) with animals

9. A classic example of a megalomaniac was   a) Wordsworth   b) Hitler
c) Robert E. Lee   d) Edgar Allan Poe

10. A national xenophobia is likely to result in   a) a laissez-faire economy
b) increased tourism   c) a persecution of those perceived as
outsiders   d) free elections

LESSON 49

The suffix -ology comes from the Greek word logos, meaning "word" or "description." In combination with other roots, -ology signifies "the study of," as in:

ethnology—study of human cultures. *A journal of ethnology publishes articles on the folkways and customs evolved by various human communities. Ethnology* is one branch of anthropology.

gerontology—study of human aging and the old. *Gerontology is becoming an increasingly important field as our population becomes relatively older. Geriatrics,* built on the same Greek *geras* (old age), is more specifically the medical study of the diseases of old age.

ophthalmology—branch of medicine concerned with the eye. *The medical student chose ophthalmology as her specialty because she was familiar with visual handicaps in her own family.*

etiology—study of causes or origins, the cause of something. *Much research is now being directed to the etiology of cancer.*

paleontology—study of prehistoric life forms through fossil remains. *As part of their training in paleontology, students uncover fossils in the field.* The *paleo* stem comes from the Greek word for "ancient," as in:

paleography—study of ancient writings. *Interpreting the signs impressed on clay tablets five thousand years ago is the province of paleography. Graph* or *graphy* means "writing," as in *telegraph,* "writing at a distance." It is a root found in many English words, including:

calligraphy—handwriting, especially when practiced as an art. *Before the printing press, calligraphy was highly regarded as a skill both practical and decorative.*

nomenclature—the names of things in any art or science, the whole vocabulary of technical terms that are appropriate to any particular branch of science. *The nomenclature of botany includes very many terms coined from Greek and Latin roots.*

orthopedics—branch of medicine concerned with bones and joints. *The setting of fractured bones is part of training in orthopedics.*

mnemonics—study or practice of aiding memory, devices such as formulas to help one remember. *Folk rhymes such as "Thirty days hath November" are mnemonics that organize information so that it is easy to recall.*

taxonomy—science or system of classification. *The taxonomy of law first separates the civil from the criminal.*

jurisprudence—philosophy or theory of law. *The courses for the most part emphasize the practical application of the law rather than jurisprudence or legal history.*

Answers to the following exercises are on page 208.

EXERCISE I Draw a line connecting each kind of knowledge or study with its object.

1. orthopedics	bones and joints
2. taxonomy	causes
3. mnemonics	folk culture
4. nomenclature	scientific terms
5. ophthalmology	old age
6. paleography	theory of law
7. gerontology	beautiful handwriting
8. jurisprudence	eye
9. calligraphy	ancient writing
10. paleontology	fossils
11. etiology	classification
12. ethnology	memory

EXERCISE II Choose the best word to complete each sentence. Write it in the blank.

1. The lives of people in a nursing home are likely to be of interest to a(n) _____ .

   calligrapher   paleographer
   gerontologist   orthopedist

2. The basketball player went to a surgeon specializing in _____ for a knee operation.

   orthopedics   ophthalmology
   mnemonics   gerontology

3. The way food is produced and distributed within a particular culture is of interest to _____ .

   ethnologists   calligraphers
   taxonomists   paleontologists

4. One of the concerns of _____ is the evolution of primitive visual sign systems into complete written languages.

        paleontology   nomenclature
        mnemonics   paleography

5. One task of _____ is to analyze the social theory that underpins a legal system.

        orthopedics   nomenclature
        ophthalmology   jurisprudence

6. After a thorough examination, the _____ recommended an operation to remove the cataracts.

        etiologist   paleontologist
        ophthalmologist   orthopedist

7. The traditional _____ of life into two major kingdoms—animal and plant—cannot accommodate many microscopic organisms.

        calligraphy   taxonomy
        jurisprudence   ethnology

8. The law has a highly specialized _____ ; part of the work of the beginning law student is to memorize this vocabulary.

        jurisprudence   paleography
        nomenclature   gerontology

9. _____ is a skill requiring patience and manual dexterity.

        Taxonomy   Calligraphy
        Mnemonics   Etiology

10. Theorizing about the structure, habits, and evolutionary relationships of extinct life forms is the work of _____ .

        ethnology   ophthalmology
        paleography   paleontology

11. Discovering the _____ of a disease is a crucial step in its prevention.

        etiology   ethnology
        taxonomy   gerontology

12. She purchased a book on _____ in the hope of improving her memory, but then she forgot where she left the book.

        jurisprudence   nomenclature
        mnemonics   etiology

EXERCISE III Circle the letter of the best choice to complete each sentence.

1. As their names suggest, both paleographers and paleontologists a) are students of human culture b) are concerned with ancient things c) must be trained as biologists d) must be trained as linguists

2. Botanical taxonomy is organized in part by a) committee b) genre c) glossary d) genus and species

3. Etiological myths are myths that purport to a) explain the origins of things b) predict the end of the world c) give the nomenclature of a culture d) describe legal obligations

4. Gerontologists study   a) extinct organisms   b) prehistoric cultures   c) attitudes toward aging   d) ancient writing

5. A professional calligrapher must know   a) a variety of scripts   b) bone structure   c) the theory of vision   d) every aspect of the culture she studies

6. Mnemonic formulas usually rhyme because   a) verse sounds poetic   b) verse is easier to remember than prose   c) they are set to music   d) verse is more arcane

LESSON 50

Here are a few of the many words in English that have been adopted from the names of people and places.

stentorian—very loud, booming. *One fan, a man with a stentorian voice, could be heard clearly above the crowd.* According to Homer, the Greek herald Stentor had a voice equal to that of fifty men.

spartan—very simple and hardy, disciplined, self-denying. *In addition to the usual classes, the military school imposed a spartan regimen of physical training.* A city-state of ancient Greece, Sparta was famed for its highly disciplined and warlike culture.

mesmerize—hypnotize, transfix, render motionless. *Deer are sometimes hit by cars when they become mesmerized by the headlights.* Mesmer was an eighteenth-century German physican who became famous treating patients by hypnotic suggestion.

bowdlerize—censor, expurgate, remove supposedly offensive or obscene passages. *The lyrics of the song were bowdlerized for performance on television.* Thomas Bowdler was an Englishman who in 1818 edited Shakespeare's works, deleting all the parts he considered unfit for family reading.

chauvinist—person motivated by zealous and unreasoning patriotism, an extreme nationalist, a person unreasonably devoted to his or her own group. *"My country right or wrong" is the slogan of a chauvinist.* Nicolas Chauvin was a French soldier, a follower of Napoleon, who become notorious for his extreme nationalism. In recent years, *chauvinism* has broadened to include all kinds of irrational devotion, such as to one's race or sex.

narcissism—excessive self-love, especially love of one's own body or appearance. *Adolescents frequently have a narcissistic preoccupation with their own looks.* Narcissus was the young man in Greek mythology who fell in love with his own reflection in a pool and so pined away.

quixotic—foolishly idealistic, unrealistically hopeful or romantic. *Their hopes of founding a utopian community of perfect harmony proved quixotic.* The word comes from *Don Quixote*, a novel by Cervantes, a Spanish contemporary of Shakespeare. Don Quixote, the deluded hero, is a country gentleman who, having read too many romantic tales of knighthood, sets out to perform chivalric deeds, his ideals ever blinding him to the true nature of what he finds.

draconian—very harsh, cruelly severe. *The inhabitants suffered under the governor's draconian tyranny.* Draco was an early ruler of ancient Athens. The laws he codified have not survived, but they were reputed to be very severe, prescribing the death penalty for even minor offenses. The name Draco, appropriately enough, means "dragon."

martial—military, warlike, suited to war. *The sculpture depicted the emperor in a martial attitude, dressed in armor with sword drawn.* Martial literally means "belonging to Mars", the Roman god of war.

protean—able to take many forms, very versatile or variable. *An actor with a protean talent is able to impersonate many different kinds of characters.* In Greek myth, Proteus was the Old Man of the Sea who herded seals for Poseidon. He could change his shape at will, but if one could hold onto him through all his metamorphoses, he could be forced to reveal the future.

Answers to the following exercises are on page 208.

EXERCISE I Synonyms. Draw a line connecting each word with the word or phrase that means most nearly the same.

1. narcissistic	shape-changing
2. spartan	very loud
3. martial	ruggedly disciplined
4. bowdlerized	overly nationalistic
5. stentorian	cleaned up
6. protean	hypnotized
7. quixotic	extravagantly idealistic
8. chauvinistic	appropriate to war
9. draconian	inhumanly harsh
10. mesmerized	self-regarding

EXERCISE II Fill in the blanks from the list of words below.

draconian	protean
bowdlerized	spartan
mesmerized	quixotic
chauvinistic	narcissistic
stentorian	martial

1. Renaissance nobles were expected to train themselves in _____ studies such as swordplay and fortifications.

2. What we call love is a _____ feeling, expressing itself in a vast variety of forms.

3. Grimm's fairy tales are often published in _____ versions in which their original violence is considerably toned down.

4. A law that demands death for stealing a loaf of bread is truly _____.

5. They lived in a _____ style, laboring hard and surviving on meager fare.

6. Her attitude is so _____ she takes it for granted that other cultures have nothing to offer.

7. For a moment he had a _____ vision of himself appearing like a knight in shining armor to save the day.

8. The _____ tones of the speaker boomed out across the open-air assembly.

9. One can become _____ staring at a monotonously moving object such as a pendulum.

10. He is a _____ man who believes no one is as handsome as himself.

EXERCISE III. Circle the letter of the best choice to complete each sentence.

1. A male chauvinist feels that   a) women are different   b) men are superior to women   c) monogamy is wrong   d) a strong defense is the highest priority

2. Originally, people were mesmerized as part of   a) a legal penalty b) military training   c) a medical treatment   d) an augury

3. A protean problem   a) cannot be solved   b) demands a simple solution c) is mythological   d) has many manifestations

4. A narcissist likes to look   a) at movies   b) at the stars   c) at paintings d) in mirrors

5. A stentorian voice is   a) grating   b) hoarse   c) hard to ignore d) inaudible

6. A spartan individual is not   a) self-indulgent   b) reflective   c) hardy d) flaky

7. Martial arts are those suited to   a) women   b) battle   c) marriage d) Greeks

8. A quixotic plan is likely to   a) succeed   b) be complex   c) founder d) garner broad support

9. Draconian laws are generally   a) treated with contempt   b) unenforceable c) feared and hated   d) lenient

10. One who bowdlerizes is probably   a) a prude   b) a poet   c) illiterate d) salacious

The following words are also derived from proper names. Using your dictionary, fill in the blanks with the original names. Make sure you know what each word has come to mean.

boycott	_____
maudlin	_____
bedlam	_____
mentor	_____
maverick	_____
daguerreotype	_____

REVIEW TEST 5

1.   *He said very modestly that he was loath to kill them, if he could help it; but that those two were incorrigible villains, and had been the authors of all the mutiny on the ship. . . .*

                                                                     —Daniel Defoe

Incorrigible villains are   a) criminals manqué   b) neophytes   c) megalomaniacs   d) miscreants

2.   *For my part, I abominate all honorable respectable toils, trials, and tribulations of every kind whatsoever.*

                                                                    —Herman Melville

Abominate means   a) hate with a passion   b) revere   c) exhort others to   d) avoid

3.   *I wanted . . . to surrender personally all that remained of him with me to that oblivion which is the last word of our common fate.*

                                                                   —Joseph Conrad

The oblivion referred to is   a) a reminiscence   b) a state of being utterly forgotten   c) a sepulcher   d) quixotic

4.   *An old-fashioned man would have lost his senses or died of ennui before this.*

                                                                —Henry David Thoreau

The old-fashioned man would have died of   a) fear   b) boredom   c) exhaustion   d) a pathological condition

Questons 5 and 6.

     I discerned he was now neither angry nor shocked at my audacity.

                                                                —Charlotte Brontë

5. Another word for discerned would be   a) conjectured   b) learned   c) hoped   d) perceived

6. Audacity is a kind of   a) emotional trauma   b) rudeness   c) daring boldness   d) euphoria

Questions 7 and 8.

     If I have not therefore importuned you on this head, you will impute it only to my fear of offending the lady, by endeavoring to hurry on so

164

blessed an event, faster than a strict compliance with all the rules of decency and decorum will permit.

—Henry Fielding

7. To importune is to a) pester with pleading b) mollify c) petition in writing d) notify

8. To impute something is to a) proscribe it b) peruse it c) ascribe it d) recommend it

Questions 9 and 10.

He began his lecture by a recapitulation of the history of chemistry. . . . He then took a cursory view of the present state of the science and explained many of its elementary terms.

—Mary Shelley

9. The last thing the lecturer does is introduce his students to a) the chronology of chemistry b) the nomenclature of his science c) contingent facts d) an interpolation

10. A cursory review a) is necessarily frenetic b) is banal c) covers only salient points d) covers esoteric knowledge

Questions 11-13.

These objections were eagerly embraced and as petulantly urged by the vain science of the Gnostics. As those heretics were, for the most part, averse to the pleasures of sense, they morosely arraigned the polygamy of the patriarchs, the gallantries of David, and the seraglio of Solomon. The conquest of the land of Canaan, and the extirpation of the unsuspecting natives, they were at a loss how to reconcile with common notions of humanity and justice. . . . The Mosaic account of the creation and fall of man was treated with profane derision by the Gnostics, who would not listen with patience to the repose of the Deity after six days' labor. . . .

—Edward Gibbon

11. In their attitude toward physical pleasure the Gnostics were a) encumbered b) nebulous c) enigmatic d) austere

12. The Gnostics' reaction to the Biblical account of the creation was one of a) advocacy b) contempt c) nascent understanding d) profound respect

13. According to this passage, the natives of Canaan were a) tyros b) the victims of genocide c) xenophobic d) chauvinists

14.   *There is no better, there is no more open door by which you can enter into the study of natural philosophy than by considering the physical phenomena of a candle.*

—Michael Faraday

By phenomena Faraday means a) existence b) process of creation c) processes or occurrences d) rare events

Questions 15 and 16.

> *The choleric City Captain seems impatient to come to action. . . . His martial finery, as he marches along, inspires him with an unusual elevation of mind . . . by which he looks up at the balconies with the fierceness of a Saracen conqueror: while the phlegmatic Alderman, now become venerable both for his age and his authority, contents himself with being thought a considerable man. . . .*
>
> *—Bernard Mandeville*

15. The captain's appearance is   a) ceremonial   b) warlike   c) spartan
    d) understated

16. As a phlegmatic man, the Alderman is   a) aged   b) optimistic
    c) ludicrous   d) slow to anger

17.
> *Most of the confidences were unsought—frequently I have feigned sleep, preoccupation, or a hostile levity when I realized by some unmistakable sign that an intimate revelation was quivering on the horizon. . . .*
>
> *—F. Scott Fitzgerald*

Levity here suggests: a) lack of attention   b) melodrama   c) a flippant
attitude   d) silence

Questions 18 and 19.

> *Recently many of our best naturalists have recurred to the view first propounded by Linnaeus, so remarkable for his sagacity, and have placed man in the same Order with the Quadrumana, under the title of the Primates.*
>
> *—Charles Darwin*

18. The problem of how to classify man biologically is a question of
    a) gesticulation   b) ethnology   c) paleography   d) taxonomy

19. To Darwin, Linnaeus was notable for his   a) caution   b) great
    wisdom   c) self-discipline   d) ability to foresee the future

20.
> *Could this be he who, of late, with sour visage, and in snuffy habiliments, administered . . . the Draconian Law of the academy?*
>
> *—Edgar Allan Poe*

The laws of the academy are   a) concerned with education   b) stuffy
c) egregiously harsh   d) arcane

Answers to the above questions are on page 209.

LESSON 51

The words in this lesson and the next are adjectives.

adroit—skillfull, clever in dealing with people or situations. *An adroit politician can push his own program without personally alienating or unnecessarily antagonizing his opposition.*

assiduous—extremely careful, attentive, or persistent. *The couple were assiduous followers of the most popular nighttime soap.*

desultory—without definite goal, plan, or enthusiasm. *After a brief and desultory attempt to clean her room, she went to the movies.*

fulsome—overly flattering, lavish to the point of being disgusting. *Such fulsome praise is more appropriate to a fan letter than to a supposedly objective report.* Many people now use *fulsome* more broadly to mean simply "full, abundant," without a pejorative overtone. However, in formal usage it's better to give the word its narrower sense and avoid ambiguity.

glutinous—gluey, gummy. *The resin flowed from the tree, thick and glutinous.*

gullible—easily fooled or cheated. *When they're allowed to win a few dollars at first, gullible victims will assume that the game isn't rigged.*

inchoate—yet unformed. *The conferees speculated on the inchoate state of the universe in the first nanoseconds after the Big Bang.*

inert—motionless, without power to move or interact. *The actor lay sprawled on the stage, so inert he appeared dead.* Inert gases, such as helium and neon, are those with a great degree of stability.

intrinsic—part of the essential nature of something. *Unlike gold, paper money has no intrinsic value; for convenience, society merely agrees to let it represent wealth.*

macabre—having to do with death in a gruesome or eerie way. *Macabre tales of vampires have persisted in folklore for hundreds, if not thousands, of years.*

plebeian—of the common people and therefore coarse or crude. *We prefer plebeian hamburgers to the picky elegance of nouvelle cuisine. Plebs* was the Roman word for the common people; etymologically, *plebeian* expresses an antidemocratic disdain.

retentive—able or tending to retain, especially knowledge. *For someone so young, my sister had a remarkably retentive mind; she could recall minor incidents from months before.*

Answers to the following exercises are on page 209.

EXERCISE I Antonyms. Draw a line connecting each word with the word or phrase most nearly its *opposite*.

1. desultory	clumsy
2. intrinsic	interactive
3. adroit	purposeful
4. inchoate	suspicious
5. assiduous	added later
6. glutinous	carelessly sloppy
7. inert	forgetful
8. macabre	aristocratic
9. fulsome	nonadhesive
10. retentive	restrained
11. plebeian	cheerfully lively
12. gullible	fully formed

EXERCISE II Choose the best word to complete each sentence. Write it in the blank.

1. The author's memory for the period of his imprisonment was so
_____ that he could repeat whole conversations he had heard
in languages he did not even understand.

      inchoate   fulsome

      retentive   glutinous

2. He was so _____ in his duties that his employers had no
complaints.

      assiduous   plebeian

      intrinsic   macabre

3. The landscape seemed lifeless, _____; from the porch to the
horizon nothing moved.

      adroit   intrinsic

      inert   assiduous

4. They went on a _____ shopping expedition, browsing from
counter to counter without any clear idea of what they were looking for.

      glutinous   retentive

      macabre   desultory

5. The pudding stuck to the pan in a _____ and unappetizing mass.

      gullible   fulsome

      plebeian   glutinous

6. *The Twilight Zone, Tales from the Darkside,* and similar programs present
_____ stories designed to send a shiver of horror through
their fans.

      inchoate   inert

      macabre   adroit

7. We believe some fundamental rights are _____ to human beings:
they cannot rightfully be conferred or canceled by government action.

      glutinous   intrinsic

      desultory   retentive

8. With so little experience of the world, even intelligent children are _____ and easily misled.

adroit   gullible
inert   assiduous

9. As Democratic senators sat in stony silence, the applause of the Republicans became even more _____.

retentive   desultory
inchoate   fulsome

10. The idea was still _____, just a hazy notion that she had filed away in the back of her mind.

inchoate   plebeian
inert   intrinsic

11. Matthews was an experienced executive, and _____ enough to avoid being fired in the corporate shakeup.

glutinous   macabre
adroit   gullible

12. The headmaster was an old-fashioned snob who considered an Australian accent too _____ for refined ears.

gullible   fulsome
plebeian   desultory

EXERCISE III Circle the letter of the best choice to complete each sentence.

1. A glutinous substance feels   a) smooth   b) sticky   c) fuzzy   d) hot

2. If a person goes about a task in a desultory way, it will not be accomplished   a) openly   b) at all   c) willingly   d) efficiently

3. An inert object is incapable of   a) burning   b) being lifted   c) moving under its own power   d) being understood

4. An adroit maneuver is likely to be   a) grisly   b) peculiar   c) violent   d) successful

5. One who despises plebeian tastes is likely to consider himself   a) a radical   b) an average joe   c) unfortunate   d) superior to the common herd

6. A person can develop an unusually retentive mind by   a) training himself to remember details   b) socializing widely   c) taking too many drugs   d) reading

7. An inchoate feeling can't be   a) nostalgic   b) clearly verbalized   c) forgiven   d) expressed indirectly

8. A truly macabre decor might remind one of   a) a crypt   b) home   c) a foreign land   d) a country inn

9. A gullible character is   a) heroic   b) always suspicious   c) easily made a fool of   d) enviable

10. An assiduous student probably spends a lot of time   a) earning money   b) in the infirmary   c) calling home   d) in the library

11. One intrinsic quality of a gem is its   a) hardness   b) setting   c) sentimental value   d) current market value

12. Fulsome praise is to be expected from a   a) rival   b) flatterer   c) stranger   d) cynic

LESSON 52

anticipatory—tending to anticipate or take the future into account. *The government imposed controls as an anticipatory measure to forestall devaluation.*

auspicious—favorable, predicting a prosperous or happy future. *The voyage had an auspicious beginning, with clear skies and a fresh wind.* The Latin root of *auspice* ("favorable sign") means to foretell the future by observing the behavior of birds.

celestial—of the heavens or sky. *In celestial navigation one can determine one's position and course by observing the stars and other heavenly bodies.*

onerous—burdensome, too heavy or troublesome. *Caring for aging parents can become an onerous responsibility, especially for a young adult.*

optimal—best, most desirable. *Under optimal conditions, the plant will continue to bear fruit until the first heavy frost.*

pernicious—deadly, exceedingly harmful. *AIDS is a pernicious disease; at this time the long-term survival rate is zero.*

potable—safe or suitable for drinking. *The tap water was brownish but potable.*

purulent—producing or consisting of pus. *When the wound became purulent, the medic applied wet compresses.*

raucous—disagreeably loud, strident, disorderly. *The audience, most of whom had the film memorized, was so raucous that we couldn't hear the dialogue.*

robust—vigorous, healthy, full of strength or flavor. *By dawn the ranch house was filled with the robust smells of coffee and bacon.*

rudimentary—fundamental, primitive, undeveloped. *The ancient archaeopteryx had rudimentary wings; it was capable of gliding but not of sustained flight.*

supine—lying face up; more loosely, too passive, lacking will or energy. *She fell asleep supine in the sun, a hat over her face.*

Answers to the following exercises are on page 209.

EXERCISE I Fill in the blanks from the list of words below.

anticipatory	auspicious
celestial	onerous
optimal	pernicious
potable	purulent
raucous	robust
rudimentary	supine

1. In the _____ classroom situation, each child achieves the best he is capable of.

2. The teaching load was so _____ that the union threatened to strike unless the teachers were given more free periods for preparation.

3. I found him _____ in the porch hammock, snoring peacefully.

4. The Black Death was the most _____ plague in Europe's history; it killed off more than half the population.

5. The community had to use bottled water until the well water was once again deemed _____.

6. The _____ crowing of the grackles was enough to wake the dead.

7. The wound was deep but not _____; it was clean and free from infection.

8. The boy's knowledge of engines was _____; he understood the principles involved but he didn't know how to make repairs.

9. Astrologers believe that people's lives are influenced by _____ events.

10. Soothsayers consulted their almanacs to determine the most _____ day for the wedding.

11. The more _____ strategy took into account population shifts projected over the next twenty years, shifts that other proposals ignored.

12. With excellent muscle tone, a slow pulse, and low blood pressure, the athlete was as _____ as most men thirty years younger.

EXERCISE II Synonyms. Circle the letter of the word or phrase closest in meaning to the given word.

1. celestial: a) enormous   b) flavorful   c) heavenly   d) star-studded

2. optimal: a) pure   b) sunny   c) free to choose   d) most favorable

3. auspicious: a) productive   b) backward-looking   c) auguring well   d) enjoying someone's protection

4. anticipatory: a) looking ahead   b) open to all   c) official   d) democratic

5. pernicious: a) feared   b) deadly   c) underhanded   d) apprehensive

6. purulent: a) pornographic   b) producing pus   c) medical   d) disgusting

7. onerous: a) hard to comprehend   b) ancient   c) heavy to carry   d) single

8. robust: a) hearty   b) smelly   c) fluffy   d) bland

9. potable: a) edible   b) carry-on   c) drinkable   d) liquid

10. rudimentary: a) decadent   b) unnecessary   c) cultural   d) basic

11. supine: a) overactive   b) reactive   c) flat on one's back   d) dead to the world

12. raucous: a) noisy   b) out of control   c) placid   d) rocky

EXERCISE III Circle the letter of the best choice to complete each sentence.

1. A rudimentary tail probably   a) is very long   b) occurs only as a result of genetic mutation   c) is used as a defense   d) does not show a high degree of specialization

2. The word *purulent* can be most literally applied to   a) a sore   b) an editorial style   c) a personality type   d) a social class

3. An executive seeking to develop an anticipatory approach to marketing would be especially interested in   a) insurance against lawsuits   b) past performance of the product   c) predictions of future trends   d) cutting costs

4. A robust wine is   a) full-bodied   b) aged   c) sparkling   d) white

5. For optimal performance, a car must be   a) driven fast   b) kept well-tuned   c) leased   d) freshly painted

6. The celestial realms are   a) in the tropics   b) overhead   c) submerged   d) in the underworld

7. Raucous behavior is to be expected   a) from swans   b) from rabbits   c) at wild parties   d) at elegant boutiques

8. A pernicious infestation of a field spells   a) a bumper crop   b) little insect damage   c) dry weather   d) crop failure

9. Doing work that is too onerous leads eventually to   a) boredom   b) exhaustion   c) a promotion   d) overconfidence

10. An example of a potable substance is   a) apple juice   b) motor oil   c) a sponge cake   d) a sponge

11. A supine position suggests   a) a lack of resistance   b) mental illness   c) alertness   d) brute strength

12. Auspicious flight conditions include   a) a safe landing   b) a clear weather forecast at takeoff   c) a change in destination   d) ice on the wings

LESSON 53

The words in Lessons 53, 54, and 55 are all verbs.

assuage—lessen the pain or distress of something, ease the severity of. *A heartfelt apology can do wonders to assuage wounded pride.*

chronicle—record a history continuously and in time order. *The news media chronicled the scandal as it unfolded day by day.*

cosset—treat indulgently, pamper. *The parents cosset the girl, letting her have whatever she wants, no matter how rudely she demands it.*

embellish—ornament, make more pleasing by adding decorative details. *The patchwork quilt was embellished with a variety of intricate stitching.*

fathom—measure the depth of; understand. *I can't fathom what drove her to get herself fired the first day on the job.* The noun *fathom* is a unit of measure for water depth; it is equal to six feet. To *fathom* is literally to measure water depth, or figuratively to "get to the bottom" of something.

foment—encourage, incite, especially something destructive or disruptive, such as rebellion. *The administration itself fomented discontent by refusing to explain or justify its policies.*

hobnob—socialize, associate with as a friend. *On sunny days the retired men would hobnob on the benches in front of the post office.*

inveigh—rail, bitterly protest. *In unusually strong language, the editorial inveighed against continued American support for the South African regime.*

pillory—hold up for public ridicule or contempt. *Ford's accidents and slips of the tongue made him an easy target; comedians had a field day pillorying his frequent blunders.* A pillory is a wooden frame in which public offenders, locked by the hands and head, were once exposed to the mockery (and hurled garbage) of the public.

scruple—refrain or hesitate because of principles. *Believing it wrong to inform on fellow students, Ted scrupled to report on the drug dealing he'd witnessed in the dorm.*

Answers to the following exercises are on page 209.

EXERCISE I From the following list of verbs, pick a term to match each action described in the sentences below. Write the verbs in the blanks.

assuaged	chronicled
cosseted	embellished
fathomed	fomented
hobnobbed	inveighed
pilloried	scrupled

1. He stirred up the demonstrators until they broke windows and overturned cars.

   _____

2. From the beginning of the Christian era to the twelfth century, monks at Canterbury, Winchester, and other centers kept records of events in England.

   _____

3. A frequent partygoer, Sabrina enjoyed socializing with a broad assortment of people. _____

4. By satirizing her peculiar appearance and ignoring her ideas, the press made the activist a laughingstock. _____

5. He felt guilty that he wasn't helping his pal, but he just couldn't bring himself to steal the test answers. _____

6. The crew took a sounding to determine if the channel was deep enough.

   _____

7. She made the story more interesting by adding details she could not possibly have known. _____

8. The old woman fed the cat salmon and let it sleep on her pillow.

_____

9. A couple of aspirin soothed the pain. _____

10. The senator protested vehemently against allowing the president to place himself above the law. _____

EXERCISE II Antonyms. Circle the letter of the word or phrase most *opposite* in meaning to the given word.

1. hobnob: a) abstain from drinking b) love indiscriminately c) snub d) accept correction gracefully

2. pillory: a) elicit admiration for b) question closely c) refuse medication d) conspire against

3. assuage: a) wake up b) make sting c) remain motionless d) rekindle

4. scruple: a) act unethically b) act without thinking c) act a part d) act normally

5. chronicle: a) leave unmeasured b) leave unrecorded c) grow younger d) chastise

6. embellish: a) remove the dye from b) be disdainful of c) deflate d) strip bare of ornament

7. fathom: a) sail smoothly b) be at anchor c) fail to comprehend d) fail to notice

8. inveigh: a) ignore b) support warmly c) shirk d) regard doubtfully

9. foment: a) discourage from acting b) cook without leavening c) take pride in d) feel hopeless

10. cosset: a) play with b) please c) take to heart d) demand much of

EXERCISE III Circle the letter of the best choice to complete each sentence.

1. The word *chronicle* in a title implies that the events described a) are purely fictitious b) are recounted in the order they happened c) mix fact and fiction d) concern royalty

2. A person who foments rebellion is a) a peacemaker b) invested in maintaining the status quo c) an innocent bystander d) an agitator

3. One embellishes a design by a) reproducing it b) enlarging it c) adding things to it d) simplifying it

4. Writers pillory thinkers whose ideas they a) respect but disagree with b) agree with c) despise d) are uninterested in

5. Inveighing carries a tone of a) levity b) bitterness c) gentle humor d) reconciliation

6. Cosseting is the treatment usually associated with a) a pampered pet b) a farm animal c) an equal partner d) underlings

7. One can often fathom another person's feelings by   a) criticizing them harshly   b) putting oneself in the other person's shoes   c) refusing to consider them   d) speaking soothingly

8. One can assuage a parent's fears by   a) calling home when one is late   b) always staying out late   c) getting caught in a lie   d) pleading the Fifth

9. A person who likes to hobnob needs   a) hobbies   b) a boat   c) many friends   d) a lot of money

10. A man who scruples to cheat on his income tax   a) plans ahead   b) tells white lies   c) is likely to be caught   d) answers the questions honestly

LESSON 54

abrogate—do away with or make ineffective, usually by authoritative or official action. *The regime abrogated civil liberties in the name of national security.*

delegate—give a task or entrust responsibility to another person. *The chairwoman delegated to her assistant the job of collecting teacher evaluations.*

deplete—use up or lessen critically; used of essential resources. *Forecasters predicted that oil reserves would soon be depleted and prices would skyrocket.*

disclaim—deny, formally renounce claim to. *The adviser disclaimed any responsibility for the decision.*

efface—make inconspicuous or eliminate by wearing away. *The fine details of the carving had been effaced by exposure to the weather.* Figuratively, a person who makes himself inconspicuous is often called "self-effacing."

enumerate—count, list items one after another. *The plaintiffs' complaints were enumerated in the brief.*

mortify—humiliate, embarrass severely. *Roy was mortified to find that the whole class was laughing at his predicament.*

preempt—take the place of as more important, take precedence over. *The regularly scheduled program was preempted by coverage of the crisis.*

rebut—contradict, show the falseness of an argument or accusation. *The leader of our debating team cited the conclusions of researchers to rebut the generalizations of the other side.*

retrogress—move backward, return to an earlier condition. *Because of a poor harvest, conditions in the villages had retrogressed and hunger was again common.*

sublimate—redirect energy from a primitive or unacceptable expression to a more socially acceptable expression. *The little boy's romantic love for his mother is eventually sublimated into interests beyond the family circle.*

Answers to the following exercises are on page 209.

EXERCISE I Choose the best word to complete each sentence. Write it in the blank.

1. I cannot precisely _____ all the times he called me, but I know he did so several times that week.

   rebut   efface
   enumerate   retrogress

2. His inner conflict has been constructively _____ into a passion for social justice.

   rebutted   abrogated
   depleted   sublimated

3. The Supreme Court can _____ a law by declaring it unconstitutional.

   abrogate   mortify
   efface   deplete

4. Over the long vacation, the child's reading skills did not improve; in fact, they _____ to a second-grade level.

   mortified   disclaimed
   retrogressed   enumerated

5. Since he was reluctant to _____ work, he wasted a lot of time on clerical tasks that could have been handled by a secretary.

   delegate   enumerate
   preempt   sublimated

6. A long period of stress and overwork can _____ your energy and leave you susceptible to infection.

   sublimate   deplete
   retrogress   delegate

7. Although the boy was very polite about it, Tiffany was _____ when he turned her down for the date.

   abrogated   retrogressed
   mortified   delegated

8. I couldn't tell how old the coin was, for the date had been completely _____.

   rebutted   effaced
   preempted   disclaimed

9. If you ignore the charges instead of _____ them, people may believe you're guilty and trying to stonewall.

   enumerating   rebutting
   abrogating   delegating

10. She _____ her share of the inheritance, renouncing it for the sake of the deceased's children.

    mortified   preempted
    disclaimed   depleted

11. The aide _____ his boss by leaking the news before the boss made his formal announcement.

    preempted   sublimated
    disclaimed   effaced

EXERCISE II Synonyms. Draw a line connecting each word with the word or phrase that means most nearly the same.

1. mortify   obliterate
2. rebut   count in a list
3. preempt   use evidence to contradict
4. disclaim   divert energy to an acceptable outlet
5. deplete   exhaust a resource
6. delegate   embarrass utterly
7. enumerate   backslide
8. efface   disavow
9. abrogate   officially make no longer in effect
10. retrogress   assign to a subordinate
11. sublimate   take the place of

EXERCISE III Circle the letter of the best choice to complete each sentence.

1. Once our firewood supply is depleted, we'll a) stay warm   b) have to cut more   c) have to stack it   d) sell off the surplus

2. The president abrogated the arms control agreement by a) consulting Congress about revoking it   b) signing it   c) campaigning for its ratification   d) exceeding the number of warheads allowed under it

3. Since my favorite program was preempted, I a) didn't get to see it   b) taped it   c) watched it with friends   d) chose not to watch it

4. In her dream she was mortified to find that she a) ruled the world   b) was flying   c) was naked in a train station   d) was desperately fleeing monsters

5. In sublimation, unacceptable impulses are diverted into a) sexual frustration   b) political crimes   c) jokes   d) constructive work

6. If a situation has retrogressed, there has been a) a slipping back into an earlier state   b) no change   c) remarkable progress in a short time   d) degeneration into complete chaos

7. Though he disclaims all knowledge of the affair, the commission believes he a) did not act alone   b) knew nothing   c) is taking too much responsibility   d) must have known about it

8. The stranger was so self-effacing that   a) no one even learned his name   b) no one else could make himself heard   c) everyone laughed at him   d) he terrified everyone

9. The general delegated the task to a) the army chief of staff   b) his aide   c) the wastebasket   d) himself

10. In enumerating items, one a) puts them in alphabetical order   b) justifies them   c) lists them   d) displays them

11. In rebutting an argument, one a) offers a counterargument   b) remains proudly silent   c) resorts to violence   d) fights dirty

LESSON 55

covet—desire what belongs to someone else, especially in a blameworthy way. *The tenth commandment prohibits coveting thy neighbor's property.*

delude—deceive, mislead by creating a false opinion or judgment. *The con artist deluded the victim into thinking that he would get rich quick.*

dispatch—send away or off, especially on official business. *The president dispatched a personal envoy to conduct secret negotiations. Dispatch* can also mean "kill with promptness and efficiency," a kind of permanent sending away: *The hero dispatched three of his opponents without working up a sweat.*

elucidate—make clear by analyzing or explaining. *The poet's notes elucidated some of the obscure passages. Elucidate,* like *lucid,* is derived from the Latin word *lux,* "light."

enjoin—command or prohibit urgently or by powerful authority. *Because of his history of violent behavior, the man was enjoined by the court from seeing his estranged wife.* The noun form is *injunction.*

forbear—hold back, restrain oneself from some action. *He could not forbear giving his opinion, although he knew it would not be welcome.* The past tense is *forbore.* Do not confuse this verb with the noun *forebear,* meaning "ancestor."

ostracize—exclude, bar from a group by general consent. *Children of that age are often highly conformist and will ostracize a classmate whose appearance or manners are different.*

recant—publicly or formally withdraw an opinion, repudiate a formerly stated belief. *To save himself from persecution, Galileo officially recanted his discovery that the earth moves.*

resurrect—bring back to life, raise from the dead, either figuratively or literally. *The group resurrected some old ballads that had been popular during the fifties.*

revile—abuse verbally, out of anger or hatred. *She reviled him so thoroughly that I never again mentioned his name in her hearing.*

supplant—take the place of, especially by force or because of superior qualities. *The generals had gradually supplanted the aged and enfeebled dictator and were running the country in all but name.*

Answers to the following exercises are on page 210.

EXERCISE I Circle the letter of the best choice to complete each sentence.

1. Being publicly reviled is likely to make a person   a) cooperative
   b) ecstatic   c) humiliated and defensive   d) bored and sleepy

2. A hunter is most likely to dispatch a deer with   a) a message   b) a rope
   c) binoculars   d) a rifle

178

3. To elucidate a situation, one must first   a) recount it   b) disown it
   c) understand it   d) enunciate it

4. One recants an opinion that one   a) does not recall   b) finds inspirational
   c) no longer holds   d) has always discredited

5. In many myths, divine heroes such as the Egyptian Osiris are resurrected
   after   a) losing their memories   b) dying   c) defeating their rivals
   d) long travels

6. Supplanted by a new arrival, a person is likely to feel   a) superfluous and
   resentful   b) cheerful and optimistic   c) overconfident   d) appreciative

7. If one forbears doing something, one   a) accomplishes it quickly   b) does
   a sloppy job   c) procrastinates   d) doesn't do it

8. An individual who is ostracized becomes   a) popular   b) a usurper   c) an
   outsider   d) a power behind the throne

9. A deluded person is the victim of   a) a false belief   b) false arrest
   c) discrimination   d) insecurity

10. An injunction is   a) a social gaffe   b) an official order   c) a verbal
    command   d) a promise

11. Coveting another person's property is usually considered   a) trespassing
    b) wrong   c) illegal   d) sensible

EXERCISE II Antonyms. Circle the letter of the word or phrase most *opposite*
in meaning to the given word.

1. ostracize: a) conform   b) be alert   c) welcome eagerly   d) formally
   reprimand

2. forbear: a) soften   b) rush to action   c) be descended from   d) recall

3. covet: a) recoil from   b) be open about   c) strip   d) share

4. supplant: a) search and destroy   b) preserve and bolster   c) divide and
   conquer   d) rip up by the roots

5. elucidate: a) endanger   b) turn off the lights   c) refine   d) muddle

6. delude: a) free from misconception   b) lead astray   c) impose by force
   d) make light

7. resurrect: a) look to the past   b) blaspheme   c) consign to the grave
   d) insist upon

8. enjoin from: a) resign   b) suffer through   c) plead for   d) reconsider

9. revile: a) dislike   b) scan quickly   c) butter up   d) tone down

10. recant: a) refuse to sing   b) recite from memory   c) be able   d) stick to

11. dispatch: a) propagate an idea   b) ignore   c) receive a message
    d) attack

EXERCISE III From the following list of verbs, pick a term to match each action described below. Write the verbs in the blanks.

elucidated   forbore
reviled   dispatched
enjoined   coveted
resurrected   recanted
ostracized   deluded
supplanted

1. In a complete turnabout, he repudiated his liberal record and pledged himself to support the ultraconservative movement. _____

2. Instead of accepting herself, she jealously craved everything her older sister enjoyed—her looks, her talents, her boyfriends. _____

3. While he was away, the man who sublet his apartment also took over his girlfriend. _____

4. Furiously angry, he verbally cut his former friend to ribbons. _____

5. In reissuing the neglected early novels, the publisher breathed new life into the author's reputation. _____

6. I resisted the impulse to help her, knowing that the only way she would learn would be by doing it herself. _____

7. For me, the review shed light on how such a badly crafted film could be so popular. _____

8. Her pride blinded her: she thought she was much more talented an artist than she really was. _____

9. A particularly bad-tempered elephant will often be shunned by the herd. _____

10. The colonel sent an urgent message by courier. _____

11. The planning board prohibited developers from converting any more factories until the economic impact could be studied. _____

LESSON 56

Eleven more adjectives:
affable—easy to get along with, friendly and pleasant. *A kind face and an affable, confident manner are more reassuring to patients than framed diplomas.*
avid—very enthusiastic, greedily eager. *An avid collector of Americana, he would go to ridiculous lengths to acquire a rare political campaign button.*

heinous—shockingly evil. *His crimes were so heinous that in prison he had to be protected from his fellow inmates.*

loquacious—talkative, tending to talk a lot, easily, and glibly. *Well informed, opinionated, and loquacious, she was ideally suited to be a college lecturer.*

puerile—childish and therefore silly, lacking depth or interest. *Critics railed against the puerile fare offered nightly by the networks.*

pugnacious—belligerent, tending to get into fights. *Donald is a pugnacious and short-tempered duck.*

querulous—full of complaints, habitually fretful. *Unlike some older people, she was never querulous; we were shocked when she was admitted to the hospital.*

sardonic—mocking, bitterly derisive, usually said of people's words or facial expressions. *The older boy affected a sardonic manner in order to appear worldly and superior.*

surreptitious—stealthy, done secretly. *A surreptitious peek into the playroom assured her that the children were playing happily.*

taciturn—inclined to be silent, tending not to talk. *Her father was so taciturn that even after a long absence he barely inquired how she was.*

trenchant—to the point, penetrating, perceptive. *The moderator's trenchant comments kept the discussion focused on the main issue.*

Answers to the following exercises are on page 210.

EXERCISE I Circle the letter of the best choice to complete each sentence.

1. A taciturn manner is ill-suited to   a) a night watchman   b) a cowboy   c) a word processor   d) a television personality

2. A pugnacious attitude seems appropriate to   a) a prizefighter   b) a driving instructor   c) a bartender   d) a nurse

3. A trenchant argument is   a) fundamentally unsound   b) prejudiced   c) long-winded   d) difficult to refute

4. An avid reader is the sort who   a) reads only what is assigned   b) reads everything, including cereal boxes at breakfast   c) prefers television to books   d) knows several languages

5. Trapped in an elevator with a loquacious stranger, you can expect to   a) be left alone   b) fear for your life   c) be regaled with elevator stories   d) be appealed to for help

6. A sardonic look is what one expects from   a) a child opening birthday presents   b) the world-weary hero of a romantic novel   c) a preacher asking for a donation   d) a woman embracing her long lost sister

7. To move surreptitiously, it helps to   a) tiptoe   b) carry your own luggage   c) wear combat boots   d) flap your arms

8. A person who is always querulous never seems   a) available   b) inconsiderate   c) satisfied   d) restless

9. An affable co-worker is likely to   a) greet you pleasantly each day   b) always be on time   c) ask a lot of personal questions   d) be unpredictable

10. Many people believe heinous actions merit   a) raises   b) the death penalty   c) emulation   d) gratitude

11. An example of a puerile attitude is a) We can compromise. b) Take my money, just don't hurt me. c) When the going gets tough, the tough get going. d) If you don't play my way, I'll take my ball and go home.

EXERCISE II Antonyms. Circle the letter of the word or phrase most *opposite* in meaning to the given word.

1. affable: a) expensive b) silent c) pugnacious d) dishonest

2. surreptitious: a) unconcealed b) unknown c) querulous d) boisterous

3. heinous: a) small-scale b) morally admirable c) physically attractive d) despicable

4. puerile: a) adulterated b) mature c) sterile d) futuristic

5. taciturn: a) written b) spoken c) bumbling d) loquacious

6. querulous: a) stoical b) impersonal c) providing answers d) painful

7. avid: a) emotional b) disheartened c) uninterested d) thoughtless

8. sardonic: a) cynical b) chattering c) inexpressive d) sweet in manner

9. trenchant: a) soaring b) sinking c) meandering d) commonplace

10. pugnacious: a) peace-loving b) enormous c) obnoxious d) volatile

EXERCISE III From the following list of adjectives, pick a term to match each action or person described below. Write the adjectives in the blanks.

affable	avid
heinous	loquacious
puerile	pugnacious
querulous	sardonic
surreptitious	taciturn
	trenchant

1. They sneaked up the drive and into the sleeping house, careful to make no sound. _____

2. A fanatic follower of the team, he attended every home game. _____

3. Her infantile mannerisms and little-girl voice became less appealing as she grew older. _____

4. He took offense easily and got involved in barroom brawls several times a year. _____

5. The words spill out of her like a flood when the dam breaks; no one else can get a sentence in. _____

6. The terse style of the essay is suited to its sharp insights. _____

7. His calm and easygoing manner made him universally liked. _____

8. She rarely spoke; she could spend hours working alongside others and never volunteer a single comment. _____

9. The viciousness of the attack turned the stomachs of even hardened police veterans. _____

10. He fretted continuously about his aches and pains, complaining that he was being neglected. _____

11. Harsh disappointments had left her with a jaundiced view of love; she mocked the very idea of romance. _____

LESSON 57

The words in this lesson and the next are nouns.

antithesis—opposite, complete contrast. *Her new neighbor was urbane and charming, the antithesis of the bumbling yokel she had expected.*

demeanor—a person's outward appearance or manner. *Scrooge's demeanor was so crotchety and forbidding that almost everyone left him alone.*

ferment—condition of unrest, upheaval, often used of positive but disorganized growth. *Artists and intellectuals congregated in the capital; the city was in a ferment of progressive enthusiasm.*

glut—oversupply. *The glut of fresh produce at this season drives prices down.*

impunity—freedom from punishment. *Since the city cannot collect fines against them, diplomats park illegally with impunity.*

interdiction—formal prohibition. *Because of the danger from terrorist kidnappers, travel to Lebanon was placed under interdiction by the state department.*

knell—ringing of a bell to mark a death or disaster; used figuratively, often in the phrase *death knell*, to mean a signal marking the passing of something. *The closing of the factory was the death knell to the community.*

penury—utter poverty. *He grew up on welfare on Chicago's South Side, but he rose from penury to become a wealthy and successful publisher.*

perdition—utter moral destruction or misery, hell. *She damned him to perdition for his callous disregard for human life.*

prerogative—right or privilege conferred by a certain position or status. *As a student, it is your prerogative to have the case reviewed by a panel of administrators, faculty, and students.*

reverie—daydream, state of dreamy thoughtfulness. *The music sent her into such a reverie that she didn't realize how much time had passed.*

squalor—state of utter disarray, filth, and neglect caused by poverty. *The appeal for aid included photos showing the pathetic squalor in which the children lived.*

Answers to the following questions are on page 210.

EXERCISE I Circle the letter of the best choice to complete each sentence.

1. The knell alerted villagers that   a) a town meeting was in session   b) the church was on fire   c) the king was dead   d) visitors had arrived

2. The science of biology was in such a ferment that it seemed   a) new breakthroughs were reported daily   b) no one was interested in going into the field   c) a repressive atmosphere was to blame   d) there was nothing new to discover

3. His driving was reckless; he endangered lives with impunity because   a) he couldn't see well   b) he was too ignorant to know any better   c) no local cop dared give him a ticket   d) he drank too much

4. Wishing to escape penury, he dreamed of   a) falling in love   b) returning home   c) hitchhiking around the world   d) winning the lottery

5. In a reverie, one's mind   a) wanders pleasantly   b) goes blank   c) experiences total recall   d) is like a steel trap

6. To learn a man's demeanor, you must   a) read his résumé   b) know him intimately for many years   c) spend five minutes in his company   d) know his family

7. One of the prerogatives of old age is   a) Alzheimer's disease   b) the sense that time passes faster   c) the fountain of youth   d) the right to bore your grandchildren with the same old stories

8. An interdiction on reporting antigovernment unrest is intended to   a) suppress the news of such unrest   b) alert foreign journalists to the extent of the problem   c) foment revolution   d) appease opposition

9. Squalor is what one expects to see in   a) a historic monument   b) a wealthy suburb   c) a shantytown   d) a major department store

10. A kind and considerate man, he lived in perdition because he   a) was rarely ill   b) was tormented by a guilty conscience   c) was always misplacing things   d) couldn't afford a better neighborhood

11. The old models are a glut on the market; you can hardly   a) give them away   b) find them anymore   c) compete with them   d) afford them

12. The antithesis of his father, the son was   a) a real chip off the old block   b) so different he thought he was adopted   c) eager to fill his father's shoes   d) the image of his old man at eighteen

EXERCISE II Synonyms. Draw a line connecting each word with the word or phrase that means most nearly the same.

1. perdition	appearance
2. antithesis	overabundance
3. glut	solemn ringing of a bell
4. squalor	hell
5. impunity	official ban
6. demeanor	exemption from punishment
7. knell	pennilessness
8. reverie	daydream

9. penury   opposite
10. ferment   filth attendant on poverty
11. prerogative   disorderly growth
12. interdiction   right due to status

EXERCISE III Fill in the blanks from the list of words below.

impunity	interdiction
squalor	demeanor
perdition	antithesis
prerogative	ferment
glut	penury
death knell	reverie

1. Although they lived in _____, the children were well cared for; their clothes were patched but always clean.

2. With the _____ of oil on the market, profits are low and there's no incentive for new exploration.

3. Though I knew he was irked by social banalities, his _____ was unfailingly polite.

4. With junked cars in the yard, the roof caving in, half-starved mongrels and flies everywhere, the scene epitomized _____.

5. It was a time of intellectual _____, when ideas seemed the most powerful weapons and we were swept up by idealist crusades.

6. The sociopath believed that he would never be caught and that he could therefore commit his crimes with _____.

7. A bout with mononucleosis sounded the _____ to his hopes of returning to college.

8. The boy was gazing out the window, oblivious to the teacher's question, lost in a _____ about his future stardom.

9. On the rebound, he looked for a woman who would be the _____ of his first wife.

10. The church placed under _____ all artificial means of birth control.

11. Her wealth and status were no comfort to her, for she lived in a _____ of self-loathing.

12. As a newly naturalized citizen, it is my _____ to vote in the general election.

LESSON 58

anomaly—something that doesn't conform to the norm, something strange, irregular, hard to classify. *The platypus is an anomaly; although it's classed as a mammal, it has a bill like a duck and lays eggs.*

antidote—a remedy that counteracts the effects of something, such as a poison. *The first-aid kit should include a dose of antidote to snake venom.*

brethren—brothers, usually used formally of the members of a sect or association. *The preacher exhorted the assembled brethren to stick to their principles.*

camaraderie—friendly group spirit, feeling of comradeship. *The volunteers relished the camaraderie that grew as they learned to appreciate each other's unique talents.*

compunction—feeling of guilt or distress over one's actions. *Believing that their victims were creatures without souls, the soldiers were able to kill without compunction.*

exponent—someone who explains or advocates. *As an exponent of a healthy lifestyle, she placed great importance on diet.*

fiasco—utter failure. *The play was a fiasco; despite all the money spent on promotion, it closed after the first night.*

languor—weariness of mind and body. *Although the fever had passed, the patient suffered from such languor that for days he was barely able to crawl out of bed.*

pauper—very poor person, especially one completely dependent on charity. *The author died penniless and unknown and was buried by the city in a pauper's grave.*

penchant—a liking or inclination. *Hitchcock had a penchant for appearing as a passerby in his own films.*

perquisite—privilege or benefit in addition to regular salary. *Traveling by company jet is a perquisite of a vice-presidency.* Perquisites are sometimes referred to as *perks*.

predator—hunter, especially an animal that kills and devours prey. *Elephants fear no predators except man.* The act of preying upon is called *predation* or *depredation*.

Answers to the following exercises are on page 210.

EXERCISE I Synonyms. Circle the letter of the word or phrase that means most nearly the same as the given word.

1. perquisite: a) liability   b) inherent right   c) coffee maker   d) benefit besides wages

2. antidote: a) counteractive agent   b) virus   c) opposition d) predecessor

186

3. exponent: a) loner   b) advocate   c) exhibitionist   d) performer

4. brethren: a) fellow members   b) forebears   c) circle of acquaintances
     d) employers

5. penchant: a) wistfulness   b) necklace   c) preference   d) retirement
     income

6. fiasco: a) mural   b) disastrous flop   c) Italian wine   d) crowning glory

7. predatory: a) instinctual   b) manipulative   c) preying on others
     d) required by law

8. anomalous: a) inconsistent with the usual pattern   b) undeserved
     c) law-abiding   d) undiscovered

9. compunction: a) timeliness   b) remorse   c) tardiness   d) pickiness

10. languor: a) hypertension   b) length of time   c) feeling of inertia
     d) excessive heat

11. camaraderie: a) sense of good-fellowship   b) solitude   c) enjoyment
     d) warlike attitude

12. pauper: a) sick person   b) destitute person   c) prostitute   d) farmer

EXERCISE II From the following list of nouns, pick a term to match each
description given below. Write the nouns in the blanks.

penchant	fiasco
pauper	camaraderie
languor	antidote
perquisite	predator
anomaly	compunction
brethren	exponent

1. Before air conditioning, nothing could be accomplished in the summer
   months; the heat was so oppressive that most people slept through the
   middle of the day.
   _____

2. His campaign for governor ended in disarray when he was indicted on
   racketeering charges.   _____

3. They credited their survival to the intense loyalty each felt for his buddies in
   the platoon.   _____

4. The members of the club addressed each other as "brother."
   _____

5. Besides his salary, he was entitled to purchase company products at a large
   discount.   _____

6. She was a street person who owned nothing but her shopping cart and the
   clothes on her back.
   _____

7. Although she felt some guilt about their fate, she called the ASPCA to
   remove the alley cats.   _____

8. She had such a fondness for gossip that she couldn't survive a day without a phone. _____

9. The economist was one of the chief proponents of supply-side theory. _____

10. The wolf returned twice more to feed on stray livestock. _____

11. Our theory could not explain the rate at which the galaxy appeared to be moving.

_____

12. One treatment for clinical depression is increased doses of sunlight.

_____

EXERCISE III Circle the letter of the best choice to complete each sentence.

1. The term *brethren* assumes that all the members of an association   a) agree on all issues   b) are male   c) are of the same religion   d) are competent in their field

2. A man with a penchant for reading is likely to   a) be ill-informed   b) have a library card   c) move his lips when he reads   d) be illiterate

3. Camaraderie is likely to develop among   a) casual acquaintances   b) competitors   c) aliens   d) cooperating fellow workers

4. In a state of languor, a person wants to   a) do nothing   b) do aerobics   c) quarrel   d) work constructively

5. The result was an anomaly. On all her other tests she did mediocre work;   a) she was absent for this one   b) on this one she excelled   c) this one showed slight improvement   d) this one was no different

6. Responsible for a fiasco, a person is likely to feel   a) exultant   b) touched   c) demoralized   d) mildly encouraged

7. An antidote acts against   a) its own best interests   b) a poison   c) invasive procedures   d) the liver

8. An exponent of yoga   a) promotes its practice   b) is uncertain of its benefits   c) practices it secretly   d) believes it to be hype

9. A person suffers compunction because of   a) poor diet   b) too little companionship   c) outlandish beliefs   d) a troubled conscience

10. Predators move in   a) herds   b) flocks   c) packs   d) baby strollers

11. The value of perquisites   a) can be measured in karats   b) is listed on the stock exchange   c) is incalculable   d) can be considered additional income

12. A pauper is without   a) remorse   b) the means to live decently   c) feelings of rage   d) intelligence

LESSON 59

Here are ten words and phrases that have been borrowed more or less unchanged from other languages:

carte blanche (French, blank card)—full authority to use one's own discretion. *The students have carte blanche in choosing their courses, as long as they accumulate enough credits for a major.*

deus ex machina (Latin, god from a machine)—in a story, a contrived ending that resolves a conflict in a sudden and unrealistic way. *The revelation that the heroine is really the millionaire's daughter is the kind of convenient deus ex machina that one never encounters in real life.* In ancient Greek and Roman drama, an actor impersonating a god would literally be lowered by a crane to resolve the outcome of a play.

double entendre (French, double meaning)—a verbal expression that can be interpreted two ways, one of which is usually risqué. *In Renaissance poetry, die is often a double entendre meaning both literally to die and to have a sexual climax.*

farrago (Latin, mixed fodder for cattle)—jumble, confused mixture. *The thesis had a few solid insights, but they were buried in a farrago of illogical arguments and groundless speculation.*

memento mori (Latin, remember that you must die)—a reminder of mortality. *Saint Jerome is usually pictured with a human skull on his desk to serve as a memento mori.*

peccadillo (Spanish, little sin)—a minor sin or offense. *Jennifer's one incident of drunkenness was a mere peccadillo compared to her brother's frequent binges.*

rapport (French, harmony)—feeling of sympathy, of being in harmony. *At first his officemate seemed cold and distant, but they developed a rapport as they discovered mutual interests.*

segue (Italian, there follows)—transition, originally from one musical passage to another. *The segue to the second movement was marred by the cellist's dropping her music. Segue* can also be used as a verb: *Her harangue gradually segued into an appeal for spare change.*

weltschmerz (German, world pain)—melancholy, depression caused by the failure of the world to live up to an ideal. *At twenty-two I fell into the kind of weltschmerz typical of sensitive young people who discover that the world isn't eager to worship their talents.*

zeitgeist (German, time spirit)—the spirit of the times, the general cultural climate of an era. *Commentators summed up the zeitgeist of the seventies in the phrase "the me generation."*

Answers to the following exercises are on page 210.

EXERCISE I Synonyms. Draw a line connecting each word with the word or phrase that means most nearly the same.

1. carte blanche   disappointed idealism
2. weltschmerz   hodgepodge
3. segue   temper of the age
4. peccadillo   smooth transition
5. zeitgeist   sympathetic identification
6. deus ex machina   death's head
7. memento mori   moral slip
8. farrago   free rein
9. double entendre   tacked-on ending
10. rapport   double meaning

EXERCISE II From memory, try to complete the following sentences with words or phrases from this lesson. The first letter of each answer is given before the blank. Write your answers in the blanks.

1. The painting was a huge, wild [f] _____ of tumbled shapes and garish splashes of color.

2. With his health deteriorating daily, he needed no external [m] _____ to remind him of death's approach.

3. His [w] _____ was obvious from his melancholy sighs and brooding silences.

4. The conclusion was a [d] _____, a happy ending inappropriate to the tragic tone of the story.

5. A difficult moment in classroom management is the [s] _____ from one kind of activity to another.

6. The [z] _____ of the Victorian nineteenth century was, at least on the surface, confident, progressive, and optimistic.

7. The parents overreacted, making a federal case out of a typical childish [p] _____.

8. A comic seductress par excellence, Mae West made every line sound like a [d] _____, and it usually was.

9. The child felt a [r] _____ with the psychologist and was soon confiding in her about his fears.

10. When he took us to dinner, my grandfather gave us [c] _____ to order whatever we wished.

EXERCISE III Circle the letter of the best choice to complete each sentence.

1. A deus ex machina is used   a) as a hoist   b) to confuse an audience   c) at the end of the story   d) as a starting point

2. A legal peccadillo would probably be   a) incarcerated   b) a misdemeanor   c) a state law   d) a felony

3. With carte blanche, one has   a) a blank slate   b) a full plate   c) authority to make decisions   d) cash

4. An agent who is in rapport with his client   a) should quit   b) is likely to lose the client   c) is guilty of malpractice   d) understands the client's needs

5. Weltschmerz is   a) a sentimental sadness   b) a type of sausage   c) an unprovoked attack   d) a foreign accent

6. *Segue* is a term borrowed from   a) law   b) the theater   c) French   d) music

7. A double entendre is   a) a facial grimace   b) an ambiguous expression   c) a high-calorie dessert   d) an architectural feature

8. A farrago resembles   a) a stew   b) whitewash   c) a tango   d) a fedora

9. The zeitgeist of an era affects   a) Germans only   b) only people with spiritual beliefs   c) everyone in a culture   d) only the educated

10. A memento mori is a   a) souvenir   b) gruesome joke   c) happy mood   d) grim reminder

LESSON 60

The words in this lesson are all borrowed from characters, places, or stories.

adonis—an extremely beautiful young man. *The casting director is looking for an adonis; acting ability is secondary.* The Adonis of Greek myth was a beautiful youth beloved by both Aphrodite, the goddess of sexual love, and Persephone, the queen of the underworld.

aegis—shield, protection or sponsorship. *Late in his career, Leonardo da Vinci traveled to Rome, where he worked under the aegis of Leo X.* The original Greek aegis was the breastplate or shield of Zeus, the king of the gods, and his warrior daughter, Athena.

braggadocio—vain, arrogant boasting. *The runner was extremely talented, but his insults and braggadocio made him unpopular with the crowd.* In the 1594 poem *The Faerie Queene,* Edmund Spenser invented the character Braggadochio as the personification of idle boasting.

cavalier—offhanded, given to dismissing things too lightly, disdainful of others' concerns. *In this state no serious candidate can afford to be cavalier about farm subsidies. Cavalier implies an aristocratic kind of disregard. In the English Civil War of the mid-seventeenth century, cavalier ("knight")* was the name given to courtiers who supported the king.

chimerical—wildly and improbably imagined, belonging to a grotesque illusion composed of incongruous parts. *The treatise, which claimed to be scientific, was filled with illustrations of chimerical creatures.* In Greek myth, the Chimera was a female monster—part lion, part goat, and part serpent.

cornucopia—abundance, inexhaustible supply of good things. *The shop was a kaleidoscope of colors and a cornucopia of delicious treats.* A cornucopia (Latin for "horn of plenty") is literally a curved horn spilling out grain and fruit. As a symbol of plenty, it is sometimes associated with Thanksgiving.

gargantuan—enormous, of colossal size. *Remains of a gargantuan ape have recently been uncovered in Vietnam.* Gargantua is the name of a good-natured giant in French folklore. He was made famous as a character of stupendous size and appetites in the sixteenth-century works of Rabelais.

manna—unexpected or miraculous nourishment, a sudden and unlooked-for gain, relief, or pleasure. *The unexpected inheritance was manna to the struggling student.* In the Bible, manna is the mysterious food that appears daily to sustain the Israelites in the wilderness.

pander—pimp, go-between, person who profits by catering to the sexual needs or weaknesses of others. *The company acts as a pander, exploiting the insecurities of the public in order to sell its product. Pander* can also be used as a verb: *The madam pandered to the bizarre tastes of her clientele.* Pandarus is the go-between of medieval romance who brings Cressida and her lover Troilus together.

saturnine—emotionally cold, somber or morose in disposition. *A quiet, methodical life without emotional entanglements appealed to the man's saturnine temper.* The influence of the planet Saturn was once supposed to make people gloomy and slow to change.

sybarite—person given over to luxury and sensual pleasures. *The founder of the Playboy empire, Hefner became America's most famous sybarite.* The inhabitants of the ancient city of Sybaris, founded by Greeks in southern Italy, were famous for their wealth and luxury.

Answers to the following exercises are on page 211.

EXERCISE I Synonyms. Draw a line connecting each word with the word or phrase that means most nearly the same.

1.	gargantuan	fantastic
2.	pander	sensualist
3.	adonis	fruitful abundance
4.	saturnine	huge
5.	braggadocio	sullen
6.	cavalier	procure sexual favors
7.	chimerical	overly casual
8.	sybarite	bragging
9.	manna	protection
10.	aegis	unexpected benefit
11.	cornucopia	gorgeous man

EXERCISE II Choose the best word to complete each sentence. Write it in the blank.

1. There was no evidence of any such conspiracy; it was merely the
_____ product of a fevered imagination.

saturnine   chimerical
cavalier   sybaritic

2. He was a(n) _____, so beautiful that he upstaged all the women he dated.

aegis	manna
cornucopia	adonis

3. Her slow, one-step-at-a-time, _____ disposition drove her hyperactive co-worker crazy.

saturnine	gargantuan
pandering	cavalier

4. Although the basketball coach was a tall man, he was dwarfed by the _____ height of his players.

chimerical	saturnine
adonis-like	gargantuan

5. The community attacked the pornographer as a(n) _____ who exploited and twisted the natural sexual curiosity of his young customers.

chimera	adonis
pander	braggadocio

6. The concert series was performed under the _____ of the state council on the arts.

aegis	pander
cornucopia	sybarite

7. A devoted _____, he built a palace designed to enhance his luxurious life-style.

cavalier	sybarite
adonis	pander

8. A _____ attitude toward safety rules eventually results in avoidable accidents.

manna-like	saturnine
cavalier	gargantuan

9. Aunt Rae's kitchen always seemed to me a _____ of cookies and pies.

cornucopia	manna
sybarite	braggadocio

10. Under all the _____, the contestant was deathly afraid of failure.

braggadocio	cornucopia
chimera	aegis

11. Praise from his grandparents was rare; it came like _____ to a starving man.

a gargantua	braggadocio
an aegis	manna

EXERCISE III Circle the letter of the best choice to complete each sentence.

1. Rory was cavalier about money; he   a) was always careful to count his change   b) never knew where it went   c) could account for every penny he spent   d) dreamed of being rich

2. The aegis of the foundation was expressed in the form of   a) an application   b) a revocation   c) an installation   d) a grant

3. Naturally saturnine, Isabel had trouble   a) controlling her temper   b) being spontaneous   c) astrologically   d) shutting up

4. A sybarite is likely to be fond of   a) pursuing arcane studies   b) running marathons   c) hot tubs and gourmet foods   d) hospital volunteer work

5. A gargantuan statue needs to be displayed   a) in a large space   b) to adults only   c) from one angle only   d) on a shelf

6. The Sphinx was a chimerical creature   a) of enormous size   b) once common in the Middle East   c) part woman and part lion   d) and therefore easily tamed

7. A cornucopia symbolizes   a) a rich harvest   b) the unpredictability of nature   c) death   d) marriage

8. An adonis may remind one of the cliché   a) too smart for his own good   b) silent as the tomb   c) strong as an ox   d) tall, dark, and handsome

9. A pander is   a) a kind of bear   b) morally reprehensible   c) a form of begging   d) very young

10. Manna comes to people   a) who don't deserve it   b) as a blow   c) who plan wisely   d) as a welcome surprise

11. Braggadocio is typical of a   a) routed team   b) sore loser   c) tactless winner   d) disgruntled crowd

Gods, Planets, and Personalties

We have in English several adjectives borrowed from names of classical gods. In Lesson 50 we saw that *martial,* "warlike," comes from Mars, the god of war. Since the planets were named for various deities, the planets themselves were thought to share in divine attributes. A person supposedly influenced astrologically by Saturn would be saturnine, and so forth. Using your dictionary, determine which heavenly bodies gave us the following adjectives. Make sure you know what each adjective means.

venereal   _____
mercurial   _____
jovial   _____
lunatic   _____

REVIEW TEST 6

Questions 1 and 2.

> *These Great Pirates . . . were the antithesis of specialists. They had high proficiency in dealing with celestial navigation, the storms, the sea, the men, the ship, economics, biology, geography, history, and science. The wider and more long distanced their anticipatory strategy, the more successful they became.*
>
> *—R. Buckminster Fuller*

1. The Great Pirates knew how to navigate   a) by approximation
   b) instinctually   c) by the stars   d) because of their formal education

2. From this description, you can assume that the Great Pirates
   were   a) desultory managers   b) avid students of practical affairs
   c) panders   d) given to weltschmerz

Questions 3 and 4.

> *Her grandfather's ability to formulate and give a voice to her own inchoate thoughts always comforted her.*
>
> *—David Freeman*

3. Her thoughts were   a) fantastic   b) misshapen   c) still vague
   d) macabre

4. Her grandfather was able to   a) elucidate her thoughts   b) abrogate her
   feelings   c) rebut her ideas   d) recant his beliefs

5.
> *She almost taunted Fleda with supineness in not getting something out of somebody—in the same breath indeed in which she drenched her with a kind of appreciation more onerous to the girl than blame.*
>
> *—Henry James*

The appreciation given the girl is   a) to the point   b) very burdensome
   c) unexpected   d) realistic

Questions 6 and 7.

> *He sat, smiling, but in an inert, heavy way, his limbs seeming, even from where she sat across the room, cold and confused.*
>
> *—Doris Lessing*

6. The man appears   a) motionless   b) like an adonis   c) robust   d) asleep

7. His attitude might be called   a) sublimated   b) raucous   c) sardonic
   d) saturnine

Questions 8 and 9.
> *He would have told his story about the day the swarm of bees flew through the window, and if he was in a good mood he would have embellished it by imitating the bees, running from one side of the room to the other, flapping his arms, and buzzing until he was breathless.*
> —*Paul Theroux*

8. The man described is definitely *not*   a) loquacious   b) taciturn   c) affable
   d) in rapport with his friends

9. To embellish a story is to   a) make it ridiculous   b) act it out   c) add
   things to it   d) leave out facts

10.
> *Who would have expected so gay a host to become the exponent of pessimism?*
> —*Will Durant*

That Voltaire, the subject of this observation, became a pessimist strikes the
author as   a) chimerical   b) a fiasco   c) an anomaly   d) heinous

11.
> *Alas! with all her reasonings, she found that to retentive feelings eight years may be little more than nothing.*
> —*Jane Austen*

The heroine's feelings   a) are auspicious   b) are a farrago   c) have become
purulent   d) have not been effaced by time

12.
> *Peacock was also a loyal friend who did not scruple to pillory his friends in his inimitable novels.*
> —*M. H. Abrams*

Peacock had   a) a trenchant style   b) no compunction about ridiculing his
friends   c) the aegis of powerful friends   d) a rudimentary mind

13.
> *An American multimillionaire . . . has everything that money can buy but little peace of mind. In his hideous Hearstlike castle in Southern California he broods on the approach of death and perdition.*
> —*Anthony Burgess*

The man described   a) lives in penury   b) is pugnacious   c) expects
damnation   d) expects resurrection

Questions 14 and 15.
> *Birds of prey hovered here and there in the shadows, or fled from their nests on the top of the rocks. There were sparrow-hawks with white breasts, and kestrels, and down the slopes scampered, with their long legs, several fine fat bustards. I leave anyone to imagine the covetousness of the Canadian at the sight of this savory game.*
> —*Jules Verne*

14. The birds mentioned are   a) pernicious   b) puerile   c) plebeian
     d) predatory

15. We can assume that the Canadian was   a) hungry   b) afraid of birds   c) a
     bustard   d) a conservationist

Questions 16 and 17.
> *He was angry with himself for being young and the prey of restless,
> foolish impulses, angry also with the change of fortune which was re-
> shaping the world about him into a vision of squalor and insincerity. Yet
> his anger lent nothing to the vision. He chronicled with patience what
> he saw, detaching himself from it and testing its mortifying flavour in
> secret.*
>
> *—James Joyce*

16. We can assume that the hero   a) records what he sees   b) is reviled by the
     world   c) is insincere   d) sees the world as a cornucopia

17. The hero's change of fortune has apparently been   a) a memento mori
     b) like manna   c) a knell to his hopes   d) a deus ex machina

18.
> *To have that sense of one's intrinsic worth which constitutes self-re-
> spect is potentially to have everything: the ability to discriminate, to love
> and to remain indifferent.*
>
> *—Joan Didion*

One's worth, according to Didion, is   a) conferred by society
     b) discriminatory   c) inseparable from the self   d) potential rather than
     actual

Answers to the above questions are on page 211.

ANSWERS

LESSON 1

I.   1. c   2. a   3. b   4. d   5. b   6. d   7. b   8. c   9. b   10. a
II. 1. c   2. a   3. c   4. d   5. a   6. c   7. b   8. d   9. b   10. a
III. 1. expose to view   2. social butterfly   3. make inevitable   4. uphold the honor of   5. in paraphrase   6. preventive   7. curved

LESSON 2

I.   1. making like something else   2. kind of comparison   3. impossible to call back   4. deliberately misleading   5. hobby   6. resemblance   7. perfect reproduction   8. summoning up   9. clamorous   10. appearance of accuracy   11. line of work
II. 1. avocation   2. verisimilitude   3. facsimile   4. irrevocable   5. assimilating   6. vocation   7. evocative   8. simile   9. equivocal   10. similitude   11. vociferous
III. 1. b   2. a   3. d   4. c   5. d   6. d   7. a   8. b   9. c

LESSON 3

I.   1. d   2. a   3. b   4. c   5. b   6. b   7. a   8. b
II. 1. b   2. d   3. c   4. a   5. b   6. c   7. c   8. a   9. d   10.b
III. 1. caustic   2. rabid   3. myopic   4. abrasive   5. insular   6. scabrous   7. profound   8. volatile

LESSON 4

I.   1. b   2. c   3. b   4. d   5. a   6. d   7. c   8. a   9. c   10. a   11. c
II. 1. maelstrom   2. apprehension   3. espousal   4. breach   5. confluence   6. urbanity   7. consonance
III. 1. b   2. d   3. a   4. c   5. a   6. a   7. c   8. b   9. d

LESSON 5

I.   1. b   2. c   3. a   4. b   5. a   6. c   7. b   8. b   9. d   10. b   11. a
II. 1. hypocrisy   2. petulance   3. acumen   4. lassitude   5. temerity

6. mettlesome 7. sobriety 8. veracity 9. fortitude 10. Diffidence
11. contrition
III. 1. acumen 2. contrition 3. diffidence 4. fortitude 5. hypocrisy
6. lassitude 7. mettle 8. petulance 9. sobriety 10. temerity
11. veracity

LESSON 6

I. 1. d 2. a 3. b 4. b 5. d 6. a 7. c 8. d 9. a 10.d
II. 1. incumbent 2. martinet 3. connoisseur 4. savant 5. curmudgeon
6. vixen 7. pedant 8. novice 9. misogynist 10. skeptic
III. 1. a 2. d 3. b 4. a 5. d 6. c 7. c 8. d 9. b 10. a

LESSON 7

I. 1. unemotional 2. besieged 3. penniless 4. joking 5. peevish
6. inactive by choice 7. very overweight 8. too demonstrative 9. lost
in thought 10. disobedient 11. overjoyed 12. like an uncle
II. 1. corpulent 2. impecunious 3. beleaguered 4. jubilant 5. facetious
6. effusive 7. pensive 8. indolent 9. avuncular 10. dispassionate
11. splenetic 12. contumacious
III. 1. a 2. b 3. a 4. c 5. d 6. c 7. d 8. b 9. b 10. a
11. c 12. a
IV. 1. a 2. c 3. d 4. d 5. c 6. b 7. a 8. c 9. c 10. b
11. d 12. c

LESSON 8

I. 1. b 2. d 3. a 4. b 5. c 6. b 7. a 8. a 9. c 10. d
11. b 12. c
II. 1. impeccable 2. obligatory 3. mellifluous 4. recumbent 5. ephemeral
6. putative 7. moribund 8. specious 9. superfluous 10. germane
11. feasible 12. inherent
III. 1. d 2. c 3. c 4. b 5. a 6. b 7. c 8. b 9. a 10. d
11. a 12. c

LESSON 9

I. 1. d 2. a 3. c 4. c 5. b 6. d 7. d 8. a 9. c 10. a
11. b 12. c
II. 1. nullified 2. obliterated 3. jettisoned 4. mitigate 5. construe
6. abated 7. procrastinate 8. debilitating 9. exacerbated 10. berated
11. impeachment 12. recapitulate
III. 1. abated 2. berated 3. construed 4. debilitating 5. exacerbated
6. impeached 7. jettisoned 8. mitigated 9. nullified 10. obliterated
11. procrastinating 12. recapitulated

LESSON 10

I. 1. imputed 2. prevaricating 3. impugning 4. rescinded 5. matriculate
    6. extricating 7. bequests 8. regaled 9. perambulating 10. enunciate
II. 1. d 2. a 3. c 4. a 5. b 6. c 7. d 8. c 9. b 10. a
III. 1. stick to the truth 2. keep as one's own 3. slur one's words
    4. promulgate 5. praise 6. bore 7. be sedentary 8. become enmeshed
IV. 1. b 2. a 3. c 4. d 5. c 6. a

REVIEW TEST 1

1. b 2. d 3. a 4. c 5. b 6. d 7. c 8. a 9. b 10. a
11. b 12. c 13. a 14. d 15. b 16. c 17. a 18. c

LESSON 11

I. 1. b 2. d 3. d 4. a 5. b 6. a 7. c 8. c 9. b 10. d
II. 1. heterogeneous 2. regenerate 3. genocide 4. genre 5. degenerated
    6. progenitor 7. generic 8. engendered
III. 1. b 2. b 3. a 4. c

LESSON 12

I. 1. malady 2. benediction 3. volition 4. benign 5. malefactor
    6. factotum 7. benevolent 8. malicious 9. benefactor 10. malaise
II. 1. b 2. d 3. c 4. a 5. b 6. a 7. c 8. d 9. c 10. a
    11. c 12. d

LESSON 13

I. 1. d 2. d 3. c 4. a 5. b 6. d 7. c 8. b 9. c 10. a
    11. a 12. d
II. 1. capricious 2. vicarious 3. ubiquitous 4. insidious 5. vacuous
    6. stringent 7. incorrigible 8. meticulous 9. conciliatory 10. fastidious
    11. turgid 12. soporific

LESSON 14

I. 1. d 2. a 3. d 4. b 5. d 6. a 7. c 8. d 9. b 10. a
    11. b 12. a
II. 1. a 2. b 3. b 4. d 5. c 6. b 7. d 8. a 9. c 10. b
    11. a 12. c
III. 1. supercilious 2. truculent 3. recalcitrant 4. imperturbable
    5. gregarious 6. obstreperous 7. credulous 8. dexterous 9. lethargic
    10. formidable 11. amenable 12. parsimonious

LESSON 15

I. 1. c 2. a 3. d 4. b 5. b 6. d 7. d 8. b 9. a 10. b
   11. a 12. c 13. b
II. 1. vapid 2. cursory 3. impromptu 4. salutary 5. complacent
   6. blatant 7. estranged 8. peremptory 9. imponderable
   10. ingenuous 11. contentious 12. efficacious 13. adamant
III. 1. b 2. a 3. d 4. d 5. c 6. b 7. c 8. a

LESSON 16

I. 1. a 2. c 3. c 4. b 5. c 6. b 7. b 8. d 9. a 10. b
   11. c
II. 1. d 2. c 3. a 4. b 5. c 6. d 7. a 8. b 9. c 10. b
   11. c
III. 1. augmented 2. quibbled with 3. denigrated 4. excoriated
   5. circumvented 6. evinced 7. militated against 8. promulgated
   9. comprised 10. expedited 11. annulled
IV. 1. c 2. c 3. b 4. a 5. d

LESSON 17

I. 1. a 2. d 3. b 4. b 5. d 6. a 7. c 8. d 9. b 10. a
   11. b 12. a
II. 1. fail to notify 2. cleanse 3. restore wealth to 4. be unable to put a
   price on 5. give honor to 6. thank 7. refuse to confer 8. obfuscate
   9. lose an asset 10. threaten 11. keep a promise 12. recall the past
III. 1. explicating 2. wheedling 3. prognosticating 4. apprising
   5. stigmatizing 6. reneging 7. upbraiding 8. desecrating 9. parlaying
   10. appraising 11. parleying 12. marauding
IV. 1. a 2. c 3. b 4. a 5. d 6. b

LESSON 18

I. 1. a 2. d 3. a 4. b 5. b 6. c 7. b 8. b 9. c 10. c
   11. d 12. a
II. 1. defiled 2. palpitating 3. capitulation 4. ululations 5. wrested
   6. flailing 7. resuscitated 8. ameliorated 9. obviate 10. inculcating
   11. Beguiled 12. enervated
III. 1. ameliorated 2. beguiled 3. capitulate 4. defiled 5. enervated
   6. flailed 7. inculcate 8. obviated 9. palpitating 10. resuscitated
   11. ululating 12. wrest

LESSON 19

I. 1. b 2. a 3. c 4. b 5. d 6. c 7. a 8. d 9. c 10. c
   11. b
II. 1. proclivity 2. chicanery 3. surveillance 4. opprobrium 5. affinity
   6. travesty 7. incidence 8. equanimity 9. rationale

          10. juxtaposition 11. liaison
III. 1. affinity 2. chicanery 3. equanimity 4. incidence 5. juxtaposition
      6. liaison 7. opprobrium 8. proclivity 9. rationale
      10. surveillance 11. travesty
IV. 1. b 2. d 3. d 4. a 5. c 6. b

LESSON 20

I.   1. a 2. c 3. c 4. d 5. d 6. b 7. b 8. a 9. a 10. d
      11. a 12. b 13. b 14. d
II.   1. unique 2. eminent 3. inferred 4. flouted 5. averse 6. adverse
      7. flaunted 8. ambivalent 9. implied 10. imminent 11. disinterested
      12. ambiguous
III. 1. a 2. d 3. c 4. c 5. b

REVIEW TEST 2

    1. c 2. d 3. b 4. c 5. a 6. c 7. b 8. c 9. d 10. a
    11. c 12. b 13. a 14. c 15. a 16. c 17. d 18. a 19. c 20. b

LESSON 21

I.   1. meddler 2. street ragamuffin 3. fool 4. exposer of graft
      5. marriage partner 6. foul brute 7. serf 8. teller of
    anecdotes 9. pursuer 10. outcast
II.   1. d 2. c 3. c 4. a 5. d 6. b 7. a 8. d 9. a 10. c
III. 1. raconteur 2. consort 3. muckraker 4. wiseacre 5. interloper
      6. pariah 7. thrall 8. nemesis 9. gamin 10. yahoo

LESSON 22

I.   1. tribunal 2. dichotomy 3. hegemony 4. chronological
      5. bibliography 6. quorum 7. referendum 8. schism 9. epitome
      10. archives 11. precedent
II.   1. c 2. a 3. d 4. a 5. a 6. b 7. c 8. c 9. d 10. a
      11. a
III. 1. precedent 2. epitome 3. archives 4. hegemony 5. referendum
      6. bibliography 7. schism 8. quorum 9. chronology 10. tribunal
      11. dichotomy

LESSON 23

I.   1. b 2. a 3. b 4. c 5. d 6. b 7. a 8. b 9. a 10. c
II.   1. vacillates 2. inundated 3. metamorphosis 4. belie 5. allusion
      6. ensconced 7. satiety 8. reminiscences 9. commiseration
III. 1. alluding 2. belied 3. commiserate 4. disparage 5. ensconced
      6. inundated 7. metamorphose 8. reminisce 9. satiate 10. vacillate

LESSON 24

I.   1. b 2. a 3. c 4. d 5. c 6. a 7. b 8. b 9. c 10. a
II. 1. traversed 2. proscribed 3. vilified 4. corroborated 5. emanated
     6. stultified 7. ascribed 8. dissembled 9. inured 10. ossified
III. 1. exalt 2. sensitize 3. be forthright 4. make brilliant 5. dispute
     6. require legally 7. soften 8. go back to a source
IV. 1. ascribed 2. corroborate 3. dissemble 4. emanate 5. inure
     6. ossify 7. proscribed 8. stultified 9. traversed 10. vilified

LESSON 25

I.   1. a 2. d 3. b 4. c 5. b 6. b 7. c 8. a 9. d 10. c
     11. b
II. 1. malleable 2. torrid 3. luminous 4. fetid 5. resonant
     6. palatable 7. impervious 8. gossamer 9. Effervescent
     10. verdant 11. dulcet
III. 1. malleable 2. luminous 3. impervious 4. verdant 5. palatable
     6. fetid 7. dulcet 8. effervescent 9. torrid 10. gossamer
     11. resonant
IV. 1. b 2. d 3. a 4. d 5. a 6. b 7. c

LESSON 26

I.   1. c 2. d 3. a 4. b 5. b 6. d 7. c 8. a 9. c 10. d
     11. c
II. 1. inveterate 2. succulent 3. Multitudinous 4. pandemic 5. sentient
     6. sonorous 7. sable 8. palpable 9. pristine 10. execrable
     11. endemic
III. 1. full of juice 2. touchable 3. full sounding 4. long prevalent in one
     place 5. conscious 6. prevalent over a large area 7. very bad 8. of
     great number 9. unspotted 10. deeply ingrained 11. black

LESSON 27

I.   1. a 2. b 3. c 4. c 5. a 6. d 7. b 8. b 9. a 10. c
     11. b 12. d
II. 1. laudable 2. reticent 3. laconic 4. laudatory 5. voluble
     6. tacit 7. obdurate 8. fallible 9. dilatory 10. culpable
     11. archaic 12. tractable
III. 1. invariably correct 2. expeditious 3. frank 4. spelled out
     5. condemning 6. voluble 7. laudable 8. contemporary 9. tractable

LESSON 28

I.   1. melancholy 2. sanguine 3. suave 4. proficient 5. insolent
     6. choleric 7. ascetic 8. gauche 9. phlegmatic 10. blasé
     11. obsequious 12. ebullient
II. 1. c 2. d 3. a 4. b 5. c 6. b 7. a 8. d 9. a

III. 1. ascetic 2. ebullient 3. proficient 4. choleric 5. suave
6. sanguine 7. melancholy 8. obsequious 9. gauche 10. phlegmatic

LESSON 29

I. 1. a 2. d 3. d 4. c 5. b 6. b 7. a 8. c 9. b 10. d
11. c 12. b
II. 1. b 2. a 3. c 4. d 5. b 6. c 7. b 8. a 9. d 10. c
III. 1. de facto 2. alter ego 3. alumnus 4. per annum 5. modus vivendi
6. sine die 7. ad hoc 8. modus operandi 9. moratorium
10. bona fide 11. de jure

LESSON 30

I. 1. d 2. b 3. a 4. c 5. b 6. a 7. c 8. b 9. d 10. a
11. c 12. d
II. 1. gratis 2. non sequitur 3. emeritus 4. sine qua non 5. errata
6. placebo 7. pro forma 8. tabula rasa 9. status quo
10. mores 11. quid pro quo
III. 1. c 2. c 3. a 4. c 5. b

REVIEW TEST 3

1. a 2. a 3. b 4. c 5. b 6. a 7. d 8. b 9. a 10. b
11. a 12. c 13. b 14. a 15. c 16. a 17. d 18. c 19. a 20. b

LESSON 31

I. 1. temple to all the gods 2. newsstand 3. burial vault 4. fortress
5. vault of heaven 6. ancient trash heap 7. unexplored land 8. area
isolated within a larger one 9. foyer 10. place for safekeeping
II. 1. d 2. a 3. b 4. c 5. a 6. b 7. d 8. c 9. b 10. a
III. 1. vestibule 2. sepulcher 3. kiosk 4. bastion 5. midden
6. pantheon 7. repository 8. enclave 9. terra incognita 10. firmament
IV. 1. b 2. c 3. c 4. a 5. c

LESSON 32

I. 1. d 2. c 3. c 4. d 5. b 6. c 7. a 8. b 9. c 10. b
11. d 12. a
II. 1. a 2. d 3. c 4. d 5. c 6. b 7. a 8. c 9. b 10. d
11. c 12. a
III. 1. philologist 2. diva 3. entrepreneur 4. choreographer
5. ombudsman 6. emissary 7. lapidary 8. steward 9. milliner
10. curator 11. thespian 12. pedagogue

LESSON 33

I.   1. c 2. d 3. b 4. a 5. a 6. d 7. c 8. b 9. a 10. d
     11. d
II. 1. paragons 2. zealots 3. ingrate 4. mendicants 5. heretic
     6. charlatan 7. nonagenarian 8. altruist 9. sycophants
     10. dilettante 11. tyro
III. 1. c 2. c 3. b 4. d 5. b 6. a 7. d 8. b 9. b 10. c
     11. a

LESSON 34

I.   1. d 2. c 3. a 4. b 5. c 6. c 7. d 8. a 9. b 10. d
     11. c 12. a 13. c
II. 1. littoral 2. palliative 3. dormant 4. vernal 5. sidereal
     6. somatic 7. deciduous 8. egregious 9. mundane 10. feral
     11. internecine 12. sedentary 13. diurnal
III. 1. d 2. a 3. c 4. b 5. c 6. d 7. a 8. b 9. d
     10. b 11. a 12. a 13. d

LESSON 35

I.   1. d 2. a 3. c 4. b 5. d 6. a 7. d 8. d 9. b 10. d
     11. a 12. c
II. 1. baleful 2. turbid 3. ostensible 4. exemplary 5. propitious
     6. redolent 7. unctuous 8. somnolent 9. limpid 10. circumspect
     11. incendiary 12. hallowed
III. 1. b 2. d 3. b 4. d 5. d 6. a 7. b 8. b 9. c

LESSON 36

I.   1. d 2. c 3. b 4. a 5. a 6. b 7. c 8. c 9. a 10. c
     11. d
II. 1. sloppy in social matters 2. health-giving 3. taciturn 4. beneficial
     5. gullible 6. invisible 7. auguring good fortune 8. petty
     9. cautious 10. like a Pollyanna 11. from a single source
III. 1. astute 2. cynical 3. detrimental 4. eclectic 5. garrulous
     6. impetuous 7. magnanimous 8. Noxious 9. punctilious
     10. sinister 11. tangible

LESSON 37

I.   1. b 2. d 3. a 4. c 5. a 6. b 7. d 8. b 9. a 10. a
     11. d
II. 1. extirpating 2. recoup 3. sloughed off 4. predisposition
     5. behooved 6. obtruding 7. deracinated 8. acquiesced in
     9. expunged 10. bifurcated 11. accrue to 12. eradicating
III. 1. c 2. a 3. b 4. d 5. b 6. c

LESSON 38

I. 1. b 2. c 3. d 4. d 5. b 6. b 7. a 8. d 9. c 10. b
11. a 12. c
II. 1. c 2. a 3. d 4. b 5. b 6. c 7. a 8. d 9. d 10. a
11. c 12. c
III. 1. speak to the point 2. conceal 3. accuse directly 4. abide by the law
5. enrage 6. expand 7. clarify
IV. 1. appended 2. curtail 3. divulge 4. envisage 5. gallivanting
6. insinuating 7. maundered 8. obfuscated 9. placated 10. requited
11. stipulated 12. transgresses

LESSON 39

I. 1. social know-how 2. government overthrow 3. as a body 4. obsessive
idea 5. mortal stroke 6. rabble 7. rationale 8. stunning success
9. pet dislike 10. untrue story 11. slight upset 12. end of a story
13. hands-off policy
II. 1. canard 2. laissez faire 3. en masse 4. bête noire 5. coup
6. coup d'état 7. canaille 8. contretemps 9. savoir-faire
10. raison d'être 11. coup de grâce 12. dénouement 13. idée fixe
III. 1. c 2. b 3. a 4. d 5. b 6. a 7. d 8. b 9. c 10. b
11. b 12. b 13. d

LESSON 40

I. 1. c 2. a 3. b 4. b 5. c 6. a 7. d 8. a 9. c 10. a
11. d 12. c
II. 1. au courant 2. faux pas 3. éclat 4. précis 5. sobriquet
6. soupçon 7. élan 8. ambiance 9. coterie 10. ingénue
11. manqué 12. rapprochement
III. 1. b 2. c 3. d 4. b 5. a 6. c 7. b 8. d 9. a 10. b
11. b 12. d

REVIEW TEST 4

1. c 2. b 3. a 4. c 5. d 6. b 7. a 8. b 9. d 10. b
11. c 12. a 13. d 14. b 15. d 16. a 17. b 18. d

LESSON 41

I. 1. c 2. a 3. c 4. b 5. d 6. b 7. c 8. a 9. c 10. a
11. b
II. 1. arbiter 2. necromancer 3. dipsomaniac 4. miscreant 5. demagogue
6. kleptomaniac 7. virtuoso 8. egotist 9. neophyte 10. philistine
11. epicure
III. 1. c 2. b 3. d 4. b 5. a

LESSON 42

I. 1. d 2. c 3. d 4. a 5. b 6. a 7. c 8. a 9. b 10. d
11. a
II. 1. chagrin 2. histrionics 3. vertigo 4. sagacity 5. ennui
6. audacity 7. rancor 8. foible 9. mendacity 10. derision
11. levity
III. 1. good will 2. timidity 3. triumph 4. foolishness 5. understated
manner 6. truthfulness 7. normal sense of balance 8. seriousness
9. enthusiasm
IV. 1. foible 2. sagacity 3. vertigo 4. ennui 5. Mendacity 6. rancor
7. Histrionics 8. derision 9. chagrin 10. levity 11. audacity

LESSON 43

I. 1. d 2. a 3. b 4. c 5. c 6. d 7. a 8. b 9. c 10. b
II. 1. empathy 2. pathology 3. austerity 4. brevity 5. dilemma
6. euphoria 7. longevity 8. euphemism 9. oblivion
10. enigma 11. idiosyncrasy
III. 1. shortness 2. typical of a disease 3. emotional identification
4. quirk 5. unpleasant choice 6. substitute word 7. strictness
8. forgetfulness 9. length of life 10. emotional high 11. puzzle
IV. 1. a 2. d 3. b 4. d 5. b 6. d 7. a 8. c 9. a

LESSON 44

I. 1. b 2. a 3. d 4. c 5. c 6. b 7. a 8. c 9. c 10. d
11. b 12. d
II. 1. sequestered 2. deviate 3. discern 4. vitiated 5. conjecture
6. simulate 7. cumbersome 8. festered 9. abominate
10. mollify 11. temporizes 12. decimated
III. 1. b 2. a 3. c 4. d 5. a 6. b 7. b 8. d 9. b 10. d
11. b 12.c

LESSON 45

I. 1. c 2. b 3. b 4. a 5. c 6. d 7. d 8. a 9. c 10. a
II. 1. importuning 2. perusal 3. censured 4. incites 5. relegated
6. designated 7. interpolations 8. exhorts 9. intercede with
10. abdicated 11. gesticulated
III. 1. edit out 2. commend 3. skim rapidly 4. take on responsibility
5. promote 6. refuse to speak up for 7. dissuade
IV. 1. b 2. c 3. a 4. d 5. b

LESSON 46

I. 1. deleterious 2. nascent 3. adept 4. salient 5. ersatz

6. nebulous   7. clandestine   8. spurious   9. banal   10. esoteric
II. 1. a   2. b   3. c   4. d   5. b   6. b   7. d   8. d   9. a   10. c
     11. a   12. b
III. 1. nascent   2. adept   3. ludicrous   4. arcane   5. salient   6. nebulous

LESSON 47

I. 1. subliminal   2. contingent   3. viable   4. mordant   5. portentous
    6. untenable   7. asinine   8. frenetic   9. resilient   10. indigenous
II. 1. intelligent   2. without bite   3. doomed   4. calm   5. auspicious
    6. unconditional   7. obvious to the senses   8. not springy   9. indefensible
    10. imported
III. 1. c   2. a   3. c   4. b   5. b   6. c   7. d   8. c   9. b   10. a

LESSON 48

I. 1. abnormal sense of power   2. fear of open space   3. abnormal fear of
    illness   4. standard for judgment   5. observable occurrence   6. fear of
    strangers   7. movement of bodies at a distance   8. summary
    9. overabundance   10. unreasoning fear
II. 1. plethora   2. telekinesis   3. hypochondriac   4. phobias   5. xenophobic
    6. phenomenon   7. agoraphobia   8. megalomania   9. synopsis
    10. criteria
III. 1. d   2. d   3. b   4. b   5. a   6. a   7. d   8. c   9. b   10. c

LESSON 49

I. 1. bones and joints   2. classification   3. memory   4. scientific terms
    5. eye   6. ancient writing   7. old age   8. theory of law   9. beautiful
    handwriting   10. fossils   11. causes   12. folk culture
II. 1. gerontologist   2. orthopedics   3. ethnologists   4. paleography
    5. jurisprudence   6. ophthalmologist   7. taxonomy   8. nomenclature
    9. Calligraphy   10. paleontology   11. etiology   12. mnemonics
III. 1. b   2. d   3. a   4. c   5. a   6. b

LESSON 50

I. 1. self-regarding   2. ruggedly disciplined   3. appropriate to war
    4. cleaned up   5. very loud   6. shape-changing   7. extravagantly
    idealistic   8. overly nationalistic   9. inhumanly harsh   10. hypnotized
II. 1. martial   2. protean   3. bowdlerized   4. draconian   5. spartan
    6. chauvinistic   7. quixotic   8. stentorian   9. mesmerized   10. narcissistic
III. 1. b   2. c   3. d   4. d   5. c   6. a   7. b   8. c   9. c   10. a

REVIEW TEST 5

1. d 2. a 3. b 4. b 5. d 6. c 7. a 8. c 9. b 10. c
11. d 12. b 13. b 14. c 15. b 16. d 17. c 18. d 19. b 20. c

LESSON 51

I. 1. purposeful 2. added later 3. clumsy 4. fully formed 5. carelessly sloppy 6. nonadhesive 7. interactive 8. cheerfully lively
9. restrained 10. forgetful 11. aristocratic 12. suspicious

II. 1. retentive 2. assiduous 3. inert 4. desultory 5. glutinous
6. macabre 7. intrinsic 8. gullible 9. fulsome 10. inchoate
11. adroit 12. plebeian

III. 1. b 2. d 3. c 4. d 5. d 6. a 7. b 8. a 9. c 10. d 11. a
12. b

LESSON 52

I. 1. optimal 2. onerous 3. supine 4. pernicious 5. potable
6. raucous 7. purulent 8. rudimentary 9. celestial 10. auspicious
11. anticipatory 12. robust

II. 1. c 2. d 3. c 4. a 5. b 6. b 7. c 8. a 9. c 10. d 11. c
12. a

III. 1. d 2. a 3. c 4. a 5. b 6. b 7. c 8. d 9. b 10. a 11. a
12. b

LESSON 53

I. 1. fomented 2. chronicled 3. hobnobbed 4. pilloried 5. scrupled
6. fathomed 7. embellished 8. cosseted 9. assuaged 10. inveighed

II. 1. c 2. a 3. b 4. a 5. b 6. d 7. c 8. b 9. a 10. d

III. 1. b 2. d 3. c 4. c 5. b 6. a 7. b 8. a 9. c 10. d

LESSON 54

I. 1. enumerate 2. sublimated 3. abrogate 4. retrogressed 5. delegate
6. deplete 7. mortified 8. effaced 9. rebutting 10. disclaimed
11. preempted

II. 1. embarrass utterly 2. use evidence to contradict 3. take the place of
4. disavow 5. exhaust a resource 6. assign to a subordinate 7. count
in a list 8. obliterate 9. officially make no longer in effect
10. backslide 11. divert energy to an acceptable outlet

III. 1. b 2. d 3. a 4. c 5. d 6. a 7. d 8. a 9. b 10. c 11. a

LESSON 55

I. 1. c 2. d 3. c 4. c 5. b 6. a 7. d 8. c 9. a 10. b 11. b
II. 1. c 2. b 3. a 4. b 5. d 6. a 7. c 8. c 9. c 10. d 11. c
III. 1. recanted 2. coveted 3. supplanted 4. reviled 5. resurrected
6. forbore 7. elucidated 8. deluded 9. ostracized 10. dispatched
11. enjoined

LESSON 56

I. 1. d 2. a 3. d 4. b 5. c 6. b 7. a 8. c 9. a 10. b 11. d
II. 1. c 2. a 3. b 4. b 5. d 6. a 7. c 8. d 9. c 10. a
III. 1. surreptitious 2. avid 3. puerile 4. pugnacious 5. loquacious
6. trenchant 7. affable 8. taciturn 9. heinous 10. querulous
11. sardonic

LESSON 57

I. 1. c 2. a 3. c 4. d 5. a 6. c 7. d 8. a 9. c 10. b 11. a
12. b
II. 1. hell 2. opposite 3. overabundance 4. filth attendant on poverty
5. exemption from punishment 6. appearance 7. solemn ringing of a
bell 8. daydream 9. pennilessness 10. disorderly growth 11. right
due to status 12. official ban
III. 1. penury 2. glut 3. demeanor 4. squalor 5. ferment 6. impunity
7. death knell 8. reverie 9. antithesis 10. interdiction 11. perdition
12. prerogative

LESSON 58

I. 1. d 2. a 3. b 4. a 5. c 6. b 7. c 8. a 9. b 10. c 11. a
12. b
II. 1. languor 2. fiasco 3. camaraderie 4. brethren 5. perquisite
6. pauper 7. compunction 8. penchant 9. exponent 10. predator
11. anomaly 12. antidote
III. 1. b 2. b 3. d 4. a 5. b 6. c 7. b 8. a 9. d 10. c 11. d
12. b

LESSON 59

I. 1. free rein 2. disappointed idealism 3. smooth transition 4. moral
slip 5. temper of the age 6. tacked-on ending 7. death's head
8. hodgepodge 9. double meaning 10. sympathetic identification
II. 1. farrago 2. memento mori 3. weltschmerz 4. deus ex machina
5. segue 6. zeitgeist 7. peccadillo 8. double entendre 9. rapport
10. carte blanche
III. 1. c 2. b 3. c 4. d 5. a 6. d 7. b 8. a 9. c 10. d

LESSON 60

I.   1. huge   2. procure sexual favors   3. gorgeous man   4. sullen
5. bragging   6. overly casual   7. fantastic   8. sensualist   9. unexpected
benefit   10. protection   11. fruitful abundance
II. 1. chimerical   2. adonis   3. saturnine   4. gargantuan   5. pander
6. aegis   7. sybarite   8. cavalier   9. cornucopia   10. braggadocio
11. manna
III. 1. b   2. d   3. b   4. c   5. a   6. c   7. a   8. d   9. b   10. d   11. c

REVIEW TEST 6

1. c   2. b   3. c   4. a   5. b   6. a   7. d   8. b   9. c   10. c   11. d
12. b   13. c   14. d   15. a   16. a   17. c   18. c

BASIC VOCABULARY FOR THE HUMANITIES

The glossaries that follow define 330 more words and phrases—all terms that you are likely to encounter in college humanities courses. The first glossary gives some basic vocabulary for the social sciences. These are terms frequently used in anthropology, sociology, psychology, economics, politics, and history courses. The second glossary comprises vocabulary for the arts—music, dance, drama, fine arts, and cinema. Finally, the last glossary defines basic terms in language and literature—the basic vocabulary you will need to know for English, comparative literature, foreign language, and linguistics courses.

You will find that some of the words below seem more technical or specialized than others. Many of them you probably already know, at least vaguely. Familiar or not, all are typical of what you can expect to find in introductory courses at the college level. Where applicable, literal translations of borrowed terms are given in parentheses.

110 USEFUL TERMS FOR THE SOCIAL SCIENCES

aberrant—differing from what is typical or normal. Something that differs from a norm is an *aberration*.

affect—in psychology, a feeling or emotion. The adjective form is *affective*.

affidavit—a sworn statement in writing, usually witnessed by a notary public. *Affidavit* is Latin for "he has sworn."

affiliation—in social psychology, the tendency of people to associate with each other or band together.

agenda—a list of things to be done, for instance at a meeting.

agrarian—having to do with the farming and ownership of land, agricultural.

allocate—to distribute according to a plan, to set aside for a purpose, as in: *The new* *serum was allocated among the states in proportion to their population. The budget allocates funds for research.*

amnesty—legal pardon (usually for a large group), official promise not to prosecute offenses against the government.

antebellum—literally, before the war. In American history, of the period before the Civil War, especially in the South.

apartheid—(separation) the official South African policy of strictly segregating and discriminating against nonwhites.

appreciation—an increase in value.

arraign—to bring before a court of law, formally accuse.

artifact—man-made object, any material object created, modified, or used by humans.

attribution—the process of inferring the motives and feelings of others on the basis of their behavior.

authoritarianism—an attitude or practice marked by strong leadership, unquestioning obedience, and the suppression of opposition and individual freedom.

autocracy—a government of absolute rule by one person, a dictatorship. *Autocratic* is used more loosely to mean "dictatorial, making decisions or giving orders without consulting others."

autonomy—self-rule, self-government.

beneficiary—one who benefits, especially one who receives a payment or inheritance.

bourgeoisie—the middle class, between the working class (proletariat) and the aristocracy. In Marxism, the bourgeoisie is the class of capitalists. The adjective is *bourgeois.*

bullion—gold and silver as raw materials and the basis of a monetary system.

cadre—a framework, a skeleton organization, the core group of an organization, often used in a military context.

caste—a rigid system in which a person's social position is strictly defined and hereditary and in which upward mobility is impossible. India traditionally has an elaborate caste system.

charisma—the personal magnetism of a leader that inspires complete devotion in followers. *Charisma*, originally meaning "divine gift," was first used of religious leaders; now political leaders as well can be *charismatic.*

coalition—a temporary union of groups for a specific purpose.

cognition—the process of perceiving or knowing. The adjective is *cognitive.*

collusion—conspiracy, a secret agreement to commit an illegal or fraudulent act.

commodity—an item of commerce, anything that is bought or sold.

consanguinity—blood kinship, relationship through a common ancestor.

consensus—agreement of opinion.

constituency—body of voters, the voters or residents who make up a unit for political representation.

deindividuation—loss of the sense of personal responsibility. The experience of deindividuation leads people to do things in groups that they wouldn't do alone.

demography—the statistical study of populations and their characteristics. Demography, a specialization within sociology, aims to chart social trends through vital statistics.

deposition—the written testimony of a witness taken under oath for use in a court proceeding.

depreciation—a loss in value or drop in price, often because of age or wear.

deviance—failure to conform, state of being significantly different from others.

divest—to strip, deprive, for instance of authority, rank, or privileges. The noun for a divesting is *divestiture*.

dogma—the defining tenets or doctrines that make up a belief, such as a religion or ideology.

dossier—an official file on a subject or person.

egalitarian—of the belief that humans are all equal in their social and political rights, equalitarian.

electorate—the body of persons entitled to vote in an election.

embargo—a governmental restriction or prohibition of trade, especially with a foreign nation.

enculturation—the learning process by which the infant human animal becomes a competent member of his culture.

endogamy—in anthropology, a rule of some cultures requiring that a person marry within a given group, for instance a social class or kinship group.

ethnocentrism—the belief that one's own culture is the measure by which other cultures are to be judged, the judging of other societies by the particular values of one's own.

ethnography—the branch of cultural anthropology that records the customs and way of life of particular groups.

exogamy—in anthropology, a rule of some cultures requiring that a person marry outside of his group.

expenditure—a spending or using, as of time or money.

forum—place for public business or discussion.

gerrymander—to redistrict a voting area so as to create a political advantage for one party over another. *Gerrymander* was coined from Elbridge *Gerry* (a governor of Massachusetts) and *salamander* (after the shape of one of his districts).

gestalt—everything that makes up a person's perceptual field, the entire context of experience in which a person judges and acts.

gross—a total income or profit before expenses.

heterodox—not orthodox, not conforming, especially in religious belief.

hierarchy—an arrangement of a group by degrees of authority and power.

holocaust—great or complete destruction of a population, a devastation, especially by fire. Capitalized, *Holocaust* now usually refers to the extermination of Europen Jews by the Nazis during World War II.

ideologue—one who believes in and propagates a social doctrine or system of economic and political beliefs, such as socialism or laissez-faire capitalism. Such a doctrine or set of beliefs is an *ideology*.

imperialism—in international affairs, the act of creating and maintaining an empire, for instance by colonizing other nations and controlling raw materials and markets.

incentive—something that encourages or motivates action, as for instance the expectation of payment is an incentive to work.

inquest—judicial investigation to determine facts and discover if there are grounds for prosecution.

jingoism—the advocating of a warlike foreign policy, chauvinism. Jingoism connotes a kind of extreme and trigger-happy patriotism.

liability—a debt, something disadvantageous.

libido—in psychology, human sexual or creative energy, psychic energy in general.

mandate—a specific order, authoritative command, especially the supposed wishes of a constituency regarded as an order to their representatives to implement some program.

matrilineal descent—in anthropology, the cultural practice of tracing descent through females only.

megalopolis—urban sprawl, an area such as the northeastern United States where increases in population have created a continuous urban expanse out of what were formerly distinct cities.

meritocracy—an ideal of social organization in which a person's class or status is determined solely by merit, an extreme open-class system.

militant—defiant, ready to fight for a cause.

mobility—freedom or ease of movement. *Upward mobility* is the movement from a lower social class to a higher one.

moiety—(half) in anthropology, a major subdivision of a population according to kinship. In some cultures, the total society is thought of as being made up of two groups, each of which is a *moiety*.

monetary—of money, particularly, concerning the actual currency of a nation.

monotheism—belief in one God.

municipal—having to do with the local government or administration of a town or city.

neolithic—of the New Stone Age, the period in prehistory following the paleolithic period, in which humans used polished stone tools and domesticated animals.

nepotism—the giving of jobs to relatives, favoritism to one's family in making appointments.

net—profit or income left after expenses are deducted.

occidental—western, pertaining to the western hemisphere or the culture of Europe or the Americas. *Occidental* is the opposite of *oriental*.

oligarchy—political rule by a small group.

ordinance—a city statute.

paleolithic—of the Old Stone Age, the prehistoric period before the neolithic period but after the eolithic one.

partisan—devoted or committed to a party or cause, especially blindly or unreasonably so.

patrilineal descent—in anthropology, the cultural practice of tracing descent through males only.

pecuniary—financial, concerning money, especially personal finances.

per capita—(by head) by the number of people. For example, the per capita income of a given country is the average income for every man, woman, and child.

plebiscite—the deciding of a political question by a direct ballot of all eligible voters.

pluralism—the public policy of tolerating or fostering cultural differences within a society instead of forcing conformity to a single cultural norm. In America, for instance, the printing of official notices in languages other than English is an example of pluralism.

pogrom—(in Russian, devastation) an organized massacre or persecution of a minority group, used originally to refer to the massacres of Jews in Czarist Russia.

polity—the political or governmental organization of a state.

proletariat—the industrial working class, considered as the labor force that produces wealth.

proponent—an advocate, person who propounds (sets forth) an idea or belief.

protocol—a rigid code of correct procedure, especially in diplomacy.

putsch—(in German, a push) a revolt, minor rebellion, especially an unsuccessful one.

ratify—to give formal approval to something, for instance a constitutional amendment.

recidivism—tendency to repeat antisocial behavior, especially the chronic relapse into criminal activity.

reciprocal—working both ways, giving and receiving, mutual. In social psychology, reciprocity is our tendency to like people who, we think, like us.

remuneration—reward, payment, as for work done.

restitution—payment for loss or damage inflicted, a making good.

revenue—income, particularly the income a government receives from taxes.

scapegoat—a person or group singled out to take the blame for others or for some misfortune.

sect—a group of people who share a belief, especially a small group within a religion or one that has broken with an established church, a denomination.

secular—not religious, worldly.

sedition—the act, regarded as a crime, of inciting people to rebel against a government.

shibboleth—password, identifying phrase of a group or movement. For instance, ''power to the people'' was a popular shibboleth of the 1960s.

specie—coin, as opposed to paper money.

subpoena—a legal writ summoning a person to appear in court.

subsidy—financial aid granted by the government.

taboo—something forbidden by cultural rules. Breaking a taboo is often thought to produce punishment automatically.

territoriality—the theory that some animals regard certain places or territories as their own and defend them against intruders. Most psychologists do not believe that humans are territorial by instinct.

theocracy—(god-rule) unity of church and state, government by religious leaders.

topography—the physical features of the earth's surface—hills, lakes, cities, and so on—in any given region.

totem—an animal or other natural object considered the symbol and blood relation of a family or clan.

utopian—(from *Utopia*, ''no place'') of an ideal society. A *utopian community* is a visionary group dedicated to creating an ideal or perfect society.

vendetta—a blood feud in which one family seeks revenge against another for the murder of one of its members.

vigilante—person who takes the law into his own hands, one who acts extralegally to enforce his own notions of justice.

110 USEFUL TERMS FOR THE ARTS

a cappella—(chapel-style) without accompaniment, said of choral music performed without instrumental accompaniment.

acoustics—the science of sound, especially musical sounds; the way sound is affected by a particular hall, theater, or other physical environment.

adagio—(in Italian, at ease) in music, a slow tempo.

aesthetics—the study of beauty, philosophical theories concerning beauty and the nature of the arts. Also spelled *esthetics*.

afterimage—the visual image that lingers briefly in perception after the stimulus (the object perceived) has been removed. Also called *persistence of vision*, the phenomenon of the afterimage makes possible the illusion of moving pictures.

air—in music, a song or tune.

allegro—(in Italian, happy) in music, a fast tempo.

alto—a low-pitched female voice, the part below mezzo-soprano in choral music. Also *contralto*.

andante—(in Italian, walking) a moderately slow musical tempo, faster than adagio but slower than allegro.

animation—in cinema, the creation of cartoons by photographing a series of drawings so that the drawn figures or objects appear to move.

aria—(in Italian, air) a song, especially in an opera, for a solo voice with instrumental accompaniment.

arpeggio—(in Italian, harplike) in music, the playing of the notes of a chord in succession instead of together.

atelier—(in French, studio) the studio or workshop of an artist.

atonal—without a tonal center or definite key, said of some twentieth-century music in which all twelve tones of the chromatic scale are given equal weight.

auteur—(in French, author) the director of a film as the "author," a director who puts his or her personal stamp on a film despite the fact that a film is a cooperative production.

avant-garde—innovative, in the forefront of the arts, vanguard.

baritone—a male voice pitched lower than tenor but higher than bass.

basilica—in architecture, an ancient structure consisting of a long hall flanked by colonnades and used as a public building or church.

bass—a low-pitched male voice, normally the lowest voice part in choral music.

bebop—a style of jazz popular after World War II and characterized by elaborate and dissonant solo improvisations. Also *bop*.

bel canto—(in Italian, beautiful song) a virtuoso style of singing cultivated especially in the eighteenth century for Italian opera.

cadence—a progression of chords that produces a sense of temporary or final ending.

cantata—a musical composition for voices and instruments in several movements or sections. Bach's cantatas using religious texts are probably the most well known.

caricature—a distorted or exaggerated sketch, usually meant to satirize or ridicule.

carol—a traditional English song, and probably dance, using a refrain. Today we associate carols with Christmas but they were originally composed for joyful occasions throughout the year.

caryatid—a pillar carved in the shape of a female figure, found in some ancient Greek architecture.

celluloid—a trade name for the substance of which photographic film is made.

chamber music—instrumental music for a small ensemble with one instrument for each part.

chiaroscuro—(in Italian, light-dark) a style of painting developed in the Italian Renaissance in which the contours of figures seem to merge with the shadows of the background.

choral—of a chorus or choir, sung in more than one part.

cinematography—the art of shooting film.

cinéma vérité—(in French, film truth) a school of filmmaking that aims to document actual situations and events as they occur, rather than working from a script with professional actors.

clef—(key) the symbol at the beginning of a staff of written music that indicates what pitches the lines and spaces of the staff represent.

collage—(in French, paste-up) a picture created by assembling and arranging objects, for instance scraps of material and paper pasted together on a canvas and then painted.

conservatory—a school or studio for the teaching of the arts, especially music.

crescendo—in music, a gradual getting louder.

decrescendo—in music, a gradual getting softer.

diatonic—in a major or minor scale rather than a chromatic one, using only the eight tones of a normal major or minor scale.

diminuendo—in music, a getting softer or diminishing, a decrescendo.

dramaturgy—the art of writing and producing plays.

dynamics—in music, relative loudness and softness.

emulsion—the chemical solution that fixes an image on film.

engraving—the process of printing designs from carved or etched plates, generally of metal or wood.

ensemble—a group of musicians who perform together; also, the degree of success with which the performers blend and balance their sound.

equestrian statue—a statue of a figure on horseback.

etch—to draw a design in acid on a metal plate in order to produce engravings.

étude—(in French, a study) a musical composition designed as an exercise for students.

facade—the front of a building.

falsetto—the soft, nasal voice that a male singer can produce above his normal range.

fanfare—a musical flourish of trumpets.

forte—(in Italian, loud) in music, loud.

fresco—a painting in watercolors executed on wet plaster.

fugue—a musical composition in several parts in which the theme, or tune, is repeated throughout by various voices in succession.

gouache—a kind of paint made of opaque colors prepared with water and gum.

green room—in a theater, a room where the actors wait when they are offstage.

harpsichord—the most popular keyboard instrument of the Baroque period. The harpsichord resembles the piano except that when keys are pressed its strings are plucked rather than struck to produce sounds.

homophonic—a term to describe music characterized by a single melodic line supported by subordinate sounds, such as chords.

icon—an image or picture, especially a sacred image, as of a saint.

iconography—the study of images, particularly the interpretation of symbolic images in painting.

improvisation—the spontaneous invention of music as one plays, rather than the re-creation of music already written. Today improvisation is practiced most often in jazz.

intonation—in music, accuracy of pitch, being in tune.

kitsch—(in German, trash) a term to describe a work which is presented as fine art but which is in fact vulgar, pretentious, and tasteless.

kore—(in Greek, maiden) a primitive Greek sculpture of a young woman. The male equivalent is called a *kouros* (youth).

largo—(in Italian, broad) in music, a very slow tempo.

leitmotiv—in opera, a short musical theme associated with a particular character, place, or idea. A leitmotiv will recur in various forms at appropriate moments.

lithograph—a method of printing by drawing a design in grease on a stone or metal plate.

madrigal—a type of Renaissance vocal music in several parts. The texts of madrigals usually concern love.

maestro—(in Italian, master) a term of respect for a distinguished and accomplished artist.

masque—a Renaissance theatrical work combining music, poetry, and lavish spectacle.

metronome—a mechanical device to indicate the speeds at which musical compositions are to be performed.

mezzo-soprano—in choral music, a female voice pitched between soprano and alto.

mime—in theater, to act out or mimic something, especially to act out a part by movement alone, without words.

mise en scène—(in French, staging) the set or backgrounds used in the production of a play or film.

modulate—to adapt or vary in pitch, intensity, volume, or musical key.

monody—music performed by one singer rather than a chorus.

monotone—single pitch, a maintaining of one pitch.

montage—in art, a picture made up of pictures or materials assembled from several sources; in cinema, the cutting from image to image within a scene.

musicology—the study of music and music history.

nocturne—a painting or musical composition that depicts a night scene or suggests a dreamy, nighttime mood.

operetta—(in Italian, little opera) a light theatrical piece with music, including singing and dancing, and spoken dialogue. Operettas are usually musically simpler than operas.

optics—the science of vision and the physical properties of light. The adjective is *optical*.

opus—(in Latin, work) any musical composition.

orchestration—the instrumentation or arrangement of a piece of music for performance by an orchestra.

overture—an instrumental introduction to some sort of stage production, such as an opera.

panorama—a picture that presents a 360° view, a view in all directions around the spectator.

pantomime—a theatrical piece without words, expressed entirely in gestures and movements.

pas—(in French, a step) a dance step or progression of steps.

patron—a financial supporter of the arts and artists.

peripheral vision—perception of objects at the edges of one's field of vision.

perspective—the art of representing three-dimensional space on a two-dimensional surface.

polyphonic—a term to describe music characterized by independent melodic lines occurring simultaneously.

prelude—a musical introduction.

proscenium—the front part of a stage; the arch, curtain, and part of the stage visible to the audience when the curtain is closed.

protégé—person supported, protected, or helped by a patron or other person of power or authority.

relief—a sculpture in which figures are not freestanding but project from a flat surface. The greater the projection, the higher the relief.

representational—in art, representing or depicting the appearance of something, making a likeness or image of something, as opposed to *abstract* or *nonrepresentational*.

revue—a theatrical show consisting of a series of musical numbers and skits, often comic or satirical.

scat—a lively type of jazz singing that uses nonsense syllables.

scenario—the outline or plot of a play or film, including the order of scenes and the appearances of the characters.

skit—a brief and comic theatrical piece, a theatrical sketch.

sonata—a musical composition for instruments, usually in four movements. The sonata has been a major form from the mid-eighteenth century to the present.

soprano—a high-pitched female voice, the highest part in choral music.

spectrum—the range of visible light considered in order of wavelength from the shortest (violet) to the longest (red).

stele—a stone pillar, usually engraved with writing or a design and used as a marker or monument.

tableau—a picture, often a scene represented by living, silently posed figures.

tempera—a type of paint made by mixing egg yolk with colors.

tempo—(in Italian, time) the speed at which a musical piece is performed. The plural is *tempi.*

tenor—a high-pitched male voice, the part between alto and baritone in vocal music.

vaudeville—a variety show, a theatrical entertainment of specialty acts of a type popular in the early twentieth century.

ziggurat—a type of Sumerian pyramid, a man-made mountain predating the pyramids of Egypt.

110 USEFUL TERMS FOR LANGUAGE AND LITERATURE

abridge—to shorten a text by taking out material and condensing.

acronym—a word formed from the initial letters of other words, for example NASA (*N*ational *A*eronautics and *S*pace *A*dministration).

affix—a verbal element added to a word to change its meaning. Prefixes and suffixes are types of affix.

allegory—in fiction, the representation of abstract ideas or qualities as actions and characters. Allegorical characters frequently have names like Mr. Worldly, Wiseman or Hopeful; such fictions often teach a moral.

alliteration—the repetition of an initial sound, as in "nattering nabobs of negativism."

annotate—to provide explanatory notes to a text.

anonymous—bearing no name, unsigned, with author unknown.

anthology—a published collection of works or parts of works by an author or several authors.

archetype—an original model on which copies are made, the essential and universal pattern for a whole category of similar events, characters, or situations.

bard—a poet, from the class of ancient Celtic poets who sang accompanied by the harp. Shakespeare is sometimes referred to as *the Bard*.

belles-lettres—(in French, beautiful letters) literature as a fine art.

blank verse—unrhymed iambic pentameter verse, the meter of Shakespeare's plays and Milton's *Paradise Lost*.

burlesque—a mocking or broadly comic imitation of something serious, a parody.

cant—jargon, secret slang, empty talk.

canto—a large subdivision of some long poems, equivalent to a chapter in a novel.

catharsis—(in Greek, a purging) in Aristotle's literary theory, the emotional purging or release that is the function of tragedy to produce.

cliché—an overworked, predictable, and therefore uninteresting expression or idea.

cognate—(born together) coming from the same source, related through a common origin, said of words and languages.

colloquial—of speech and informal writing, conversational.

connotation—any meaning, idea, or association suggested by a word beyond its strict or explicit definition.

couplet—a self-contained verse unit of two lines, rhymed or unrhymed.

decadence—a period of decay, a falling off from an earlier achievement, energy, or mastery.

decorum—in literature, fitness or propriety, for instance the appropriateness of the style of a piece of writing to its subject.

denotation—the strict, explicit meaning of a word, a dictionary definition.

diacritical marks—marks printed above or below letters to indicate pronunciation, for instance the accent marks used in French and Spanish.

dialect—a major subdivision of a language. Speakers of different dialects of the same language can usually understand each other to some extent.

dialogue—in dramatic literature, speeches of conversation for two or more characters.

didactic—intended to instruct, said of some literary works.

dirge—a lament for the dead, a funeral hymn.

discourse—in general, all communication in language.

doggerel—trivial, inept, singsong verse.

elegy—usually, a lyric poem on death or some other somber or tragic subject.

ellipsis—the leaving out of a word or passage in a text. In writing, an ellipsis is indicated by spaced periods: "Now we are engaged in a great civil war, testing whether that nation . . . can long endure."

elocution—the style or art of speaking, especially in public.

emendation—a change or correction in a text.

encomium—a formal praising, a panegyric.

epic—a long narrative poem recounting the exploits of larger-than-life characters in important and heroic actions.

epigram—an extremely short, pithy poem, usually satirical or ironic in tone.

epigraph—a quotation used as a motto to introduce a book or chapter of a book.

epilogue—something that follows the main body of a text as a summing up or further comment. In drama, epilogues are traditionally addressed to the audience by one of the characters and sometimes invite the audience to applaud.

epistle—a letter, particularly a long or formal one.

epitaph—the inscription on a tomb or gravestone.

epithet—a descriptive name given to a person, for instance Charles *the Simple* or William *the Conqueror*.

eulogy—a spoken or written praise, particularly the praise of a person who has died.

exegesis—an interpretation or explanation of the meaning of a text, especially a passage from the Bible.

farce—an absurd or ridiculous comedy, a play of silly complications and broad humor.

homily—a discourse on a moral problem, a sermon.

homonyms—words pronounced the same but meaning different things and often spelled differently, for example *seen* and *scene*.

hyperbole—obvious exaggeration as a figure of speech. "He was as big as a house" is an example of hyperbole.

iamb—in poetry, a metrical foot made up of an unstressed syllable followed by a stressed one.

idiom—in language, a customary expression, especially a customary but nonliteral or illogical way of expressing something. In English, for instance, a plane *takes off;* to say that it *takes up* would be *unidiomatic*.

invocation—a calling upon a divine power for aid. Many poems begin with an invocation in which the poet asks for inspiration, often from a muse.

irony—saying the opposite of what one means, or conveying a meaning different from and usually opposed to the surface meaning. The simplest kind of irony is, for example, when one calls a stupid idea "brilliant" or a blizzard "lovely weather."

lampoon—a satirical attack, usually on an individual.

lexicographer—a dictionary writer or compiler.

lexicon—a dictionary, a list of words used in a particular context, such as the vocabulary of a given author.

linguistics—the scientific study of language.

lyric—a poem, usually fairly short, of a musical, emotionally expressive, or subjective character. The lyric is one of the major categories of poetry, along with narrative and dramatic.

marginalia—notes written in the margins of a book.

meter—the rhythm pattern of a given verse.

metonymy—a figure of speech in which one thing is substituted for another thing with which it is actually associated. Saying "the Pentagon announced . . ." instead of "a military spokesman announced . . ." is an example of metonymy.

mimetic—imitating, representing, from the Greek term *mimesis,* "imitation" in a broad sense. *Mimesis* has been a central concept in literary theory since Plato and Aristotle.

monologue—in drama, an extended speech by one person alone, with or without an audience.

narrative—story or plot, in the broadest sense; of literature in which story-telling seems a prominent element.

neologism—(new word) a new word, a word just coined or used in a new sense.

novella—a prose fiction shorter than a novel.

occasional—composed for a particular occasion, as for instance an ode written for a specific celebration.

ode—a lyric poem usually composed in a complex stanza form and generally intended to praise or commemorate.

paean—a hymn or song of thanksgiving, praise, or triumph, originally to the god Apollo.

pagination—the numbering and marking of pages in a book.

palindrome—a word or phrase that reads the same frontwards and backwards, such as *Madam I'm Adam.*

panegyric—a speech or poem praising highly or unreservedly a group, person, or event.

paradox—an internal contradiction, a statement that appears to contradict itself or that at first appears untrue but is in fact valid. "This sentence is false" is a paradox because if it's true it must be false, and if it's false it must be true. The witches' prophecies in *Macbeth* are paradoxes because they appear impossible but turn out to be true.

paraphrase—a rewording, the repetition of the meaning of something in different words.

parlance—a special idiom, a style of writing or speaking peculiar to a limited group.

parody—a written imitation that mocks or ridicules the style of the work imitated.

pastoral—a work of art, especially literature, that purports to be about simple country folk, especially shepherds, or about the simple pleasures of rustic life.

pentameter—a poetic line consisting of five feet or units. Traditionally the most popular meter in English poetry is an *iambic pentameter*—a line consisting of five iambs:

My glass | shall not | persuade | me I | am old
  1   2   3   4   5

persona—(in Latin, a person) in literature, a role or character.

personification—a figure of speech in which an idea or thing is spoken of as if it were a person, as in "Mother Nature."

poet laureate—the officially recognized or chief poet of a nation.

polemic—a controversy or dispute, especially a formal or intellectual argument.

prologue—in literature, something that precedes and serves to introduce the main body of a work.

prosody—the art of writing verse or a set of rules by which verse is composed; broadly, the study of language rhythms used for literary effects.

protagonist—the leading character in a fictional work.

quatrain—a common type of English stanza, consisting of four lines, rhymed or un-rhymed.

refrain—in a song or poem, a phrase or line repeated at regular intervals.

rhetoric—the art of persuasion by speech or writing.

roman à clef—(in French, a novel with a key) a novel portraying real-life characters and events thinly disguised by fictitious names.

satire—a literary work that exposes vice or folly by exaggerating it and holding it up to contempt.

scansion—the analysis of the rhythm of any given verse.

schwa—the name for the most common sound in the English language, the vowel sound of *but* and *a*lone.

semantic—pertaining to the meanings of words.

semiotics (or semiology)—the study of signs and sign systems. Semiotics is concerned with the way arbitrary sign systems (including language) produced by cultures convey meaning.

sociolinguistics—the study of the relation of language to society, especially to social class.

soliloquy—in drama, a speech in which a character does not address other characters but rather seems to be speaking aloud to himself.

sonnet—a type of short poem, usually fourteen lines, popular in English since the Renaissance.

stereotype—a cliché, a trite or overly conventional depiction of a character, especially a depiction that reflects and reinforces a common prejudice.

sublime—very elevated or lofty in style or content, exalted or noble, inspired.

syntax—the structure of grammatical sentences, the way in which words are ordered in an utterance.

tetralogy—a group of four related works.

tetrameter—a poetic line made up of four feet (metrical units), as for example:

I wan | der through | each char | tered street
1   2   3   4

thesaurus—a dictionary of synonyms that distinguishes shades of meaning among words with similar definitions.

transcribe—to make a written copy of.

trilogy—a group of three related works, for instance the three plays that make up Shakespeare's *Henry VI*.

triplet—a verse stanza or unit of three lines, usually rhymed.

trope—(turn) a figure of speech, a nonliteral use of language.

troubadour—a courtly poet and musician of the French Middle Ages. The poetry of the troubadours was concerned with courtly love.

verbose—using more words than are necessary, tedious because of wordiness.

vernacular—the native language of any particular place.

INDEX

plethora, 156
pluralism, 215
poet laureate, 224
pogrom, 215
polemic, 224
polity, 215
polyphonic, 220
portentous, 153
potable, 170
precedent, 71
précis, 128
preclude, 3
predator, 186
predispose, 119
preempt, 175
prelude, 220
prerogative, 183
prevaricate, 29
pristine, 84
proclivity, 59
procrastinate, 26
proficient, 89
pro forma, 95
profound, 9
progenitor, 36
prognosticate, 53
proletariat, 215
prologue, 224
promulgate, 50
propitious, 114
proponent, 215
proscenium, 220
proscribe, 77
prosody, 224
protagonist, 224
protean, 162
protégé, 220
protocol, 215
provincial, 11
puerile, 181
pugnacious, 181
punctilious, 117
purulent, 170
putative, 23
putsch, 215

quatrain, 224
querulous, 181
quibble, 50
quid pro quo, 95
quixotic, 161
quorum, 71

rabid, 9
raconteur, 68
raison d'être, 125
rancor, 137
rapport, 189
rapprochement, 128
ratify, 215
rationale, 59
raucous, 170
rebut, 175
recalcitrant, 45
recant, 178
recapitulate, 26
recidivism, 216
reciprocal, 216
recluse, 3
recoup, 119
rectilinear, 3
recumbent, 23
redolent, 113
referendum, 71
refrain, 224
regale, 29
regenerate, 36
relegate, 147
relief, 220
reminisce, 74
remuneration, 216
renege, 53
repository, 101
representational, 220
requite, 122
rescind, 29
resilient, 152
resonant, 80
restitution, 215
resurrect, 178
resuscitate, 56
retentive, 167
reticent, 86
retrogress, 175
revenue, 216
reverie, 183
revile, 178
revue, 220
rhetoric, 224
robust, 170
roman à clef, 224
rudimentary, 170

sable, 84
sagacity, 137

salient, 149
salutary, 47
sanguine, 90
sardonic, 181
satiate, 74
satire, 224
saturnine, 192
savant, 16
savoir-faire, 125
scabrous, 9
scansion, 224
scapegoat, 216
scat, 220
scenario, 220
schism, 71
schwa, 224
scruple, 173
seclude, 3
sect, 216
secular, 216
sedentary, 110
sedition, 216
segue, 189
semantic, 224
semiotics, 224
sentient, 84
sepulcher, 101
sequester, 144
shibboleth, 216
sic, 96
sidereal, 110
simile, 6
similitude, 6
simulate, 144
sine die, 93
sine qua non, 95
sinister, 116
skeptic, 17
skit, 220
slough, 119
sobriety, 14
sobriquet, 128
sociolinguistics, 224
soliloquy, 224
somatic, 110
somnambulist, 31
somnolent, 113
sonata, 220
sonnet, 224
sonorous, 84
soporific, 42
soprano, 220